For My dear aunt Mildred,
you have meant so much to
our family forever.
I love you,
Jocie
7/31/18

High praise for *Jocie*

"Jocelyn's long service on the Reform Jewish Movement's national Commission on Social Action helped shape the policy positions of the largest segment of American Jewry. This wonderful book captures for a national audience, with humor, candor, and insight, her remarkable life."
Al Vorspan, Senior Vice President Emeritus,
Union for Reform Judaism

"*Jocie* is a lovely, thoughtful account of a different time when many of us were searching and of the journey that allowed some of us risk-takers to survive in wonderful and unexpected ways. Thank you for sharing the light."
Carol Berz, LSCW, JD, PhD, Private Dispute Resolution Services, LLC, Chattanooga City Council Chair

"Come, have a conversation with Jocie Wurzburg, for that's how this charming collection reads. From suburban Jewish housewife to a leading civil rights activist in Memphis to a legal mediator, music buff, and politico, *Jocie* will engage and delight you."
Gail S. Murray, emerita professor of history, Rhodes College, and author of *Throwing Off the Cloak of Privilege: White Southern Women Activists in the Civil Rights Era*

"What a great read! Jocie's life reflects the ups and downs of our history and she tells it in the most compelling way. Highly recommend this book!"
Paula F. Casey, speaker and publisher,
The Perfect 36: Tennessee Delivers Woman Suffrage

Jocie

Jocie

Southern Jewish American Princess, Civil Rights Activist

Jocelyn Dan Wurzburg

Library of Congress Cataloging-in-Publication Data

ISBN: 978-0-9963458-5-9

Printed and bound in the United States of America by Ingram Lightning Source

First edition

Editing, layout, and design: Jacque Hillman, Jesse Hillman, and Katie Gould

Cover design: Wanda Stanfill

To contact the author, write her at wurzburg@mediate.com.

Website: wurzburgmediation.com

The HillHelen Group LLC. 127 Fairmont Ave.,
Jackson, TN 38301
hillhelengroup@gmail.com

To Richard, though the journey was from him, he made it possible
and
to Adonai
שֶׁעָשַׂנִי יִשְׂרָאֵל
who made me a Jew

Contents

Introduction

They say it is a more common phenomenon than you would think. Here is this woman standing before the Memphis City Council giving them the devil. And giving it well! And that woman is *me*, Jocelyn Maurie Dan Wurzburg. But I am overhead looking down at that woman, listening and watching her do this. And she's doing a damn good job!

It felt like an out-of-body experience, whatever that is. The right words came quickly and were delivered sharply. It was as if I were a puppet with some smart person feeding me the best answers. I've read of others expressing the same feelings, phenomenon, if you will.

The topic of this exchange was the threatened second sanitation workers strike set for July 1969. July, as in very hot in Memphis when you don't want garbage piled up on the street. July, as in flies.

I wasn't alone. Women from the more prominent east side of Memphis were there to ask — no, demand actually — that the city council and the American Federation of State, County, and Municipal Employees (AFSCME) come out from the corners into which they had backed themselves and return to the bargaining table. We told the council and the union that we were not going to tolerate a repeat of macho, political-based bargaining this time. An important person got murdered over it the last time. Memphians had needs, and so did the sanitation workers, and no one needed a garbage strike in July!

In *Jocie*, I share the adventures of how a typical Southern Jewish American Princess got converted into an acknowledged, award-winning civil rights activist. After Dr. Martin Luther King was assassinated in my town, I started calling my maid "Mrs."

— while my husband and children didn't. This is a collection of stories charting the journey of how this upper-middle-class, fifth-generation Memphis Jewish woman found herself in that situation and the divorce that followed.

Born in 1940, I hit adulthood in Memphis during its 1960s turmoil. My value system was turned upside down; I tried to straddle the life I was reared to live and the life that was revolting against it. What was the catalyst for this conversion? What were the factors that made me receptive to it? I didn't travel that journey alone. There were incredibly interesting people to help me (when the chela is ready, the guru appears) and mind-boggling incidents and situations in which I found myself.

I write about growing up with religious and class expectations. We were poor, but I didn't feel it. When my father got sick and lost his business, the family was literally in poverty — except for help from family. But my mother would dip the edge of the lettuce cup in paprika before adding a scoop of the tuna fish salad we had to eat too often.

I married exactly who I was supposed to marry. Not a wealthy, Memphis Reform Jewish doctor, but a businessman whose family had been here as long as my family had. He gave me the security and the cover that allowed me to risk change.

This is not a sad story of loss and sacrifice, although there was a lot of that and death in various forms. Au contraire. This book is a compilation of those crazy situations and funny incidents. While there was a loss of friends and family, not to mention a marriage, the balance sheet is positive. I found new insight, new friends, new values, wild adventures, and an old crush — who loves me still today.

Chapter One

'Garbage' Strike

The sanitation workers strike in 1968 marked the real beginning of my journey.

In 2014, I attended a showing of the documentary *At the River I Stand*, taken from the book of the same title by Joan Beifuss. It is an extraordinary film depicting the events that led up to the assassination of Dr. Martin Luther King.

The movie was shown at the union hall of AFSCME, the American Federation of State, County, and Municipal Employees. It was a fundraiser for the workers being locked out by Kellogg Corporation in Memphis. It wasn't a strike; it was a lockout. I supported the workers, but I really went to see this film.

The sanitation workers struck against the city when it had no death benefits for workers Robert Walker and Echol Cole, who met a horrific death on the job. It started raining. Mr. Cole took shelter in the back of the garbage compacting truck. Lightning hit the truck, the mechanism engaged, and Mr. Walker jumped in to rescue his friend. Both were crushed. One thousand three hundred employees walked off the job. They didn't have a union to back them, but they had just had enough.

I was not a union person; I, with my big mouth, just couldn't see why anyone needed to pay good money to have someone redress a grievance for them. And neither could my father-in-law, who was personally insulted that the workers at our family's business organized with the Teamsters.

"My door has always been open. I've always helped my

employees when they needed it. Why would they unionize?" he said.

Henry Loeb was our mayor at the time. Always interested in politics, I volunteered at age seventeen to run his political headquarters on Saturdays when he ran for public office the first time to turn out a Boss Crump-anointed pol. Henry would pick me up at home and drive me downtown, if I didn't have a ride or Mama's car. He had a car telephone, a novelty at the time; I had never seen one. He was elected to run public works.

As mayor, Henry, too, was personally affronted that his "boys" wanted a union. I understood unions for private businesses, but public employees? That was holding the citizens hostage. And I wrote Henry to tell him to stay the course.

Our house sat on one of the few hills in East Memphis; getting the garbage down it was a chore. I developed a healthy respect for the brawn it took to get my garbage from behind the house and down our steep driveway to the street when we were told to bring our trash to the front of the house to the "scabs" who would be running the routes. I was used to paying for brains, and all of a sudden paying for brawn was worthy.

After my wedding in 1960, I was recovering from mononucleosis and needed a maid. I called Tennessee Employment Security, which matched employers and employees. I asked what was minimum at the time and was told, "Darling, you don't need to pay minimum wage; four dollars a day and carfare is more than enough."

With complete lack of any sensitivity, we called it the "garbage" strike or "garbage men" strike. Learning to say "sanitation workers strike" was the first step we took to honor the dignity of hard-working men who had to proclaim with iconic signs "I Am A Man." As the daughter and granddaughter of advertising and PR men, I knew the "I Am A Man" signs worked. They were potent.

The movie was based on the information garnered by a few Memphians who had the foresight immediately to collect everything about the strike, the assassination, and the aftermath of all the chaos. David Yellin, a professor at Memphis State University; Carol Lynn Yellin, his wife and an author and editor with

Reader's Digest; and Joan Beifuss formed the Search for Meaning Project and collected thousands of documents, interviews, films, and photographs. The university library is the depository of this collection. Joan wrote the book, *At the River I Stand*; later, the movie was made. And seeing it took me right back to April 4, 1968.

We faced the news of the strike and our politicians' response to the events every night on our three TV channels. This was pre-cable, so the news was mostly local and pretty slanted for the city's position. That is until Dr. Martin Luther King got involved and when the first march he led got violent.

A march was scheduled for March 22, and the Black community called for a supportive citywide strike by all Black workers and a boycott of white business. Dr. King was supposed to lead it. This huge snowstorm came over Memphis and didn't move. It dumped inches and inches of snow. The city was paralyzed!

It was interesting to note that white people said, "See, Dr. King, God didn't want you to come here." I later learned that Black folk were saying, "God supports us. He didn't let anyone shop or go to work today."

Dr. King's involvement gave us national news coverage. And it wasn't very complimentary to Memphis.

I was with my daughter Cheryl in Gus Mayer's department store, buying her shoes. We were advised over the intercom system that the store would be closing and to proceed immediately with our purchases. It was too early, so we knew something was wrong. Our salesman said he heard on the radio in back that Dr. Martin Luther King had been shot.

We left quickly, anxious to get to the car radio. At that time, Dr. King had not been proclaimed dead, but the city fathers immediately placed a citywide curfew. As soon as the death announcement came through, chaos ensued, but it was remarkably nonviolent. But our city was in trouble. And I was soon to learn this tragedy would affect the whole world. This was more than a "garbage" strike, and I had a lot to learn.

AFSCME was seeking recognition, the right for the men to have organized representation to address work-related grievances. For a union to work, it had to get "check-off," a process whereby the city deducted union dues from the worker's paycheck. The city was adamant that wasn't going to happen, but of course, it was willing to deduct a United Way donation.

By the time we got home, St. Joseph Hospital confirmed Dr. King was dead. Our Black leaders wisely kept a lid on revenge violence. But Memphis was in turmoil, and so were the negotiations between the city and AFSCME.

At one point our city's ministers got involved, and our rabbi, James A. Wax, happened to be the president of the Ministerial Association at the time. He was a fierce social justice activist, and he considered this an issue of social justice. He was televised shaking his finger at the mayor, saying there was a law higher than city ordinances and that was God's law.

I had a problem with the statement: like, whose God? But I thought I should attend the monthly Saturday morning children's services at Temple the next day to be supportive of the rabbi, despite my reservations. I called and asked if the Temple was receiving threat calls. It was, so I decided to attend but leave my child at home. The attendance was sparse and devoid of children. I had to laugh at myself: I put myself on the west side of the sanctuary by the window. If anyone was going to throw a bomb into the building, it was going to be there.

The strike and the assassination were ever present in the city; we hardly spoke of anything else. Community meetings were held and attended by Memphians who had never gone to a racially integrated gathering before. My father-in-law and I went to Memphis Cares, a huge event at our football stadium. It was an eye-opener for me; I'd call it a game-changer.

Eventually, the mayor gave in and the strike ended with AFSCME being recognized and allowed to represent the sanitation workers.

Years later I went to law school and took a labor law course. My favorite professor, Steve Shields, fresh out of Yale Law, went around the room asking to learn the names of his students, if we were labor or management. Being a "W," I was last and responded, "I sleep with management, but I think I'm pro-labor."

Chapter Two

Memphis Cares

My husband's father, Reggie, and I decided to attend Memphis Cares. The city was in an uproar, and Memphis Cares was held to try to calm emotions and speak of reconciliation. With heavy police presence, the city had not had a chance to grieve respectfully for Dr. King.

The program, created by the late John T. Fisher and Nat Landau, was held at Crump Stadium, Memphis's football stadium. A speakers' platform was constructed on the fifty-yard line facing south. The south side of the stadium was totally full — and totally integrated. City leaders pleaded for racial harmony, and some spoke for recognition of the union — causing a bit of discomfort for some of the white audience. Some comments were met with rousing cheers from the Black audience.

Of all the speakers, the comments made by a Black high school mathematics teacher, Ms. Mary Collier, held me spellbound. The gist of her comments was that this was not merely a union-management fight but a fight all about race, prejudice, and discrimination.

That wasn't how I framed my reference to this conflict. I thought that outside agitators, in the form of a union from New York, were taking advantage of our poor garbage workers to line the pockets of the union bosses. I understood utterly nothing about unionism. Tennessee was a right-to-work state, and our company had never had a union. If a boss was fair, why would anyone want to unionize?

Ms. Collier was not accusatory and spoke in a mild manner

about racial prejudice institutionalized in our society. I left the event with her words resonating in my head. Later that night, I found her name in the Memphis phone book and called her.

"Ms. Collier, I heard you speak today, and you were telling us things I saw in an entirely different light. Why was this not a labor management fight? Why was this a racial issue?" I asked.

She was so patient on the phone and gently asked me if I had ever seen a Black garbage truck driver. Did I ever see a white person with a huge garbage pail on his head?

No, I hadn't. She told me that was no accident.

I thanked her for being so gracious to me and then asked her if she would be willing to come and speak with some of my friends if I held a tea. She said she would be delighted, and we made a date right then and there.

Most of my girlfriends were the women with whom I played cards or golf, pretty exclusively Jewish. About twenty showed up, but Mary Collier did not. Instead she sent Professor Elizabeth Phillips, an older white woman. She started her conversation with us, "The darkest day in the history of mankind was April 4, 1968, the date of the assassination of Dr. Martin Luther King." Then she morphed into a pro-union stance and explained why it was so important that the sanitation workers be allowed to organize.

She was talking to a room full of people who thought the darkest day in the history of mankind was the rise of Adolf Hitler; they probably never had a relative who belonged to a union. They were stunned!

I could see them looking at each other and rolling their eyes; they looked at me quizzically. When they left, I received, "Jocelyn, what are you getting yourself into? Jocelyn, you better be careful, girl." Some just looked at me and shook their heads and shrugged their shoulders.

It pretty much was a defining moment for me. My friends knew instantly, and I think I did, too, that I was taking off on an entirely different path.

I started reading the Black newspaper; listening to WDIA, a Black radio station; going to lectures; and attending racial reconciliation programs. I had so much to learn, mostly unlearning the "givens" with which I had been reared.

I attended a program put on by the National Conference of Christians and Jews (NCCJ) called "Rearing Children of Good Will." It addressed how hard it was to rear kids to be prejudice-free and how hard it was to rear a put-upon minority child with good self-esteem. The presentation was similar to a program I had seen called "The Panel of American Women."

Chapter Three

Family of Origin

I was born in 1940 in Memphis, Tennessee, on August 3. I never really got into astrology, but I have had people say, "You're a Leo. I can tell." My mother was Rose Sternberger Heyman Dan. My father was Charles Lewis Dan. I was a doted-upon only child for my first six years, and then my brother, Ray Heyman Dan, was born in 1946. Then four years later, my sister Libby — Lizbeth Faye Dan — was born.

Both my parents were born in Memphis. I'm supposed to be a fifth-generation Memphian through my mother's lineage, a designation considered "high" to my "family background-conscious" German Jewish mother, but we have five generations of my father's side buried at the Orthodox synagogue.

It's my understanding that my father dated my mother's sister, Mildred, and double-dated with his best friend, Joe, and Rose. Daddy asked Joe if maybe it would be okay to trade dates.

That would have made Daddy the first non-German Reform Jew Mother ever dated; it was an unwritten rule that Reform Temple girls did not date the Orthodox boys. Those boys probably had the reverse prohibition. Naturally, Mother and Daddy fell in love with each other.

Early memories are vague. Our house in the early 1940s backed up to Vollentine Elementary School. My strongest memory from that time is Daddy driving up to a man leading a horse on Evergreen Street and asking if he could put me on it.

Somehow, we lost that house, and when I was three, we moved

to a second-story flat in an apartment building on Stonewall between Poplar and Madison. My bed filled a small alcove, probably designed to be a breakfast nook. Daddy stuck glow-in-the-dark star constellations and moons in various phases on the ceiling.

We lived on the second floor in the front quarter of the building. The stairs ascended from the front to the rear, and at nighttime, I was afraid of the top of the stairs. I had this fear of a monster character waiting in front of our apartment door to scare me. It had a box for a head with the light bulb on top, and its arms and its legs were lightning bolts. At age twenty while traveling through Arkansas to get to Route 66 for my honeymoon trip, I saw this same character logo, my monster, up on a billboard for an Arkansas utility company. It must have gotten into my consciousness somehow at an early age.

In the building next door lived a couple named Ike and Gladys Friedman. They had two sons: One was a radio personality in Washington, and the other married a 1940s movie star, Marie Wilson. She was a beautiful blond comedienne, and Aunt Gladys kept me supplied with autographed photos of her and other celebrities. The Friedmans enjoyed me and babysat me. I was reared to call all adults "aunt" and "uncle" if they were too close to be "Mr." or "Mrs."

The help — a kinder way to refer to the Negro men and women who were servants in a white household — played an important part in my life. Mama had to work, and she did at Levy's store for women. She worked in the shoe department, and during World War II when the men were gone, she sold shoes, which was a "man's job." Mama said she thought she was the first woman shoe salesperson in Memphis.

Anise Wright was the maid. Though caring, she was not too bright and was afraid of thunder. In a storm she would grab me and dive under a large, silky-feeling duvet bed cover. At age five, I was more aware of her mental deficiencies than Mama and remember having to explain simple things to her. I had never called the maids by their last name with a proper title until 1968, the assassination date of Dr. King, so she was Anise to me then.

Anise loved the radio soap operas, so I grew up on them. I think it was *Stella Dallas*, "Can a young girl from a mining town in the West find love and happiness with the rich ...?" At one time I could recite the opening lines of all the daytime radio programs.

In the afternoons, the children's radio shows played. Captain Marvel, Superman, Wonder Woman — all with attending comic books. I sent off for a Captain Marvel decoder and awaited the secret message we had to decode at the show's end. Anise was amazed I could translate the numbers to words.

Rosalie Pulliam was a different story. She taught me a lot about household chores, utensils, and the ways of the world — the ways of her Memphis, at least. If she had an errand to do downtown, such as paying her utility bill or shopping, she was allowed to take me. She could sit at the front of the bus with me. She walked into a store barred to Black folk and, when halted, she picked me up to display, pretending she was on an errand for her white employer.

Rosalie had a daughter, Josephine, about my age, and sometimes Josephine came to work with her mother. What a treat for me — a playmate. Somewhere along the line Josephine started calling me Miss Jocelyn. That didn't feel right, but I was told that was the way it was. Rosalie was heartsick when Josephine got pregnant at a young age.

On a stroll down Stonewall, you would see a number of 1940s Ford automobiles. They were ugly, black, two-door coupes, but affordable. Daddy was a traveling advertising salesman, so we had to have a car.

You might also see a wire hanging from our living room window. Daddy made me a crystal radio. Google describes it as a simple early form of radio receiver with a crystal touching a metal wire as the rectifier, instead of a tube or transistor. It had no amplifier nor speaker; we dropped the antenna wire out of the window and had to use headphones to get sound. You could pick up a few radio stations.

Our apartment had an honest postman, thank goodness, because one year I wrote a letter to Santa Claus and used about three months of sugar and flour World War II ration stamps for postage. The postman brought the letter back to Mama.

The war was in my consciousness: Even then I knew it had something to do with Jews, although I don't think we still had family living in Europe. Surely, we must have, but none we knew about since both sides of my family had been in America for a long time. Candy bars were for the soldiers, but occasionally we had a sugarcane stalk for a candy treat. Somehow, the Mid-South Fair was allowed to make and sell cotton candy.

My cousin George Lapides was given a set of black models of German and American airplanes created by the Army Air Corps, a predecessor to the Air Force. They were used to teach the volunteer air patrol spotters what the various planes looked like from the ground against a sky. We were fascinated with them.

Besides the postman who used to deliver mail twice a day, the iceman and milkman would visit us. Milk came in recyclable glass bottles; you gave the empties to the milkman when he brought you milk with cream on top. The iceman delivered a huge, rectangular block of ice that fitted into the top cabinet of the icebox. I still use the term "icebox" in referring to the refrigerator. For a while we all called that box Frigidaire, since that was the first brand of refrigerator marketed. Many of us ask for a Kleenex when we mean a tissue.

That apartment was within walking distance to the Madison Avenue trolley line. Daddy and I would catch a streetcar to go west down to Russwood Park, which was the baseball diamond for our AA baseball team, the Memphis Chicks, as in Chickasaw Indians. I was a "Chickasaw Buddy." A big baseball fan back then, I thought behind third base was the best seat in the house.

I saw Babe Ruth once when they had big league teams playing exhibition games in smaller markets. Our team was a farm team for the St. Louis Cardinals.

For reasons I have never understood, I stayed with Aunt Mildred and Uncle Abe Lapides and my cousin George Lapides for a while in their home on Vollentine off Springdale, north of Jackson. Aunt Mildred said I lived with her for a year, but the length of time grew exaggerated as the stories were told through the years.

My parents came over every night to see me, and on Sunday nights, I sat in my daddy's lap while the entire extended family listened to Jack Benny on a real radio. The more Aunt Mildred extended the time span I stayed with her in her recounting over the years, the angrier my father got. Perish the thought he would give me up for more than a few weeks.

Memphis didn't have condos or townhouses until the 1970s. There were some duplexes, but most homes were single-family residences on large lots. Aunt Mildred had a big backyard with a chicken coop.

Aunt Mildred's help was Cookie Woolfork, a good lady and remarkable cook. Cookie would go out into the backyard, pick a chicken out of the coop, wring its neck, and fry it to perfection. The trick, she told me, was to cook the dark meat separately from the white meat. She taught us kids a lot of things about the kitchen. She trimmed the pie crust hanging over the pie plate after she patted it down to line the inside of the plate and taught us how to make cookies out of the trimmings. We would flatten them even more with a rolling pin and sprinkle them with sugar and cinnamon to bake. Cookie was also responsible for our daily dose of castor oil, which, for some reason, was supposed to be healthy for us children.

I started first grade at Idlewild School, but we moved to Berkley Street about January, facilitating a change of schools. That had me entering a class of children who had been together a year and a half already from kindergarten. Putting a six-year-old in "outsider status" was a delicate matter, one I didn't handle very well. But in retrospect, perhaps that was the genesis of my sympathy for the outsider.

Chapter Four

Berkley Street

Upon moving in 1946 to 2145 Berkley in Memphis, I was old enough to understand I was having my first brush with prejudice. While it was hard transferring to a school where children had already created their cliques and alliances, living as a Reform Jewish child on a predominantly Orthodox Jewish street had challenges. There were two Catholic families on the street, but more about them later. The Orthodox Jewish kids persecuted me, saying I was not a real Jew and there was a cross in my ark at my Temple. This was a bit of a conflict because I always thought my mother was much too snobbish about our being fifth-generation Reform Jews in Memphis. Mama looked down on these neighbors, while they were looking down on me. As I mentioned earlier, my mother married the first Orthodox Jew she ever went out with.

The neighborhood, off Springdale Street north of Vollentine, was built by a Jewish developer and intended for lower-income folks. Two streets to the north started a "colored" neighborhood, which was convenient for the Black Popsicle men and the occasional vegetable trucks that cruised Berkley.

The Orthodox synagogue was within a long walk, but the rich Orthodox Jews lived within a few blocks of it in an upscale custom-built section we called Hebrew Hills. When Memphis grew eastward and so went the Jews, many kept "Shabbat" homes to move into before sundown on Friday night so they could walk to Baron Hirsch Shul, which at the time was the world's largest Orthodox synagogue. It finally moved out east as well.

Our small house had three bedrooms, but one served as a hallway with doors on opposite walls so we could get to the kitchen without having to go through the living room and dining room. It had one bathroom to serve a family that was eventually five.

We enclosed the screened-in porch to give us an extra room. Later, Uncle Ike Heyman added a room and bath in the back so we could take him in, and Mother took care of him. He paid me a quarter to shave his head bi-weekly. Including the additions, I doubt we had 1,000 square feet.

The backyard was large, big enough for Daddy to mark off a baseball diamond with limestone powder or set up a badminton court. In 1946, it was safe enough to play outdoors after dark: Red Rover, Sling the Statue, Hide and Seek. And during the summer the Popsicle man came down the street at least once a day. A Black man would push a white cart loaded with frozen treats, which sold for about a nickel apiece.

Unpopular with the girls on the street, I was considered a "tomboy," played sports, and got along great with the boys. In fact, directly behind us was the Fox family. Andy had a basketball goal, and I was the only girl allowed to play with the boys; I was a whiz at the basketball game "three horses." Andy, Jewish, grew up to direct Catholic Charities here in Memphis.

I do remember one day using the word "exaggerate," and the girls chanting, "Jocelyn uses big words, Jocelyn uses big words," meaning to put me down. I also remember thinking that prejudice only hurts when you feel vulnerable to the slight. "Honky" doesn't do much to or for me, but I learned early that prejudice is a power thing.

The house had floor furnaces with pilot lights that Daddy had to light when we awoke on cold mornings. We would jump out of bed and run to stand on them Marilyn Monroe style, with our nightgowns blown like balloons from the warm air. In the heat of summer, a fun thing to do when home alone was to close all the doors to the hall except my bedroom and let the attic fan blow a gale through the room. We got the first window-unit air conditioner on Berkley, and I became more popular.

Judy Schwartz was a few years older and probably my favorite friend on the street. She taught me how to twirl a baton, but Daddy said, "We don't parade down a street in shorts." Judy's mother was from New York, and she married a South Georgian who sold insurance policies door to door and collected the premiums monthly on his route. All the kids loved Judy's mama.

Judy and I told Daddy we wanted to start a club and asked if he would like to be our president. He got into it, and it became CHJOJU — CH for Charles, JO for Jocelyn, and JU for Judy. But we needed to be branded. We were blindfolded, and he wrote CHJOJU with Mercurochrome on our arms, but when he touched the little glass Mercurochrome wand to our skin, he put a lit match into water. The hissing sound made us think we were actually being branded. Pre-TV, we were creative in entertaining ourselves.

Judy had a younger stepbrother, Richard, who was killed in Vietnam the week he arrived there. His death was the first time I personally knew a serviceman who died in the war. The funeral was devastating, especially when our Rabbi Wax took the opportunity to protest the war. I thought that insensitive; a mother doesn't want to hear her son died in vain.

The Melchers lived next door. They were Catholic, and one day Mike took me to vacation Bible school. I fretted because we had to be prepared with a memorized Bible verse to recite. I got up the nerve to tell Mike I didn't have a copy of the New Testament in my house. He solved my dilemma by telling me to just say, "Jesus wept," a verse all to itself.

All of the neighborhood kids participated in extracurricular activities. Mine was dancing, since we didn't have the room or the money for a piano. But that wasn't cheap because Mrs. Weakley put on these elaborate dance recitals with handmade, expensive costumes, usually worn once.

To get more bang for the buck and to keep us busy during the summer, we kids put on variety shows. We sang and danced, and anyone could come for ten cents each. Once we performed Snow White and the four dwarfs. There were only that many little boys on the street.

We had the first television on the block in 1950. Our TV was a large piece of furniture like a cabinet with a small screen. Daddy once put a variegated piece of plastic on the screen to give the illusion of color.

Kukla, Fran, and Ollie was our favorite show. It seemed bizarre to me that most of our local programming was sponsored by Garrett Snuff. Even at ten years old, I questioned Memphis's first television set owners being the right market. I guess the Condon family loved television. There was lots of wrestling on TV, too.

Directly across the street lived Sid Marcus, who was the wrestling promoter and referee in Memphis, where TV wrestling was big. Once, a huge wrestling bear in a small trailer cage was parked for days in his driveway.

I was fascinated with our one TV network televising the Joseph McCarthy hearings in 1954. The anti-communist zealot McCarthy was a household name in the early 1950s, as was Herb Philbrick, who "led three lives," one as an FBI spy. But I was glued to the McCarthy hearings on TV and understood that the senator was wrong and unfair. Even I knew he had no shame.

Before Dr. King was assassinated in 1968 and all throughout the 1950s and the early '60s, downtown Memphis was the place you went shopping. I can remember leaving my house on Berkley, turning right on Springdale, and walking about eight blocks down to Jackson Avenue. Below Vollentine, Springdale had Black residents living on the west side of the street and white residents on the east side. Nobody thought anything about letting a little ten- or eleven-year-old white girl go to town and back alone.

"Try to get home before dark" was the rule.

I could catch a bus at Jackson and Springdale with one dollar in my pocket. The bus was five cents each way, and you would meet your friends either at Britlings Cafeteria or a beautiful dining room in Goldsmith's department store. At Britlings you could get spaghetti, a blueberry muffin, and iced tea for fifty cents. You could then go by Planters Peanuts and pick up a quarter pound of pistachios for twenty cents if you didn't want popcorn. The movie would cost twelve cents, so you would have a few cents left over, saving your bus fare nickel to get home, to go to the five-and-dime store. That's where you bought your jewels, little plastic emeralds, sapphires, diamonds, and rubies we used to wager when we played a game called twenty-one. At ten, eleven, and twelve, we were gambling at blackjack.

We were poor, but we kids didn't know we were poor. I had what everybody else had, I just got mine for occasions. The girlfriends I would meet downtown could go to town and charge for a cashmere sweater; I would get mine for Christmas or for making all As.

Across the street and one house up lived Pat and Bert Malone. Sadly, I can't remember who was Pat and who was Bert, but they were the only other Catholic couple on Berkley, and they were older. They were so good to us kids. One Christmas, the wife, I think she was Pat, gave us little girls a holiday tea party. They had a decorated tree and left the curtain open for all to see.

After our snacks, our hostess sat us around the tree, and there were six identical dolls under the branches. Identical, except that one was a Negro doll baby. She called out our names, and we were to go pick out a doll to take home. She called my name fourth. I chose the Black doll. When the party was over and we were on our way out, she asked that I stay behind a minute.

She asked me, "Why did you pick the Black doll, Jocelyn?"

"I was afraid no one would pick her and she would be chosen last, and I didn't want her to get her feelings hurt," I said.

She told me she was proud of me and then as a "reward," she went into a cabinet and gave me a white doll to take home. How's that for a mixed message!

When trying to look back and ascertain the various stops I made along my journey from J.A.P. to Jocelyn, I just now recall this little test. If I was a princess, I was a kind-hearted one.

Chapter Five

A Good Little Girl

I was always considered to be a good little girl —
respectful, never got into trouble. That continued into my teenage
years and young adulthood.

I went to kindergarten at St. Mary's — the right school. I don't
remember too much about it except one embarrassing moment. I
was assigned to play the cymbals. The two cymbals I had to hold
in the air, prepared to strike, became heavy, so I let the kinder-
orchestra down when I didn't strike at the right time. I was a terrific
Jocko the monkey in the class circus. I look back and wonder
why all the little girls wanted to be beautifully costumed tightrope
walkers (across a bench a few inches off the ground) and trapeze
artists, but I wanted to be Jocko.

Then on to Vollentine Elementary situated on Vollentine Street.
In first grade, I was placed in the worst little reading circle. There
were Cardinals, Bluejays, Robins, and I was a Sparrow. I was
pegged as not too bright. But by third grade, I was an arithmetic
ace, so they didn't know what to do with me. I was assigned to the
split fifth- and sixth-grade classes for ages ten and eleven, and
that was reserved for the best students. I made all As, but I had
difficulty reading very quickly.

In the 1940s, education experimented with sight-reading, not
sounding out words. If I had previously memorized "neighbor," I
wouldn't know what to do with "unneighborly." But my real problem
was that I am an audio reader. I say all the words in my head.
Reading for me goes from eye to ear to brain, not eye to brain. I

think the world may be divided into audio and visual readers.

The good news is when I read, I comprehend everything because I explain things to myself as I read, and I retain everything because I tell myself everything. And when I read, it is like a radio show in my head, and I change voices for the different characters.

I later learned I am dyslexic, transposing "was" for "saw," for example. Law school was a bitch!

The only D I ever received was from my marvelous English teacher, Ms. Metz, at Central High. I couldn't get *Of Human Bondage* read, so I read the first and last fifty pages and left Mildred the prostitute out of the book report. The shame I had when I had to admit to her I hadn't read the book! She knew.

At Southwestern, my undergraduate school, I took reading enhancement courses. Professor Schrivner threw words up on a screen in a fraction of a second. I never saw them. I paid a huge amount of money to take an Evelyn Woods reading course, but to no avail.

I read all the time, every night for about an hour before falling off to sleep, but it's slow going. I love fiction; I've read every Richard North Patterson, Daniel Silva, and John Grisham book written. Lately everything I seem to read is political or something written by someone I know. To this day, I have never joined a book club, fearing I couldn't get the book read in time. But I digress.

Thinking about Vollentine has brought back strange memories. Once during recess, this good little girl, an embroidery buff, accidentally sewed the pattern I was embroidering onto my skirt. Then the bell rang. Afraid to be late, rather than delicately pull out the connected threads, I cut the piece off the skirt, destroying weeks of work.

I lied to a teacher once. On the way to opening class, I ran into the principal, my fifth-grade teacher who had been promoted, talking to my sixth-grade teacher, Ms. Ladd. They asked me to do the Bible assignments. Every class in the Memphis City Schools system read the same passage of the Bible every morning. I thought they were asking me to read the selection to our class. I panicked, not knowing if the assignment was from the Old Testament or the

New Testament, and I didn't know as a Jew if I was "allowed" to read from the New Testament. I said my throat was hurting a bit, and I didn't think I could do it. It turned out they were asking me to deliver the assignment to each classroom teacher, a cool job I would have loved to do.

The fifth-grade teacher was Ms. Epperson, a good teacher who read us stories aloud. She loved the prose writing of A.A. Milne in *Winnie the Pooh*, and her reading was close to performance art. And she read us Langston Hughes. Who would have thunk it! "Your arms too short to box with God." He was a great writer; I think she told us he was "colored."

We used to get a student newspaper every week called the *Weekly Reader*. It contained history cartoons, and a memory that has never left me was one showing former slaves, hat in hand, approaching the master on the porch and begging for their job back as a slave. Nothing in our elementary education told us slavery or Jim Crow was wrong. The *Weekly Reader* told us slaves were happy.

I felt it was wrong. Once when I was seven, I decided I would sit in the back of the bus to show I thought being made to sit there wasn't nice. When the bus got to the Black neighborhood and began to pick up Black passengers, I was sitting about four rows from the back on the aisle. Finally, a woman leaned over to me and said, "Little girl, I think you are wanting to be nice, but we can't sit in front of you, and we have to stand as long as you sit back here." I moved.

I had an experience in the fourth grade that I later used as an introduction to my speeches. I raised my hand in class and asked the teacher, "If an Indian moved to Memphis, would he sit in the front of the bus or the back of the bus?" She said she didn't know and that I should write to the government. I wrote to President Harry Truman. Six months later I got an 8½" x 11" trifolded pamphlet from the Department of the Interior's Bureau on Indian Affairs. It did not answer my question. So that lesson learned was: There are questions you just aren't supposed to ask.

Empathy has always been my long suit. It's a must for being a mediator. I think I developed my sense of empathy early on.

Julia Y., in our class, was a large child. Obese is probably not an exaggeration. One day our teacher, Ms. Ladd, was out of the room, and the kids passed around a pretend newspaper with hurtful headlines. "Julia Sneezes, Hurricane" and "Julia Jumps in the Ocean, Tidal Wave." A student would get the passed paper, laugh, add a comment, and pass it on for additional edits. I refused to play, which was brave in a way because I feared I would become an object of ire. I don't know how, probably from Julia, but Ms. Ladd found out about it and chastised the class. She approached me later and told me she was pleased with me that I didn't participate in the bullying. She then asked me if I could help her on Saturdays sometime to help her grade papers. I felt so special and rewarded.

In the summer, Vollentine became a Parks Commission park. Children could be dropped off in the morning and be supervised for play all day. We had a wading pool, softball diamonds, box hockey, and sing-alongs. I guess it's a liability issue, but do we ever need such a program today!

Junior High

In Memphis, junior high was seventh through ninth grade. Vollentine was a feeder school to Snowden. Snowden was the name of a prominent Memphis family; one of their heirs became my cohort in the crime of being a civil rights activist in our conservative city. Snowden was the clout school, and a big percentage of the students were Jewish. Jews and gentiles interacted at school in sports and activities and some socially, until hitting the ninth grade when sororities and fraternities took in pledges. Jews were not allowed into those clubs. So we set up our own.

The seventh-grade music teacher at Snowden took us to see *Aida* when the MET came to town. Ms. Lancaster, the ninth-grade music teacher, held an essay contest, *Why I Want to Go to the Memphis Symphony*. I didn't want to go to the symphony, but I liked essay contests. I won, I went, and I was smitten.

Memphis has a lot of classical music. A New York Philharmonic maestro, Alan Gilbert, is the son of Michael, a member of that orchestra and a Snowden classmate. One of our symphony orchestras here is IRIS, led by Michael Stern. IRIS performs about five times a year, and the musicians come from all over the country. When I met Maestro Stern, I told him I was lucky enough at Snowden Junior High to have sat on the front row when his famous father, Isaac, came to the school to talk about classical music. He was so enthralling I recall what he wore. Snowden was able to attract dignitaries to speak or perform.

It's funny how some memories stick with you: One morning my homeroom teacher, Ms. Prescott, came over and whispered that Mr. Hutchinson, the principal, wanted to see me right away. Being called to the principal's office isn't good! I sat across from him at his desk, and he lit into me.

"Jocelyn, apparently you are a person who thinks just because you make all As you can slack off and still get the same grade. That's not going to happen here. That's a flaw in your character. You've failed science, and we are not going to tolerate your laziness. You have to work hard and earn your grades. Do you understand me?"

I was shocked. "Yes, sir." I was able to hold in my tears until I got back to my desk. Ms. Prescott came over to pat my back and encourage me to do better next period.

"I don't know how to do better," I said, showing her my science folder with As on every pop quiz. It turned out that Polly DeBardelaben got my A, and I got her D.

Good news and bad news. The school was on top of its concern for the students. They checked on us, and the principal gave a damn to call me in and bawled me out. The bad news was he never apologized to me for impugning my character.

High School

Central High School's original name was The High School. Hence an athlete good enough to earn a letter received an "H" and not a "C." My great-aunt was in the first graduating class of Central, so I was a third-generation Warrior.

When I see some kids today not enjoying their educational

experience, I realize how lucky I was to have gone to a great school like Central — a good, safe environment with competent, dedicated teachers who were really concerned for our future. Central football games were held at the old Crump Stadium, which was behind and attached to Central and was Memphis's football venue for high school and college games. Central High football was our family's game of choice when not at a Chicks baseball game.

The yearbook was my thing, only because Ms. Selma Siegman announced to the whole class of women students the first week of entering Central that "tryouts for cheerleader would be held next week for everyone but Jocelyn Dan. She's going to be on the yearbook staff." She was my Sunday school teacher and had already decided my extracurricular activity!

My mother and I both had the same homeroom teacher at Central High — Ms. Laura Mauzy. And she disliked both of us intensely! Mama admitted she wasn't a serious student and used the class to flirt with her beaux, but I was one of those obnoxious goodie-goodies. Ms. Mauzy taught us math and was probably one of the best teachers I ever had. She gave pop quizzes every few days, and a correct answer was awarded with ten points. She would call out, "A great big ten for Anna Kay Robertson." She would print a tiny, little "10" on my paper and not say a word.

One night I had a fever, and Mama said I was to stay home the next day. I had a big math test and threw a fit to get to go to school. I said I would stay home only if Ms. Mauzy said I could. So Mama called her.

"Ms. Mauzy, this is Rose Dan, Jocelyn's mother. Jocelyn has fever and is insisting on coming to school for the test tomorrow ..." Mama's face turned red, her neck shrunk into her shoulders.

"Yes, ma'am. ... Yes, ma'am. ... Yes, ma' ... Yes ... Yes ... Thank you, ma'am." She hung up the phone.

"Well, what did she say?" I asked.

"She said, 'Rose Heyman, you know perfectly well I don't want that child coming to school with fever! You keep her home. You know I will let her make up the test.' She called me by my maiden name and scolded me like she used to. I'm still scared of her."

Once Ms. Mauzy asked us to list our extracurricular activities and how many nights during the week we went out. I was overprogrammed, even as a teenager, going to meetings of some sort every night: B'nai B'rith Girls, Delta Sigma Theta sorority, Sweetheart of AZA, and the board of directors of the Jewish Community Center as its youth representative. On reviewing my list, Ms. Mauzy smirked and said she wasn't amused.

Central was 12 percent Jewish, making it the school with the most Jewish students in the system. Central was considered the college prep high school, so Jewish kids came in from outside the district. But there was some anti-Semitism.

One day Ms. Raucher walked by our table in the cafeteria and asked, "Why is y'all's table of the lunchroom always so messy?" It didn't seem to be any messier than the rest of the room, but I was struck with "y'all." I realized we Jews were segregated. No Jew sat with kids at other tables.

Conscious there was anti-Semitism at school, I was confronted with a dilemma. Selection for the honor society was coming up, and we current members were to sign off on the list of prospective new members as to character. I knew my girlfriend, a Jewish girl, was being proposed, and I knew she cheated. I knew if I checked "no" for her, it would be interpreted as a character problem. If someone respected enough to be proposed by teachers had a fellow student mark "no," I feared the teachers would be looking for cheaters in the entire Jewish population of the school. If she cheated, how many others did?

I was so conflicted that I went to the director of the Jewish Community Center for advice.

He agreed there was potentially a problem, but I would have to decide what to do. It turned out I had a way out. When we met and the current members got the form, there was a column to mark "I don't know him or her." Ms. Siegman, also Jewish, was the honor society advisor-teacher. I took my list to her, and she could see I marked "I don't know her." She knew better, and she knew what I was doing. Mainly I was throwing the ball in her court. The girl made it into the honor society.

Honestly, I never cheated in school and broke up with a boyfriend when I learned he did. But once I did fib and got caught. I was asked to be in a beauty contest to select Miss B'nai B'rith, who would be sent to the City Beautiful contest. I got Mama to write a note for early dismissal for a dental appointment. Damned if I didn't win the contest and was pictured in the newspaper! Mr. King, our principal, called me down to the office.

"Now, about this dental appointment, Jocelyn?"

"Oh, Mr. King, if I told you I needed to leave school early to be in a beauty contest, you couldn't believe that!"

My yearbook activity was a learning experience. I thought I had earned editorship, but I lost to Harriett Barnes. Harriett was away the summer before our senior year, and August 25 was the deadline when the first twenty pages were due to the Dallas printers. I was in town and performed the job well. Right after school started, our teacher-advisor, Ms. Malloy, took Harriett and me to a private place and surprised us by announcing that she had made us co-editors. Dallas had been informed, and the pages denoting staff had been amended. In other words, this wasn't a negotiable rearrangement. Harriett left the meeting in tears. I told Ms. Malloy that I felt badly for Harriett; Ms. Malloy said I deserved it.

We published a pretty good yearbook and had fun doing it. I was in charge of the photography. Luckily for me, the darkroom was downstairs at the north end of the main floor, and our yearbook office was on the south end of the second floor. Lucky, because I had an excuse to go downstairs where my crush, Bobby Bostick, was the hall monitor. We only had a rainy-day sock-hop dancing relationship, since I couldn't date non-Jewish boys, but it was fun to go flirt with him every day. Never could I have imagined at the time that Robert L. Bostick Jr. would become my lifelong soulmate!

My best photo was of a perplexed class looking at the blackboard. The picture appeared to be seen from the back of the blackboard looking through a reverse image of a diagrammed sentence. I remain a shutterbug.

The last day of school before graduation, our senior class gave Ms. Mauzy a luncheon at Anderton's. I chaired the affair but told our class president not to tell her, and I wouldn't sit at the head table. During lunch, I received a note. Her handwriting was unmistakable. "Please come see me in the morning at ten o'clock."

Ms. Mauzy said she knew I had put on the luncheon. She confided that she had been in constant pain for the last number of years and probably should have quit teaching, but she couldn't bring herself to do it. Then she apologized to me.

"I've taken it out on you for no reason." She asked my forgiveness and gave me a warm handshake.

My most remembered moment at Central was Principal Robert King stopping me in the hall one day and asking what my college plans were. I told him I hoped to go to Southwestern, but my father was ill, and I could go only if I received a scholarship. He said, "Wait a minute." In a few minutes he came out of his office and said, "Let's go over and visit that school." He actually put me in his car and drove me over there. No permission from my parents, no forms to fill out. As a principal, he would be put under a jail for putting a teenage girl student in his car and driving off campus in today's world, but this was 1957.

Ms. Bess Wolfe, the admissions director of Southwestern, now Rhodes College, was waiting for us. Sputnik had gone off that morning, and we talked about the impact that would have on our country, on education, on politics, and other topics. After a pleasant visit, Mr. King said, "By the way, Jocelyn won't be able to come here if she doesn't get a scholarship. Just wanted to let you know. I've got to get her back to school."

A few days later he called me to the office to tell me I had received a scholarship to Southwestern!

College

Southwestern, a Presbyterian liberal arts college with a student population of five hundred, was a good experience for me. I was exposed to real Christianity. Between the MAN course and Senior Bible, I learned what real Christianity was — not the televangelist version, nor the Tea Party's, neither of which felt Christ-like to me, but real Christianity and the community of the church.

For the first time, I made real friends who weren't Jewish. Here I was, 50 to 100 percent of the Jewish population in any semester and delighted to be enlarging my circle of friends to include people of other religions. I still could not date outside my faith, so I dated the Jewish men in Memphis who didn't go away to college or those older than me who had returned home after graduating.

I signed up for sorority rush, but the dean of women called me into her office to let me know I wouldn't be allowed to join one, being Jewish and all.

"Oh, I know. I just wanted the experience and to let the girls know I was open to friendships," I said.

Rush was fascinating. We prospects were seated on the floor in a circle and members, in an inner circle, took turns in a clockwise motion to interview us.

Tri Delta sorority invited me back the second day. I got a midnight call from a member I knew from high school asking if I would be willing to take a pledge to the sorority in Christ's name.

"I'll do it in God's name, but doing it in Christ's name isn't valid for you or me. How did I get a recommendation?"

"We got your ninth-grade Latin teacher to write one for you."

I didn't get invited to the third day of rush.

On an errand for Mother, I stopped by a family friend's to drop something off. Evelyn Beatus asked how college was going, and I told her I was excited to be considered to be the first Jew in Tri Delta.

"Big deal! So they are considering to take in a Jew. Shame on you for being excited. If they don't take you, it's their loss." What a life lesson she gave me.

For a lot of my classmates, I was their first Jew. They had to give me "the word" and felt compelled to convert me. Eventually, I had to go to Professor Neal and ask, "How do I call them off? I'm exhausted defending my Judaism. I know they mean well, but ..."

One student asked me, "Jocelyn, where are you from?"

"Memphis."

"Well, I mean your mother."

"She's from Memphis."

Looking a bit quizzical, the student asked, "Your grandmother?"

"Memphis. I'm a fifth-generation Memphian. Why do you ask?"

"Oh, you're not really an American; you're a Jew, aren't you?"

Along with the fourth-grade President Truman story, I've used this as one of my "prejudice" stories for the Panel of American Women.

All freshmen took an extraordinary humanities course titled, politically incorrectly, Man in the Light of History and Religion. A survey of philosophy, history, literature, and religion, it exposed us to liberal arts on day one. One of the professors actually worked on the newly discovered, at the time, Dead Sea Scrolls.

I had signed up for an eight o'clock economics class with Professor Han, who voiced "er" between every syllable. I could barely stay awake. I didn't get the hang of things that first semester; I received a 2.3 GPA, but it rose to 3.2 the following semester. I also switched from econ to sociology in the second semester, and landed exactly in the right place.

Dr. Jack Conrad, more an anthropologist than a sociologist, ran the one-man department. We liked each other. We studied the culture and art of people around the world. The main takeaway was that even "primitive" cultures have socioeconomic structures that may be working better for their societies than our "advanced" culture may be working for us. Thus, it may not be too smart to judge other people by our values.

One day a noted anthropologist was visiting the campus and asked to see the anthropoids at our zoo. It was "colored" day, and it almost took an act of Congress to get him in.

Between Dr. Conrad's dedication that we could learn from all mankind and my political science professor Lowery, I left Southwestern a liberal Republican. That was not an oxymoron at the time. That pleased my father-in-law, who bragged he never voted for Roosevelt four times.

I made some wonderful women friends at Southwestern, which was a rarity for me. Most were Tri Delts: Lynn Finch, who later would take me to her farm in France; Bunky Haigler; and Maysie Cobb. Maysie had taken me to her home in Durham Estates in Mobile,

Alabama, for Thanksgiving. In helping her mother prepare, Mrs. Cobb said she would handle her antique demitasse herself. They were family heirlooms and precious to her.

After dinner, the men went into one room and the women into another. I listened in on the discussion for the men, whether rifles were still appropriate on their hunting grounds since the number of family hunting had grown so much. Perhaps everyone needed to switch to shotguns, not quite so deadly in a confined space.

Cleaning up after dinner, the maid's daughter, not knowing the demitasse were to be handled only by Mrs. Cobb, fell while carrying them on a tray and broke most of them. I saw Mrs. Cobb consoling the child, who was sobbing uncontrollably. "It's not your fault, darling. Don't worry about it. It's not important." I observed real Christianity in action. I also observed Mrs. Cobb going to her bedroom and shedding a private tear herself.

Since I married between my sophomore and junior year, my girlfriends had a place in town to stay when they had special dates. They could sign out of the dorm and not have to observe a curfew.

Later, Bunky and I put on a mini-reunion for our dear friend Maysie at her home in Macon, Georgia. Her multiple sclerosis prevented her from coming to Memphis for reunions, so we went to her. We lost Maysie and Lynn shortly after that event.

If I have a criticism for Southwestern, it is that a whole civil rights movement was going on in our country, and our school didn't acknowledge it. Nothing was ever mentioned on campus nor presented in class discussions. It was, after all, a southern conservative school, but exposure then could have shaved years off my ignorance.

All seniors must take Senior Bible, a course on the New Testament. It was interesting for me, especially since I had never read the New Testament. As a non-believer, I had a different slant on it. Jesus said, "I am the son of God, I am your brother, we are all the children of God, we are all brothers, thus we all should behave Christ-like." Sounded like the Jews' covenant with God to me.

I really took the course seriously and became upset with the final exam. There was a weird question. There were a number of Middle-Eastern names listed with the instruction to circle the places Paul visited. I thought to myself, "What a crock! Ask me what Paul said, not where the hell he said it!"

In 1982, I took a Greek island cruise and the ship made a stop at Ephesus. We walked down incredibly restored Roman ruins, and when we got to the end, we took a right and came upon a Roman coliseum. The tour guide said, "And this is the very spot where the Apostle Paul spoke to the Ephesians here in Ephesus!"

Ding-a-ling-a-ling. Ephesians! They lived in Ephesus! And I'm standing here in Ephesus! Thank you, Rhodes. Thank you, Rhodes.

Chapter Six

Daddy, Charles Lewis Dan

I adored my father! If there ever was a Daddy's girl, it was I. Daddy was brilliant, creative, fun-loving, and oh, so handsome. People would say, "Your daddy looks like a movie star." He loved music and dancing; his hobby was writing. He possessed the kind of personality that lit up any room he entered. And he adored me back.

Daddy was born in Memphis in 1916, and while his family moved to Tulsa when he was two weeks old, he moved back to Memphis about 1938. He had six brothers, all handsome men, and one sister, who was stunningly beautiful, even up into her nineties. His parents were Sol and Molly Berger Dan.

According to his obituary, my grandfather Sol was an advertising and marketing genius. Once on a bet, Sol Dan proved he could sell blankets retail in August and started the annual August blanket sale, now well-known in retail trade circles. On a roll, he also created the January white sale, a department store tradition that still exists today.

At one time, he ran a nickelodeon and emceed a vaudeville show. A "nickelodeon" was a movie theater for silent movies before talkies, and the appropriate music for the scene on the screen was provided by a scripted player piano when there wasn't a live pianist. A vaudeville show was a live performance of numerous acts. Not to the level of a Broadway show, vaudeville was a variety show, often a bit on the risqué side. Sol died in 1941, so I never knew him.

Grandma Molly was a stereotype of what a grandmother

looked like, gray hair pulled back into a bun, overweight with huge drooping breasts. I rarely saw her in anything but a house dress. With eight children, the family joked that Sol, a traveling salesman, impregnated her every time he came home. When the Dan family moved back to Memphis in the late 1930s, Grandma Molly lived in a back apartment of a "U"-shaped building on McLean. We went there on Sunday mornings for a family breakfast and, upon entering the "U," a family member would give the family whistle announcing our arrival. Then someone inside would whistle back saying, "Come on up."

Daddy did not seem to miss his Orthodox rearing too much. Mother converted him to Reform Judaism immediately; he loved all forms of treif, barbecue pork, and lobster, prohibited for Jews under the laws of kosher. While we celebrated Hanukkah, he adopted a secular version of Christmas. The storyline was that Santa Claus brought our Christmas tree with him Christmas Eve, but it had to be disassembled and out of the house the next day after Christmas morning so that Santa Claus could take the tree to children on the other side of the world. The real cause was fear that some of Daddy's family would drive down the street and see Christmas lights through the window.

My dad's crazy tradition was to go out about midnight Christmas Eve with some guy friends and steal a tree. They left a dollar, 1943 prices, but in essence, it was a theft. The men would come home and decorate the tree, including those lights that heated up the colored water contained in little glass tubes, making the tree literally bubble with colors. Then they would assemble the train set or the dollhouse in time to be ready for the big Christmas morning surprise.

Daddy had me fully convinced he was Superman. After all, like Clark Kent, he was a newspaperman. He traveled a lot for his work, but he told me that besides his job, he had a lot to do as Superman. For my sixth birthday, Daddy made me a phonograph at a local studio: It began, as did the radio program, "It's a bird. No, it's a plane! No, it's Superman! But I'm taking off my uniform and staying home today because it's my daughter Jocelyn's birthday.

She is six years old today and becoming quite a grownup young lady. While she's grown up, it still doesn't mean she can cross the street without having to hold my hand, but ..."

He taught me how to dance by standing me on his shoes as we did the rumba, samba, and foxtrot. Pre-television, we were always putting on skits at the house. Once, Daddy dressed me in black and blackface. He put on his tuxedo, and I became Eddie Jackson to his Ted Lewis, singing and soft-shoe dancing to "Me and My Shadow." I still have some one-sided, Brunswick labeled 78 vinyl Al Jolson records and the original Xavier Cugat samba album.

Daddy loved all kinds of music — jazz, pop, classical, and especially Broadway theater — and tried to expose me to it all. He was a bit displeased, however, when I was a bit older and he heard the Coasters' lyrics from my 45-record player: "You the cutest thing that I did ever see. I really love your peaches, want to shake your tree, lovey dovey," written by Edward Curtis and Ahmet Ertegun. Daddy just walked out shaking his head.

When we said my bedtime prayers, "Now I lay me down to sleep," and after we blessed every living relative, all of our friends, and the dog, I was taught to add, "and make me a sweet and smart girl tomorrow. Amen."

My father taught me it was smart to be smart. When I reached junior high, I complained to him that there were sororities, clubs, and some school-elected positions that were off limits to Jewish kids. He dismissed it out of hand.

"They can't keep you out of the honor society, can they?"

My father and I would talk — a lot. We talked about the newspaper headlines. At ten years old, I understood about the Aswan Dam, the debate over who would help Egypt build it, Russia or the West, and why it was important. He was tickled that I was interested, and he made the headlines interesting.

Daddy inherited his father's advertising gene and became a newspaper advertising representative. His clients were small-town weekly and daily newspapers in the Mid-South, papers too small and too understaffed to have their own national ad department, and his job was to get them national products' advertising such as

Kellogg's Rice Krispies for the *Oak Ridger* newspaper.

The deal back then was that there was a huge differential between the cost of running an ad in a major market newspaper and a small-town paper. The price of advertising per agate inch in a local paper may have been fifty dollars. But the national agate-inch rate might be one hundred dollars. In newspaper talk, an agate inch is a newspaper column wide and an inch in height. If Dole was willing to pay the paper the national rate to advertise pineapples, the local Clarksville, Tennessee, *Leaf-Chronicle* paper could run the ad for less cost to that newspaper. The labor wasn't union, and southern salaries were less. Thus, that was a potent ad. The price margin between the national agate-inch dollar rate and what the small-town paper's agate inch cost kept these papers thriving for decades until technology allowed the nearby large city newspapers to compose, print, and distribute their papers to these towns by morning. Daddy's business died about 1958.

Ken Howard, a partner of Daddy's, had brought a French bride to America after World War II. She created a charm school to teach children the French language and French manners. Every Saturday morning, we went to her home dressed in our best clothes for tea and instructions on the proper way to hold the teacup. We could name every item *sur la table*. I learned pretension at an early age.

A perk of Daddy's business was my going to the Tennessee Press Association meetings with him. We attended one in Gatlinburg, Tennessee, when I was fifteen years old. The editor and publisher of the Oak Ridge paper, Don McKay, said, "Jocelyn, I want to teach you a little lesson about politics."

He walked me over to Estes Kefauver, then a senator, and said, "Estes, you remember Charlie Dan's daughter, don't you?"

Kefauver commenced an "Oh, look how much you've grown and what a pretty young lady you've become."

When we left, I said, "Uncle Don, I've never met the senator before."

"That's the lesson I wanted to teach you about politics."

Daddy was a terrific public speaker and taught me the difference in writing for reading and writing for listening. It's all in the timing, he would tell me. He was also a great joke teller, teaching the difference between a clever risqué joke and simply a coarse bathroom joke, the difference between good Jewish humor and a hurtful anti-Semitic joke. A good risqué joke is: Do you know the difference between an automobile tire and 365 used condoms? One is a Goodyear and the other is a great year! An anti-Semitic joke is: Do you know the difference between a Jew and a gentile at a football game? A gentile says, "Go team, go." A Jew says, "Get that quarterback ..."

I have been known to regale folks with jokes when I get wound up. I can tell joke after joke, and people say I tell a joke pretty well. And I am pretty comfortable in front of a mic. Thank you, Daddy.

He was also a good writer. He even submitted essays to the *New Yorker* magazine, but none were accepted. He struck up a correspondence with Harry Golden, the Carolina Israelite, who authored *For Two Cents Plain*; he had complimentary things to say to Daddy. One essay was about the unsung heroes of our time, like the man who struck Casey out, and the first person to eat an artichoke. He had a unique sense of humor, and it drew people to him.

Daddy also wrote letters to the editor. One in particular was to critique Memphis's movie and book censor, Lloyd T. Binford. Mr. Binford headed a censor board to review movies with his friends in attendance in his office atop the Columbia Mutual Tower building. This was later renamed the Lincoln American Tower, where I rented half of the nineteenth floor for my law office. He disallowed any movie with Ingrid Bergman, thinking her a wanton woman; any interracial love scenes; or any movie with a train robbery, since he had been in one.

Daddy's letter said Binford was falling down on the job. He needed to ban nursery rhymes. After all, Jack and Jill fell down the hill, one tumbling down atop the other!

Paul Schwartz, the director of our Jewish Community Center; Seymour Gilman; and Daddy did the most clever thing. They were co-producers of parody skits in Memphis, mostly for fundraisers for our local philanthropic organizations. Popular Broadway plays were adapted into the charity's theme. Mother was president of the United Order of True Sisters, our country's first national Jewish women's organization. Each local chapter was assigned a woman's first name, and the Memphis chapter was called Regina. For a Regina fashion show fundraiser, the men adapted Cole Porter's *Kiss Me Kate* into song-and-dance routines. The song "Tom, Dick, and Harry" became "Hart, Schaffner, and Marx." They were well done, extremely popular, and raised a lot of money. There was no lack of talent.

One year they decided to write and produce a song-and-dance format for giving the report at the Jewish Community Center's annual meeting. They called it *I Hate Annual Meetings!* A usually ill-attended and boring meeting became a standing-room-only happening, held over for an additional run the next night.

Daddy was fond of Jack Paar and a real fan of the late-night talk show format. He and Paul Schwartz created "Late Night at the Center." Once a month, starting about ten o'clock on Saturday night, Daddy held forth, telling jokes and interviewing fellow Memphians. It, too, was a hit.

Mother and Daddy's crowd of friends took turns hosting the Treasure Hunt. The Treasure Hunt was a brain-teaser game that was played for money. Four or five people per automobile, casually dressed with running shoes, would arrive at the host house in a car equipped with telephone books, a dictionary, pencils, paper, and flashlights. There could be as many as ten to twelve teams.

The hosts would collect one dollar per person, announce the Memphis street boundaries, and hand out the first clue. The boundary might be between McLean and Perkins, between Central and North Parkway or Summer. A clue would be a picture, words, objects, and the answer was someone's name in the phone book. Under the clue would be two numbers, one the sum of the numbers in the person's telephone number and the other the sum of the numbers in the person's address. If the sums matched, you solved the puzzle. If that person lived within the boundary, you raced to that address and looked for the next clue attached to the closest light pole. If the correct person lived out of the boundary, the clue would say "down seven, left two." That would be the address seven book-listed names down and two columns to the left and that name would be in the boundary.

When you read the new clue, you signed your car captain's name on the light pole and commenced work on the puzzle. You knew how your team was doing by the number of signatures.

A clue might be an empty box of Old Spice solid deodorant. The answer was "a B O (bad odor) stick." You would find in the phone book the name "Bostick" on Perkins Road, speed to the address since it was within the boundary, and look for the new clue on a utility or light pole near the Bosticks' house. If you were hopelessly stuck, you could call the hosts, and they would give you a clue if your team was behind. The first car back to the hosts could win as much as fifty dollars, a huge amount in the 1940s and 1950s, and desserts awaited the contestants. There might be six of these games a year, and only the most clever participants would take turns creating the games.

In 1998, I uncovered a stash of Mother's memorabilia that I neglected to find when she died in 1979. It contained love letters Daddy wrote to Mama. Among them was a Mother's Day letter he wrote to her as the fetus in her womb. "HE," the fetus, said "HE" was very happy in "Mr. Joshua's nursery" but couldn't wait to finish his nine-month course of study and get big enough to come home to her.

Finding this letter was disconcerting. It was dated Mother's Day, May 14, 1939. He wrote her again May 24, 1939, and in this letter, he referenced a new kid in the nursery who he claimed would be "HIS" first cousin (George Lapides, 1939-2016). I was born August 3, 1940. Thus I wasn't conceived until November 1939. Mama must have had a pregnancy before me and lost the baby. I never knew this, and none of her friends still with us whom I queried knew anything about a miscarriage or stillbirth either. But, they added, folks didn't talk about miscarriages in those days. Cousin George was born November 1939. All the letters were signed "Charles Jr.," so my daddy, who adored me, really wanted a boy!

In 1958, when I was a high school senior, Daddy was diagnosed with four enlarged heart valves. This was way before repair of such things was developed to the art it is today. He was told he had to lead a sedentary life and that business traveling was out of the question. Besides servicing the newspapers he represented throughout the Mid-South, Daddy normally traveled to New York three or four times a year. He could no longer perform those duties and had to give up his company.

But Daddy had ideas. He tried to start a new company — with hardly any capital or cash flow. He wanted to help others develop advertising strategies.

One of the more interesting ones was designed for customers of our transit system. It was a game with prizes. A bus rider received a free "Brand-O" card, similar to a bingo card, but instead of numbers, there were pictures of products or names of companies. The Memphis Transit Authority already had inside and outside bus advertising; it was a lucrative business owned by Tom O'Brien. All O'Brien had to do was paste a code number on his ads each week, and riders would have to read the ads to get the code numbers to put on their Brand-O cards. If, as in bingo, they got a line in a row or four corners, they were winners. Imagine consumers searching for ads to read! O'Brien used the idea after it was pitched and instituted a bus advertising game idea without Daddy.

No matter how talented you are, or how good your ideas are, there are some in business who will take advantage of you if they smell that you're desperate. And that's what happened to Daddy. He was pretty down and out. Nothing was working for him. He resorted to borrowing money from family but knew that wasn't limitless.

He found solace in prescription drugs — all legally prescribed — but way too many. Handfuls of drugs to go to sleep and handfuls to wake up! His doctor took offense when I went to visit him to question the wisdom of this, but he didn't see the slurred speech and crazy talk as the family did.

I hurt Daddy's feelings so badly. His best friend and best man at his wedding owned a shoe store. In a tearful exchange, I begged Daddy to do anything but what he was doing.

"Sell shoes for Uncle Joe, Daddy," I said. "You don't have to own your own business; I don't care. We all love and need you whatever you do."

Daddy had insurance, a sizable amount that assured the family's security in his absence. Charles Dan wasn't going to sell shoes. So in 1961, at the age of forty-four, he committed suicide — while I was on my honeymoon. So talented and such a loss; I miss him all the time.

Remembering Him on Father's Day

In June 2006, I was among a few people asked to participate in writing a Father's Day article for the *Best Times*, a free monthly publication targeted to seniors that's available at stores and restaurants.

We were asked about the most important lessons we had learned from our fathers. The life lessons I learned have held me in good stead, and I have incorporated them into the peer mediation course I teach to students.

Daddy taught me:

1. Never paint yourself into a corner; you always have to leave yourself an "out."

2. Never push someone else into a corner so that the only way out is by fighting.

3. Leave all your options open. Why close one out if you don't have to? I lecture to kids that if you can make As and Bs, but make Cs and Ds, you're closing out options. The "somebodies" out there who have the power will tell you where you get to go to school; it won't be you telling them where you want to go to school.

4. Don't give up your power. Lose your cool, you lose your power.

5. Be all you can be. Don't be told by someone else what you can or can't be.

6. Run whatever you're going to say through your brain before you let it come out of your mouth.

I have trouble with the last one.

Chapter Seven

Mama, Rose Sternberger
Heyman Dan Felsenthal

Rose Heyman Dan was a smart, strong, sweet, competent woman, none of which I realized until my Daddy died and I decided to check her out. Rose was pretty and dressed attractively and appropriately; she was a proper lady at all times.

She was my mother, and I so regret to admit I didn't care for her. Probably I was jealous of my father's devotion to her. When Mama and I disagreed on anything, he would tell me, "Right or wrong, she's your mother, right or wrong." The way I translated it was "I know you're right, but I have to side with her."

Mother was sickly — a lot — with the result that, with Daddy traveling so much, I reared myself. When she was feeling better, she delighted in getting out of bed and out of the house to be with friends. Being with surly me couldn't have been much of a pleasure.

Mother quit working when Daddy was doing well, but then she was impressed into Jewish civil service as a volunteer. She was competent in whatever she undertook; she was president of the Regina chapter of the United Order of True Sisters and on the board of the Temple Sisterhood.

Her illness was constant throughout the 1950s. And sadly, she got labeled a crank. Someone let Daddy know that doctors talked behind her back, teasing about who would fall heir to her next. A psychiatrist even put her in a mental institution and gave that poor woman shock treatment. The story goes that Dr. Pasture was called late at night from the hospital after the shock procedure and was told Rose was throwing up and having diarrhea. He ordered two tablespoons of paregoric and said, "Call me in the morning." He claims he went back to bed and arose in a jolt.

"My God, she's a paregoric addict! Doctors have been ordering her paregoric all her life!" It is a form of opium.

She remained at the hospital to help her with withdrawal from the drug, but she continued with similar gastric symptoms. It was not until the 1970s that Mayo Clinic agreed to accept Mother in an experimental program. Medical science was beginning to explore lactose intolerance, and Mayo Clinic diagnosed Mother with that condition. All those years of constant pain and erroneous treatments, and it turned out she couldn't tolerate milk products. She also had a wheat allergy. I had resented her absence as a mother, and it wasn't her fault. I was so ashamed for my insensitivity toward her.

When Daddy lost his company, Mama went back to work at Levy's (then Gus Mayer's), the same store where she had sold shoes during World War II. Actually, Mama was a terrific sales lady. She sold costume jewelry, finely crafted pieces by designers such as Miriam Haskell. Pieces that sold for $20 or $30 back then now sell for $1,200 to $1,500!

When Mama was too ill to work, they let me come in her place. She didn't handle Daddy's predicament very well; she had to be feeling terribly insecure. Both sides of the family were helping us out, and it embarrassed her. But she tried to maintain her pride. She and Daddy were popular, but Mama began to refuse invitations to parties.

"We can't afford to pay back," she said.

She felt she couldn't reciprocate adequately. I used to tell her that they were so popular and attractive, people would be happy to come eat hamburgers, but she had too much pride.

While we ate a lot of tuna fish salad for dinner, Mama would take a large iceberg lettuce leaf, wet the edges, and dip them in paprika, giving the lettuce bowl a red lining. Then she would turn them over and put in a scoop of tuna fish, serving them as if she was having ladies over for luncheon. She tried so hard to be poor with dignity.

After Daddy died, I made a conscious decision that Mama was my only parent left, and I needed to make the effort to be a better daughter. And I'm glad I did. I discovered she was not a weak person; to the contrary, Mama was strong and worked so hard to be a good widowed single mom.

Mama married her distant cousin, Robert Henry Felsenthal, and moved to Brownsville, Tennessee. Robert was a bachelor, fifty-six, when he fell head over heels for my mother.

Originally from Chicago, Robert and his brother Henry Robert Felsenthal moved down to Brownsville to take over Felsenthal's Department Store, the business some of his family started about the time of the Civil War. When Robert's brother Henry was a little boy, he was on the list that Leopold and Loeb had compiled for their infamous, murderous adventure. Robert and Henry's parents were in the millinery business, and we kids have fallen heir to some old but beautiful table linens.

We visited Brownsville often as children; we had a number of relatives there and had often visited the Reform Jewish Temple there that was built before the Civil War. The stained glass windows lining the walls have our family's names noted as dedicating the art. One window is in memory of so-and-so Sternberger Felsenthal, the next in memory of so-and-so Felsenthal Sternberger. The Temple cemetery is a history lesson, and my Civil War relatives are all buried there.

Mother and Robert were married in October 1962. And they were entertained royally by Brownsville's Jewish families, now dwindling in number.

Months later, Mother decided she would entertain back. Mother did not entertain very much while married to Daddy. But in Brownsville, and married to Robert, they were among the top of that social ladder. Mother knew how to cook and how to entertain beautifully, so she blossomed as one of Brownsville's noted hostesses.

When she began to entertain, she called Elroy to engage him to serve her first party. Elroy politely said that he would not be able to help her as he was already engaged that night. So a few weeks later Mother called him back to engage him for another party in her series. Again Elroy refused, saying he had a previous engagement to work another party.

The third time when Mother called him, he again refused, and Mother said, "Elroy, I know for a fact that nobody else in town had a party the last time I called you. Why won't you serve my party?"

Elroy answered, "Mizz Rose, uz don't understand. Uz a Felsenthal and I only work for the Sternbergers."

"Elroy, my mother was Rae Sternberger!"

Elroy responded, "Oh, Mizz Rose, why didn't you tell me we was family!"

Mama was accepted immediately by the small Jewish community and took her turn as secretary of the Temple. And she was accepted by non-Jews for her cooking skills and for being a card shark. I learned Mama was a superb bridge player. Mama was brave enough to invite our Panel of American Women, the human rights organization I founded, to Brownsville. That took nerve on her part, and she was proud of me.

During a terrible Ku Klux Klan (KKK) demonstration, Mama complained to the FBI official in attendance at a cross burning on the Temple lawn. He told her she would have to address the sheriff; the FBI agent couldn't do anything about it.

She said, "The sheriff? He's one of them in the robes!"

Proud of being a southern Jew with ancestors in the Brownsville Temple cemetery with Confederate States of America designations on their tombstones, Mama became a member of the Daughters of the Confederacy. As a surprise for me, she signed me up as well.

By then, I was enmeshed in civil rights. "Mama! I'm a Golden Heritage member of the NAACP! Unsign me!"

In 1979, I made a miserable mistake. I dragged my son, Richard Jr., on a camping trip from Memphis to New Hampshire with a good friend and her son, who was his classmate. Her child was an experienced camper; Richard wasn't, and that put him in an unequal status. His father didn't want him to go and insisted Richard call him collect all along the way, three and four times a day. I felt sabotaged. I later learned that was a form of what is called parental alienation syndrome. So Richard made it to Washington, DC, where I put him on a plane to go home. I was crushed.

In a moment of inspiration, I called Mama and asked her to meet me in Toronto, Canada, and drive home with me. We could visit Libby, my sister, in Detroit.

"Only on the condition that we stop in Louisville on the way home, and let me show you off to the Kentucky family."

"Deal!"

We had a good time in Canada, and we saw Niagara Falls for our first time. But Mama wasn't well and was pushing herself hard to be a good sport. We decided she should fly to Louisville, and I would meet her there a few days later. The family was charming, and I'm glad I did it.

A few days after Mama returned home, Robert brought her to a Memphis hospital.

"I reach for something over here, but it's over there," she said. She had a brain tumor that was probably metastasized lung cancer.

Mama died that October at age sixty-one. As is the custom, the Daughters of the Confederacy sent a flower wreath. When my civil rights icons Maxine and Vasco Smith came to the funeral home, we chuckled about that wreath. And I was able to thank my son for my having some quality time with my mother.

Chapter Eight

Richard Wurzburg (1934–1992)

Richard and I married on October 29, 1960. I was married in a wheelchair, having left the hospital five days before the wedding. I caught mononucleosis from going to so many engagement parties and dinners and working. Because I was feeling such guilt for leaving our family problems to my brother, I got up early in the morning to play golf with him. Rich and I were going out, coming in to "neck" for a bit, and then I stayed up writing thank-you notes for the beautiful wedding gifts arriving every day. With my getting three to four hours of sleep each night, my mono turned into another debilitating virus; the least amount of activity exhausted me and too much activity could cause a relapse.

The doctors said I could only move once on the wedding day, so instead of going to my parents' house, I went to the Wurzburgs' home from the hospital to convalesce and have the wedding there. My mother-in-law was thrilled since Richard was an only child, and this was her only chance to put on a wedding.

By being married there, we could go that night to the Parkview Hotel, our temporary home while our apartment was being refreshed. Richard's parents owned the apartment building where we were going to be living for the next five years. It was "refreshed" very comfortably.

In July 1960, my friend Carol Underberg called me with an urgent request. "You know the open house I'm having tonight? Well, I know of sixteen guys coming, and you and I are the only girls. Promise me you are still coming."

Hum, I liked those odds. "Sure."

I got cornered at the party by four guys I did not know. One asked, "Do you play tennis?"

"Badly."

Another said, "Do you know how to bowl?"

"I know how, but I'm not really good at it."

Richard asked, "Do you water ski?"

"No, but I'm dying to learn." We made a date for Sunday week.

I wasn't quite ready when he came for me at ten o'clock, so I sent my baby sister, Libby, to greet him with a glass of orange juice. It was a cloudless July morning and hot enough that water skiing would feel good. We needed to go to his house to pick up the ski boat, so I got to meet his mother, Matil.

Our first meeting was interesting. When Richard took me in to meet her, a friend of my mother's, Dorothy Davis, was there having coffee. I shook hands with Mrs. Wurzburg and then went over and kissed Mama's friend with a greeting. "Hi, Aunt Dossy."

I later learned that Matil asked, "Well, who is she?" Aunt Dossy was shrewd. She didn't say, "Rose and Charlie Dan's daughter." She didn't say, "Rae and J.B. Heyman's granddaughter." She went back to my grandmother's maiden name and declared, "She is Rae Sternberger's granddaughter." The old Memphis Jewish family name made me immediately acceptable.

The first date was fun. We picked up another couple and went to a cabin Richard's parents had on Horseshoe Lake in Arkansas, about forty-five minutes southwest of Memphis. Richard was a great water skier and could teach it so well. I got up on the second try. The men cooked steaks while we women made a salad.

Rich asked me for a dinner date for the next Saturday, and since I told him that would be fine and it was my birthday, he said for me to pick where I wanted to go to celebrate. I chose our only Chinese restaurant; it would have been crass to pick an expensive place.

My mother told my Aunt Mildred about my date with Richard, and she immediately took me to lunch. Lord, she lobbied hard for him. "I know this family. They are lovely people. You need to give this man a chance."

At the next week's lunch she said, "Jocelyn, Richard is marriage material. Y'all would be a perfect match. Your getting married would be so helpful to your parents." (They were then in severe financial straits, so I would be one less mouth to feed.) "You wouldn't have to work. You won't need to finish college." That last point was almost a deal breaker; I wanted to finish college.

When Richard brought me home one night, I told him to be careful not to trip on some lumber I had placed in the carport.

"What are you going to do with it?" he asked.

"I'm making some bookshelves for my room." And I detailed how I was going to put some rope through a ceiling beam and then thread it through the lumber and place a knot under the wood to hold the shelves in place.

"Oh, you know how to use a drill?"

"No, I'm going to whittle the holes."

I know he thought that was crazy; he said he was handy with tools and would be happy to help me. We fell in love making bookshelves over the next three nights. He said so first, after the first month of dating, and I responded back a week or so later. He was so kind to me, and for the first time in a long time, I felt safe, secure, and loved. We were engaged six weeks after meeting and married two months later.

Mama and Daddy were pleased with my marrying Richard. I was reared to marry a wealthy Reform Jewish Memphis doctor, but a wealthy Reform Jewish Memphis businessman was just as good. I think Daddy was relieved I had married well; I was taken care of, and Aunt Mildred was right — there was one less mouth to feed and have to worry about. Besides, he liked Richard. Daddy was pretty much a straight arrow, and Richard certainly was. Aunt Mildred bought my trousseau.

Richard and I planned a honeymoon trip to the famous Greenbrier Hotel in White Sulphur Springs, West Virginia, but plans changed. When we came in one night, my folks were up and said, "Y'all need to run out to Ridgeway," the Jewish country club where the Wurzburgs belonged. The club had a "Vegas night" party. Richard, knowing we had other plans that night and couldn't go, meant to return his raffle tickets to win a free trip to Las Vegas. He was charged for them, and damn if he didn't win!

Richard's father, Reggie, came back to the bedroom where I was convalescing and said he knew someone who could play a fiddle. "Would you like some music for the wedding?" he asked.

Certainly, I would. And then I was overjoyed when he said the fiddle player was Joy Brown Wiener, concertmistress for the Memphis Symphony. He spent the afternoon finding her a thank-you present and scored big when he found a gold charm of a violin in a tiny case.

Mrs. Wiener was adorable. "I've been working on a medley of Stephen Foster songs; would you like that?"

My face must have displayed disappointment.

"No, of course not," she said.

I told her I loved the music from the Broadway play *Kismet*. "Oh, Borodin, perfect!" and it was, especially played on her Stradivarius.

At the wedding, I was allowed to get out of the wheelchair, stand up for the ceremony, and then sit back down during the reception. The ceremony was family only, and the house was decorated beautifully with flowers. I didn't see any of it until I was wheeled into the den where the vows took place that night.

Life at the Parkview Hotel, aptly named since it was located at the Overton Park entrance, was fun for the month. Richard and I had a large suite, and dinner was sent up each night. I still required bed rest and some nursing care, so I was spoiled with help. A month later, we moved into our two-bedroom apartment three blocks up the street. The rooms were spacious and, thanks to the numerous windows, they were bright. The apartment had been in the family for decades, and most Wurzburg cousins started their marriages there.

Mom had a ball decorating it. She brought photos of furniture and swatches of material for me to select upholstery and draperies. It was in conservative taste, but I liked it. However, when I first walked into my new home, my heart sank. The carpet was awful and didn't match the rest of the color scheme.

I didn't say anything. And it appeared Mom thought the same

thing and didn't say anything. She thought I had vetoed a decision, and I thought perhaps she had. Neither of us wanted to hurt the other's feelings. A few weeks later she broached the subject, saying, "The carpet surely looks different in this sunlight." I got the sample I thought we had selected, and we both laughed. They had covered the entire space with the wrong carpet, and we both were still walking on eggs trying to be so nice to each other.

College became an issue. My illness kept me out of school the fall semester of my junior year. One of my scholarships was from the Kahn trust at the Jewish Welfare Fund in Memphis. When I called to check about resuming school at Southwestern that spring semester, I was informed I had lost my scholarship.

"There's no way we can justify giving a scholarship to a Wurzburg."

"But my husband can't afford to send me to college, and my father's economic predicament is getting worse," I said.

Those words fell on deaf ears. So I enrolled in Memphis State. Four weeks into the semester, I got a call from Southwestern.

"You've been given a complete scholarship to come back to school," my math professor said.

Figuring out my new father-in-law was my patron didn't take a nuclear physicist. I never found out how many other kids to whom he had to donate a scholarship to get that phone call to happen. I waited until the next fall to start back; four weeks behind at Southwestern was too much for me to catch up.

Our courtship had been fun. We went to hear Van Cliburn, to theater, concerts, and symphony. After marriage, Richard confessed he didn't enjoy theater, concerts, or symphony. Ugh. And I can't believe I got engaged to someone before we went dancing! He wasn't very good at that. Ugh, again.

"So what do you enjoy doing?"

"Sports, hunting, fishing, target shooting." Okay, I could be a dutiful wife and take up those things. I learned to bait a live cricket or worm on a fishing hook. Richard bought me a 20-gauge Remington 1100, and I shot doves out of the sky. I took them home and learned how to cook them. We shot so much skeet and trap, 400 rounds three days a week, we started reloading our own shotgun shells.

Matil, his mom, loved theater, so we often attended together. She took me to New York a few times just for plays, and we would see eight plays in six days. I wished for a hand to hold at some theatrical moments, but here I was, at last, on the real Broadway! And she was good company.

With my illness, our Las Vegas honeymoon was delayed until June. We drove out there and were having a wonderful time. We were told to call Mr. Carl Cohen's office when we arrived at the Sands Hotel. His secretary arranged all our reservations to the various shows so "CC Good" was noted beside our name. We were always ushered down front to ringside seats.

Vegas shows are terrific fun. The first night we saw the singer Eddie Fisher when his then-wife, Elizabeth Taylor, dressed up like a waitress, dropped the whole platter of plates to interrupt the show. They had a little colloquy from the tables up to the stage, to the delight of us in the audience.

Frank Sinatra was playing at the Sands and was actually too impaired to be performing. So the entire "Rat Pack" jumped up on stage to save the show, including Peter Lawford, married to a Kennedy; Sammy Davis Jr.; Dean Martin; and Joey Bishop. They all ad-libbed with Sinatra, making the performance so special.

Afterward in the bar, they came and sat at the table next to ours. I screwed up my courage and asked if they would autograph a bar card that the Sands had on the table. I was so proud of getting all the Rat Pack on one piece of paper that I stupidly placed it on my hotel room mirror to display. It was scarfed up by the cleaning crew.

Early the next morning, we got a phone call. Daddy had taken very sick, and I needed to fly home right away. Plane reservations had been made for me, and Richard would drive home by himself. Daddy had gone into the hospital the night before, but the folks ascertained there was no way for me to get home, so there was no sense telling me until I could.

I went straight to the hospital from the airport. Daddy was in one room, and Mama was next door in another room in such stress she needed hospital care. Daddy's family was standing around, keeping vigil for him and barely disguising their disgust for Mama's weakness. Daddy had taken poison and lost consciousness. I like to think he knew I was there. Richard made it home in less than two days and in time to accompany me to Daddy's funeral.

As I said, Richard was a sweet man, highly capable with a genius IQ, and not pretentious with the wealth of his family. He worked for the family business, Wurzburg Brothers, a shipping and packaging supply company located in six states; while incorporated, all the stock was owned one-half by Richard and his father and one-half by Richard's uncle and his three children.

The business was founded in 1908, by his grandfather, so Rich was the third generation. But he was the youngest of the cousins by fifteen years. At a University of Tennessee reunion, I got him to say, "I started out as a truck dock worker and have risen to vice president — of my father's business."

Richard had gone to Pentecost-Garrison School for elementary school and then to Culver Military Academy in Indiana. He said he learned to drive a tank before he drove a car.

From there he went to the University of Tennessee, where he was selected to Omicron Delta Kappa, a leadership fraternity; joined Zeta Beta Tau Jewish fraternity; and was selected for the exclusive Scarabbean Society. I'm not sure what that did, but he was one of three men inducted that year. The other two were Johnny Majors and the dean of men. Every few years Richard would receive a black-covered pamphlet with no identification on it containing names, addresses, and phone numbers.

Rich could do everything fairly well. He would pick up a new hobby, work at getting pretty good at it, and then drop it. Bowling, golf, archery. For a first baby present, I gave him a stereo radio kit to put together, and it worked! He was a good tennis player but rarely played.

I came home one Sunday afternoon to a smoky apartment.

"It's okay," he said. "No big problem. I decided to bake you a cake, and I learned a good lesson. We have to leave at six o'clock, and I figured if it took one hour at 350 degrees, I could bake it at 425 for thirty-eight minutes."

With our honeymoon having been cut short, we went to the West Coast a year later. We were advised to go to the Purple Onion in San Francisco to see this new singing sensation. She wasn't pretty. Her high notes seemed more of a scream than a song. We both agreed this Streisand woman would never make it.

Richard was a good father — for the times. Being a great father didn't mean he would ever change a diaper. But he was proud of the kids and very hands-on with their activities. Except swimming. Richard was extremely hairy and embarrassed by it. I shamed him into going swimming with us one day, and a friend's child climbed onto his lap, grabbed a handful of hair, and said, "Uncle Richard, you look just like a monkey!"

We were a pretty good team for the first eight years. We had a nice social life, mostly with his childhood friends. I finished college, we built a house, reared three wonderful children, performed the requisite service on various boards, and did charity work. Richard did not enjoy travel, so we rarely did and only went abroad once. Most trips we took were business-related.

Building a house was a great experience. It was duplicating a market house, so we didn't get to be too creative. But I realized that I had workmen building a house they could not afford for themselves. I schmeicheled (Yiddish for "flattered") the men all the time, and asked for advice. I brought them sandwiches and booze for Christmas. On the last day of work in March, the men asked me to come upstairs to the attic. Fearing a problem, I was so surprised to see the men had made me a cedar closet for out-of-season clothes — as a gift.

Rich didn't have a notable sense of humor, so he surprised me one day when we both stepped into a full elevator. Instead of going in and then turning around toward the door, he stayed with his back to the door, facing all the people. "So I guess you're wondering why I called this meeting." I was so proud of him.

Richard was happy for me to be a stay-at-home mom and treated me to "help" so I could golf at the club, play bridge and canasta, and do my lady do-gooder things. That is, until the do-gooder things got edgy. When I got into race relations work, that was a bit too much for the family.

Actually, Richard introduced me to my first Black friend. Dr. C. Eric Lincoln was an extraordinary scholar. The Wurzburgs housed Eric and gave him a scholarship to LeMoyne College (now called LeMoyne-Owen College) in exchange for tutoring Richard and cutting the grass. He went on to become a professor of note and author of numerous books. Dr. Lincoln, while studying for the ministry and doing prison work, uncovered the Black Muslim movement. He became the leading authority on the subject.

I met Eric when he brought us a wedding gift. He was so interesting, and sociology was one of his degrees. Since that was my major, I asked my professor Jack Conrad if I could invite Dr. Lincoln to speak to our class and perhaps take him to lunch in the cafeteria. This was 1961, and restaurants were still segregated. Dr. Conrad was quite pleased. Little did I know that I was starting a shit storm.

Dean Jameson Jones called me at home and accused me of trying to hurt the school! I had suggested Dr. Lincoln address the whole student body at our morning chapel, so I guess the proposal went to his desk.

"You can't have him in the lunchroom; the help doesn't like it. We're not here to promote this man's career," Dean Jones said. I was flabbergasted.

"Dr. Jones, Dr. Lincoln doesn't need us to advance his career. This year, he is guest lecturer at Boston College. He's quite famous in academic circles. You can look him up."

When I hung up the phone, I burst into tears and drove over to Dr. Conrad's office.

Apparently, Dr. Jones looked him up!

"Jocelyn, Dr. Lincoln may speak to your sociology class, and then you can host him and six other people for lunch in the Bell Tower," said Dean Jones.

He did not apologize to me for his earlier accusations. Normally, lunch in the Bell Tower is an honor and privilege, but I knew what this really was. We were going to be hiding him. Jameson Jones must have "woke" later because he became known as a person of tolerance.

I laughingly told people that I majored in Monday-Wednesday-Friday, whatever classes were available when I had help at home. By then I'd had our first baby, Cheryl.

From the beginning of our relationship, Rich was sick a lot. Leg aches, stomachaches, headaches, none of which ever attended a diagnosis. As I began to be a stress for the family, he got sicker. He would lie in the bed in the dark for days. He asked me to lie with him, but I just couldn't for more than fifteen to twenty minutes at a time. I just couldn't. One year I kept tabs and counted him missing work 102 days. Somehow, this became my fault, and my job was to get him out of the bed and down to the office.

Finally, Dad sent him to a psychiatrist. After one session, the doctor wanted to see me. After forty-five minutes with me, I got diagnosed.

"You are an emotionally disturbed woman. It is obvious that you don't want to be a woman because you don't like to cook. You could get well if you would learn how to cook. You could start with scrambled eggs and graduate to crepes suzette in a matter of weeks."

And I was so gullible that I said, "If I'm sick, I want to get well and fast."

"Well, I can't see you because I am seeing your husband. But I can send you to a new colleague," he said.

That was Bobby Buchalter, a Temple Israel confirmation classmate who I believed was a stand-up guy. So I commenced an accelerated program of psychotherapy.

"Since you're recently graduated, you have the time for me. I want to come see you three days a week, and let's get to the bottom of this," I said.

I was heading for law school, but that didn't mean I wished I was a man. After two weeks, I proclaimed, "I don't have any aches or pains. I can eat anything that doesn't eat me first. Why am I the sick one?"

Bobby responded, "That's what we psychiatrists want to hear, our patients telling us they are better."

Richard didn't go back since I was the emotionally disturbed one.

How many women who sought to do interesting things in addition to homemaking and parenting were sent to doctors to be fixed? Back in the 1970s and '80s, there was lots of conversation about women on Valium. Damn, I wanted to go to law school, and I was labeled sick! Here the feminist movement was saying: Be all you can be and be what you want to be. And when a woman did, she was emotionally disturbed. Some marriages were casualties of the feminist movement. It was a contract thing. So many of us married under one set of rules and then wanted to change them.

A few years later, Dad sent Richard to another psychiatrist, the head of the psychiatry department at the University of Tennessee Health Science Center. After two sessions, the doctor needed to see me. I went in loaded for bear. He was a kind man, a Lebanese Christian, who didn't deserve my initial presentation: "I am totally threatened by this. I have been through this before, and I got judged as disturbed. In the meanwhile, my husband is still dysfunctional. If my presence can help my husband, I'm game, but be aware I am not going to engage in any more psychotherapy."

One night I was cleaning out a cabinet while watching a movie on television, *The Group*, based on the book of the same name by Mary McCarthy. It was about a group of women at college and was considered an early feminist book. This was not in the movie, but one of the women in the book was dating a psychiatrist med student. Her father presented himself at her door wanting to move in after Mama had kicked him out. She was complaining to her boyfriend that her father was broke and kept coming home every night with useless purchases. The med student said that was a classic symptom of manic depression (now called bipolar disorder). So there I was sitting on the floor surrounded by packages, still in their blister packs, of citizen band radio mounting kits. We had several cars, each already equipped with citizen band radios. Why did I find five more kits under the cabinet?

The next morning I called the psychiatrist. Could my husband possibly be manic-depressive? What is the difference between that and just being depressed?

"Yes, his paternal uncle had a severe case," I was told.

It turns out it is a chemical thing. Rich got tested and blood work confirmed he had mood swings. The reason it wasn't so obvious was that his rare highs were pretty inconsequential. The worst thing he did was buying things we didn't need. Like a television in every room, some of which were rarely turned on. But he was low a lot!

Even with a diagnosis, he didn't want to take lithium, a drug that chops off the highs and raises the lows. They say people with mood swings really miss their highs. The doctor had given Richard a number of options for treatment; some were out-of-town clinics like the program at Duke University. I was told it may be necessary I go with him. Time passed.

By fall 1980, I learned I had passed the bar and started looking for a job. I needed to know what was expected of me before I could take a position. I told Richard I had to know what program he was going to accept by Thanksgiving, that I couldn't hang in limbo forever. He said he was making a decision soon. I called the doctor right after Christmas to see what had been decided.

"Mrs. Wurzburg, I regret to tell you Mr. Wurzburg won't participate in any of the programs I have suggested," he said.

On New Year's Day I went up to visit Mom and Dad to tell them I was going to divorce Richard.

I was not without fault, to be sure. I was the one who wanted to change the contract, change the rules. My fantasy was that Richard would accompany me on my journey, be my partner, and encourage my change. He provided me with the luxury to change, even though he didn't want it. This begs the question: How do you divorce the really nice guy?

Our divorce was fairly civilized. Neither one of us could stomach a knock-down, drag-out. The kids had caucused and gathered us to make a proclamation: "We go with the house, and we don't care who gets it!"

By then, they were fifteen, seventeen, and twenty. I offered to help Richard find a place, and I would help him decorate it. "Over my dead body!" And he meant it. He told me he wanted the house, and if he couldn't have it, he would kill himself!

I wrote him a letter saying that it was not fair for him to threaten suicide. He saw what Daddy's suicide did to me, and surely he didn't want to do that to the kids! Richard didn't want the divorce. I don't think it was because he loved me, but he said, "Divorce is a social disgrace."

I did understand that this was entirely my doing, and moving would be devastating for him. I told him I would vacate the house if he would buy me a house around the corner in bike-riding distance for Richard Jr. The girls already had cars.

I knew what would happen if I moved out: I would get criticized for leaving my children. One afternoon, I heard some older ladies at a tea, ironically at the home of Aunt Dossy. They were talking a bit too loud. "Isn't that the girl," meaning me, "who deserted her children?"

Richard died in 1992. He killed himself.

I was away on vacation, and my brother was at the airport gate waiting for me to depart the plane. It didn't take but a few seconds to change my happy surprise about seeing him to realize his meeting me at the gate wasn't good. It had to mean something terrible. My scream, "No, I don't want to hear this!" scared the crowd gathered at the gate; the pain was instant.

Ray enveloped me with his arms and walked me over to the wall. He told me Richard had committed suicide the day before, and he was buried that morning in a private funeral. They couldn't get in touch with me; Playa del Carmen back then only had one telephone in town.

Richard had shot himself. When he was missing from work, Arlene, his third wife of just a few months, called the kids, and they met at the house. She found him in the kitchen closet and shielded the kids from seeing him. I am forever grateful to her for that. He left a briefly written note saying, "I love you all."

Ray assured me the kids were handling things as well as could be expected, so I asked to go to the in-laws first.

We went to the baggage claim, loaded the car, and were on the way to Mom and Dad's when, to my great shame, it hit me how this impacted me. I was in financial trouble! If Richard hadn't deposited my last alimony check, I would be bouncing checks all over town.

The women's movement often said: "Women are one check, from a man, away from poverty. It's either a boss or a husband."

Damn, Jocelyn, what kind of person are you? My former husband had died; my kids had lost their father. In the midst of concern for others, it didn't take forty-five minutes before it became about me. I'm not too proud of that memory.

When I got to Mom and Dad's condo, Matil's niece, Carol Ann, from Hawaii was there. Mom received my hug and sorrow; Dad was unkind. He came out of the bedroom full of venom for me. "I don't want to hear her fake it." While it was Rich's third marriage, my father-in-law blamed me. I was the ultimate person to blame because if I hadn't divorced him back in 1982, he wouldn't have committed suicide a decade later.

Carol Ann ushered Dad away and Mom apologized for him. She hugged me hard, and I left quickly; I wasn't going to be any help, and Carol Ann was there.

When I learned there were messages on Rich's answering machine, I knew exactly what happened.

Richard's second wife's children were suing him for money they thought was due their mother when their mother died. Lord, have mercy, she died six weeks after she and Rich got married. I'm the one who suggested that Richard call her for a date. They went together for about six years, and she died of a heart attack six weeks after their wedding!

The lawsuit was for their mother's share of the equity in their house. For God's sake, I cannot imagine why he didn't just pay them! But Reggie wouldn't hear of it.

Dad needed some papers for the lawsuit, and Richard couldn't find them around the house. He had called Arlene to see if she knew where in the house the document was.

Richard always knew he wasn't living up to Dad's expectations.

He didn't demonstrate the drive his father had to have to make it. But he didn't need to.

There was a message left: "Don't you even think about coming to the office if you can't find those papers!" Richard couldn't find them. A subsequent message said, "Forget it, I found them down here."

I know Rich couldn't find the papers, and he just couldn't disappoint his father one more time. And Reggie had the papers. My poor baby. My heart still hurts.

When my son, Richard Jr., was cleaning out his father's papers, he found the letter I had written Richard when he threatened to commit suicide if I didn't give him the house in our divorce. I don't know if Richard Jr. ever told his siblings. At least he and now my girls know why I was the one to leave.

Chapter Nine

Reggie and Matil

Reggie and Matil were my in-laws, Reginald and Matil Levy Wurzburg. And I really loved them. They were gracious and generous to me and taught me a lot. I called Matil Mom, and Reggie became Dad. Their backgrounds were similar; both were from Alsace-Lorraine, but the Wurzburg family when Alsace-Lorraine was German and Matil's family when it was originally French. We think her family came to America south through the port of New Orleans, which a lot of Jews did, and headed north. We possess Reggie's grandmother Henrietta's citizenship document, awarded in New York in 1874.

Reggie was a handsome man. He was about 5 feet 7 inches tall, bald with a ring of gray hair on the back of his head. He dressed nicely but was not particularly fashionable. He played golf occasionally with his elderly friends (about his speed) and fished Horseshoe Lake in Arkansas one weekday afternoon and one weekend day per week with his closer buddies. Gin games topped off the fishing jaunts. Reggie had a cabin over there that he had leased from the Snowdens since the 1930s.

Matil was fairly attractive, but not a beautiful woman. She was always well-dressed; I only saw her wear slacks one time. She went to the beauty shop twice a week and didn't begin to get strands of gray hair until her late eighties. She had ceased her Jewish civic activities by the time I met her in 1960 and enjoyed travel, decorative sewing, and entertaining her crowd with dinner parties. She embroidered tablecloths and needlepoint purses and cushions.

When Richard and I got engaged, Mom and I had lunch one day, and she said she needed to run an errand. I went with her into Freudberg's women's dress store. Matil had been there earlier and picked out numerous clothing items for me to try on. I protested to no avail. "Please let me do this. I've never had a little girl I could buy clothes for."

Matil had a maid named Maude whom she had employed since Richard was born. Maude didn't like me so much; I figured it was some dynamic of jealousy I didn't understand. Maude was brought to work each morning by Walter, who washed the folks' car each day and the car of any one of us who came by for breakfast.

The morning meal was often pork chops and "hoecakes" or crappie or bream, fish Reggie caught from Horseshoe Lake. Hoecakes, cornmeal patties seasoned with salt and pepper and fried, tasted a whole lot better than they should have.

While we ate our breakfast, Maude would go to the back, make the beds and clean the bathrooms, and, if the folks were going out that evening, Walter would take her back home.

The folks dined out a lot. Although Maude worked six days a week, rarely did a workday extend beyond ten in the morning. She would do laundry and extended cleaning the few days a week she fixed dinner. Richard and I didn't have a washing machine the first five years of our marriage, but Maude made it quite clear to Mom that her washing machine and dryer were totally off limits to me. I guess she feared she would end up doing my laundry, so we became loyal customers of a laundromat.

The seated dinner parties in their home were elegant, and we were invited to most. Mom kept accurate records of invitations she received so she would know to whom to reciprocate. And the menus were recorded so she could vary the meals from the last time she entertained.

The dining room table sat twelve, and overflow tables of six or so were set up in the living room. Reggie or Richard would sit at one and I at the other as if I were hosting. These parties were catered by Memphis's best, and servers were brought in. Mom set a *Downton Abbey*-style table with sterling and fine china. My favorite dinner partner was Dr. Phil Schirer, the bachelor ob-gyn who delivered Richard, me — and my mother.

Mom and Dad had a robbery with twenty-four place settings of Grand Baroque and forty-eight inherited place settings of Patrician flatware stolen. All of Mom's jewelry was taken as well. I never saw her cry over the loss as a monetary issue, and she never mentioned the sentimental loss. She just bought stainless steel knives and forks and continued to entertain.

I don't remember any non-Jews in attendance at these parties, which was probably good when Reggie's favorite thing to do, after the after-dinner cordials had been consumed, was to announce, "Okay, you Jews, time to go home!"

I once commented to Reggie that their friends — and most social friends were Temple Jews — were happily married. He said that was no accident; they only chose happily married people to be their friends.

Reggie was a civic leader in Memphis. The story was that his brother Abe was the face man in the business called Wurzburg Brothers, and Reggie was the nuts-and-bolts guy. It was discovered that Abe was manic-depressive, and he retreated from the business when depressed to the extent that he had pretty much retired when I came on the scene. Until that time, Abe was a beloved figure in Memphis — president of the Temple, on numerous civic and charitable boards. In his absence, Reggie got out of the office and into the community more.

The *Commercial Appeal* performed a sociometric measure to identify the fifteen most powerful people in Memphis. They were all men, and most were members of the Downtown Rotary Club. The newspaper's process was to examine all the volunteer boards in Memphis and see whose names kept coming up. And strangely enough, the same names popped up here and there. Thus they were identified as the most powerful folk in town.

When the newspaper interviewed them, they all denied they were "powerful," as if being called that was a pejorative. Their comment was: "I'm not powerful, I'm just doing my civic duty." None considered himself in a position to make change in Memphis.

Amazing, because they were the real movers and shapers.

Reggie and I got along well. We argued politically, but I think he enjoyed it. When I got into so much trouble because of my role in the sanitation workers strike (and consequently with the company), he did an extraordinary thing for me. In the midst of the chaos and the death threats, he came home from a fishing trip in Bayou La Batre, Alabama, to take me to a Rotary Club dinner dance at the Memphis Country Club. Mom and Richard were out of town, and he came home to demonstrate support for me — while in his heart of hearts, he didn't believe in what I was doing.

A funny thing happened that night. Mr. Red Adcock, publisher of the *Commercial Appeal*, enjoyed dancing with me a few times. At the end of one song, he said, "I don't understand what you've been doing with this garbage union business, but I'm proud of you for doing it. And you're a great dancer."

My daughters conference-called me one night, Mindy from the University of Tennessee, Cheryl from Tulane University where she was in grad school, with a "problem."

"Mama, we feel so spoiled and ungrateful, and we hate what this says about us, but Paw Paw just called us asking us what color Mercury Grand Marquis we want. He's buying each of us, as he says, a good, safe car. We love him for it, but Mama, we don't want a Mercury Grand Marquis. What should we do?" I told them I would look into it.

I went to the Mercury dealership to meet with Dad's salesman. I made the appointment on the pretext of looking at color charts. When I got there, I asked if we could meet privately.

"Look, I have two daughters who feel terrible about how it appears, but honestly, as much as they appreciate their grandfather wanting them to have new cars, they really ..."

"Oh, Mrs. Wurzburg, I begged him not to buy these cars! I knew they wouldn't want an old fogey car like this. Let me talk with him again and see if I can talk him into something sporty."

It worked. Mindy got a cute Oldsmobile. Cheryl called to tell me that she went into an Audi dealership in New Orleans and asked, "How much does an Audi 4000 weigh?"

The salesman said, "Little lady, that's not the right question. What you want to know is the wheel ratio to the body cam," da, da, da.

"No, sir," Cheryl said. "I have got to know exactly what the Audi 4000 weighs! My grandfather has to know exactly what that car weighs."

Cheryl got her MBA from Tulane and interviewed with Frito-Lay here in Memphis. They liked her and explained that part of her training would be for her to detail the grocery stores for a few months. That meant she would be driving a truck from the plant at about four o'clock in the morning, delivering the chips and snacks to the store, and stocking the shelves. The items weren't heavy, but this was driving into an industrial neighborhood in the dark, loading the truck, and unloading at the store shipping docks, among other tasks. Reggie was excited Cheryl got a good reception for her first job interview, but not too pleased with the store-detailing part. Since the Frito-Lay regional executive was a fellow Rotarian, Reggie called and said he would be delighted for his granddaughter to work for them, but asked if they would mind if he, at his expense, provided her with a chauffeur. Cheryl was so embarrassed she did not go back for further interviews there — or any in Memphis.

The one thing I respected most about Reggie and Matil was their philanthropy. They were generous. I asked Reggie once why he donated to the Hebrew Academy, an Orthodox Jewish day school (Yeshiva). "So Sam Margolin will give me money for LeMoyne-Owen College."

His obituary quoted a remark I heard Reggie say: "The first 10 percent you give to charity doesn't count. That's just rent you pay to God for living on earth. Charity starts after that."

I loved Reggie, but he really turned on me when Richard took his life. I still received the blame, though we had been divorced ten years.

Dad died one year after Richard on July 3, 1993, at the age of ninety-two. Mom died on July 4 a few years later.

Chapter Ten

My Kids

A long time ago, I decided the least amount of parenting may be the best amount of parenting. That was probably a justification for being a semi-absentee mother. I also justified my absence to deal with my interests by saying I was making the world a better place for my kids and all children. Well-l-l if not the world, at least Memphis.

But somehow Richard's and my three children — Cheryl Lyn, Minda Leigh, and Richard Jr. — turned out terrific. Not as liberal on all issues as I am, but if kids are going to rebel against a liberal parent, where can they go? At least they were probably placing themselves in safer situations than their crazy mama. I almost disowned Mindy when she told me she was not so sure she was for the Equal Rights Amendment, but at the moment, all three agree the election of President Donald Trump is disastrous.

Cheryl, born in 1962, traveled the world for her job. I wish I could say it was for world peace, but she was a Chase Bank loan officer for McDonald's franchise holders and suppliers. When she graduated from Vanderbilt University and then graduated from Tulane with a business MBA, she moved to Houston and went to work at the bank. One night she called me, furious:

"I have just been in an after-hours meeting, and, at its conclusion, our boss turned to me and asked me to type up notes. Mama, I don't know how to type, but one of the men does. I'm livid!"

"Cheryl, do you suppose it's because you are a woman?"

"Damn it, Mama, I don't want to hear any of your feminist shit!"

"Oh, sorry, darling. I'm sure I have to be wrong."

At Vanderbilt, Cheryl told me she had to drop her woman's study course; the professor assigned eighteen readings, and she didn't bargain for all that. She said the teacher was disappointed because Cheryl wrote in her initial essay, "My mother is a feminist who recoils at the name Marabel Morgan, author of *The Total Woman*, but isn't as far out as Gloria Steinem."

"You don't think I'm as far out as Gloria Steinem?" I asked when she read me her essay.

"Do you?"

"Well, yes."

Cheryl chaired Impact, a think tank symposium with national speakers such as California Gov. Jerry Brown, Sen. Eugene McCarthy, and then-senator Al Gore. She was selected as the student representative to the University Board of Trustees. She left for college a nail-biting, mildly shy, petite little girl. She came home for Christmas a sophisticated young woman, with long, manicured nails. That may have been a sorority thing. My little firstborn baby grew up overnight. She lived alone in a New Orleans Garden District beautifully appointed apartment for grad school. Cheryl developed style and grace in perfect taste.

She married Michael Rubenstein, a Birmingham boy who went to the University of Texas, got a law degree, and got a job at the firm that represented the bank. He and Cheryl have become big Houston civic and Jewish civic workers. I'm proud to say Cheryl inherited my father's public speaking skills and is a natural on a podium in front of a thousand people.

They picked up their baby daughter from a surrogate carrier in 2010, so at age fifty-five, Cheryl has an eight-year-old.

Cheryl and her sister, Mindy, went to horse-riding day camp and still compete in hunter classes. In fact, they have been rated one and two in the nation in their adult fence-jumping class.

Mindy is my middle child, born in 1965. She came home to Memphis from the University of Tennessee and went to work in the family business. She and her husband, Blair Parker, have a landscape architecture firm in the same office building my business resides, so I get to be with her every day. Mindy, a recent cancer survivor, is strong and savvy; she, a blond, and her sister, a brunette, are beautiful women, much prettier than their mother and father. Both have more hair on their heads than any women I've seen, so when Mindy lost hair to chemo, one hardly noticed.

Both girls and their brother, Richard Jr., born in 1967, attended a Montessori elementary school so we didn't have to bird-dog the usual grading system. They learned at their own rate. I complained to the teacher, wondering when they would learn "of" isn't spelled "uv."

She pinned my ears back, saying, "For Lord's sake, Ms. Wurzburg, Cheryl, at six years of age, just wrote a script for *The Partridge Family* TV series. I wouldn't be concerned."

After writing a TV show, Cheryl spent all day for three weeks knitting me a pair of slippers; I didn't say a word. Mindy demanded half a door be decorated for Hanukkah, so I thought I saw a bit of social justice in her.

Richard Jr. became an amateur electrical wizard. He wired up his bedroom to control his radio and TV from a control panel by his bed. He became so good at installing citizen band radios and enhancing speakers in cars that he was recommended by car dealers who said, "You're not going to believe this. But there is this fourteen-year-old boy who can do the best job in town."

After Richard Sr. and I divorced, Rich called me one day, saying, "You need to incorporate the kid. There's a Jaguar dashboard sitting on our carport floor!"

Richard Jr. became the audiovisual (AV) guy for his school. He went on to Christian Brothers College in Memphis.

Richard has two boys, Joshua and Noah, and an ex-wife. There was a terrible six-year divorce over a ten-year marriage. Divorcing smartly is my life's work, but, of course, I couldn't even help my own son. It was decided the boys should reside primarily with Richard, and these parents have reared smart, delightful young men.

Mindy meeting her husband is a fun story: Blair came to me as a client to take him to divorce mediation. When he saw my maiden name, Dan, on the door, he asked if I was related to Ray, my brother. He had gone to school with my sister-in-law, Barbie, since first grade in Charleston, West Virginia, and had used her as a real estate agent a few times. About a year later, Mindy had broken up from a long-term relationship, and I told Barbie we needed to find Mindy a new friend or I feared she would go back with her ex. Barbie said the only eligible guy she knew was Blair; would it be okay if she mentioned Mindy to him?

I said, "Yes, he's a fine man and did more for his children than the law required."

A few nights later I got a phone call from Barbie. "Why didn't you tell me Mindy knew Blair? I haven't called him yet."

"I didn't know she did," I said.

"Well, they are coming down the stairs here at the Grizzlies game. Better run."

It seemed Mindy and Blair attended the same salon, and he saw her across the room with her head wrapped up in a towel.

"She's beautiful; who is she?" he asked his operator.

"She's Mindy, and she just broke up with her boyfriend! I'll tell her operator what you said."

The operators got their emails and exchanged them with Mindy and Blair. They corresponded a bit when he asked her last name.

"Wurzburg? Are you related to Jocelyn?"

The operators were invited to the wedding. Never having been a mother, Mindy is now one of three grandmothers to Blair's granddaughter.

I'm proud of my children. They have had a lot to deal with: parental divorce, their father's suicide, and the demise of the family business after 108 years. They have handled their financial comedown with great aplomb.

Mindy, my parsimonious one, is the trustee of my alimony trust. After Wurzburg Inc. went kaput, there was family infighting that resulted in lawsuits. In the courthouse hall doing last-minute negotiations, the attorneys carried Mindy back and forth to explain how the company finances worked. They settled. Less than 4 percent of family businesses survive the fourth generation. We were no exception.

Chapter Eleven

Panel of American Women

The assassination of Dr. Martin Luther King Jr. was the most transformative event in my life, but it was my response to that dastardly action that was the game changer. That response was founding the Memphis Panel of American Women.

The first time I saw a Panel of American Women program was in the middle 1960s at my Temple. Our Temple Sisterhood invited the Little Rock, Arkansas, Panel, formed as a response to their 1958 school desegregation fallout, to give its presentation. It was amazingly potent in its simple concept. A Panel program consists of five women telling their personal experiences with prejudice. That's it! Women sharing their pain dealing with prejudice.

A Panel presentation consisted of a Catholic, a Jew, an African American, what we called a "white majority," and a moderator. Each of the first three women spoke for about five minutes on what it felt like being considered a member of a group instead of being an individual. What it felt like dealing with discriminatory comments or actions in everyday activities based on stereotypes. The main focus was racial prejudice, but couching it in prejudice toward Catholics and Jews made it more digestible to put on the table for discussion.

Catholics talked about being accused of worshiping statues, the pope's influence, and employment discrimination. Jews talked about restricted neighborhoods, clubs and organizations, and anti-Semitic comments and propaganda. The Black panelist spoke of segregation and its impact on trying to rear children with positive self-esteem when society says you're not good enough. The white majority panelist's role was crucial: "I can go anywhere and do anything my education and money will allow. And only we members of the white majority can change it for the others." The program didn't designate that category as white Protestant because that panelist was accepting personal responsibility for the prejudicial situation. She wasn't trying to blame a religious sect, nor anyone in the audience. Just herself. Back then we didn't call it "white privilege," but that's what it was.

The program was so awesome, literally. The audience was awestruck. The women were intelligent, sympathetic, yet proud, and there was nothing with which you could disagree. It was their personal stories. Everyone is an expert about themselves! They were non-accusatory; it was truly thought-provoking.

Leaving the event, I saw the Panel in the Temple library speaking with some of our leaders. I stuck my head in the door and said if they were talking about establishing a Panel in Memphis, I would like to participate.

I received a cold thank-you — "don't call us, we'll call you" kind of thank-you. I believe my Republican conservative credentials vetoed my being invited into the room.

The death of Dr. Martin Luther King was a huge consciousness-raising event for Memphis. There were responses from many sources: Memphis Cares, the creation of a Human Relations Council, and a program created by the NCCJ. I attended all of them; I so needed to understand what had happened and why.

The NCCJ program was called "Rearing Children of Good Will." It was a panel of mothers of diverse religions and was racially integrated. They were talking about prejudice and how hard it is to raise kids in that kind of environment.

I said aloud, "Oh, they're doing the Panel of American Women."

"I beg your pardon?" said the man sitting next to me.

"What this panel is doing is a program called the Panel of American Women."

"May we speak when this is over?"

And we did. Since I believe that everything is timing and

synchronicity, I wasn't surprised to learn that the man who heard my muttering was Wallace P. Bonifield, director of the NCCJ. Bless his heart, he had just come on duty April 22, a few weeks after the assassination. I told him about the stunning program I had heard a few years earlier presented by a group called the Panel of American Women from Little Rock. One was named Brownie. Bonifield called the NCCJ chapter in Little Rock, which put him in touch with Brownie Ledbetter, who had him call the original founder of the Panel of American Women, Esther Brown of Kansas City, Missouri.

Esther Brown (1917-1970)

About seventy-five Panels across America came into being as a result of a program Esther created for a Brotherhood Month celebration at her synagogue. The program was so successful the panelists repeated the newly created program in their churches. Then out-of-towners in those audiences took the program back to their hometowns. It spread like wildfire. Our Memphis Panel in 1968 made it seventy-six.

Bonifield invited Esther to Memphis and asked me if I would take her to lunch. He would gather some NCCJ participants to meet with her afterward in the Union Planters Bank boardroom. Some had been in the "Rearing Children of Good Will" program.

Esther was extraordinary. She was a friend of the Brown family, as in *Brown v. Board of Education*, and had helped raise money for the lawsuit.

She told me Memphis was ripe for the program. I asked her how it was funded. It didn't need much, and they asked for honoraria to pay for babysitters.

I noticed what looked like a hospital wristband on her arm. "Oh, I'm in the hospital for cancer and just slipped out to fly down here today. I will slip back in this afternoon," she said.

When I asked Esther how she funded going around the country and starting these Panels, she said she got a few human relations grants in Kansas City, but she was using the money to travel.

"I'm dying, so what are they going to do to me!" she said.

"How did you balance this activity and rear a family?" I asked.

"Oh, I neglected them — and everyone has turned out fabulous! And my husband has been real supportive."

I was smitten.

Esther was attractive, inventive, and quick. She spoke to the group in glowing terms about how these Panels across the country were raising consciousness about the effects of prejudice. The program was a mild introduction to the subject, but it was so interesting to hear women tell these stories in such a non-threatening way, with only self-accusations. The women were dressed in heels and hose, and some still wore gloves. It's hard to be threatened by a woman in gloves. And sometimes those white gloves felt like handcuffs.

After giving their talks, the panelists were then open to answer questions. "What is kosher? Do Catholics practice idolatry? How would you feel about interracial dating?" In fact, the national office created a marketing pamphlet titled *Everything You Ever Wanted to Know About Other Races and Religions, But Were Afraid to Ask!* as a takeoff on the popular sex book.

Esther told anecdotes of post-presentation reactions and even of action it spurred the church or organization audience to do. The Panels were a program chair's delight. Rotary Clubs, Kiwanis, churches, and school classrooms could engage a Panel for a guaranteed successful event that didn't cost very much. If honoraria weren't available, the Panels went anyway.

Esther said she was there to recruit a Panel for Memphis. She needed about thirty to fifty women so there would be enough members in each category to fill speaking engagements at any given time. "And Jocelyn here will be your coordinator."

That was a shock to me; I'd only been with this woman for a little less than two hours. "Jocelyn will do all the work. You don't have to do anything but show up and give your talk when she calls you. Each Panel is run by a benevolent dictator, and Jocelyn will be yours. I will send her all the organizing materials, and I promise you this will be one of the most exciting experiences you will ever have," Esther said.

About ten of the twenty women the NCCJ had assembled signed

up for the Panel. Esther left to catch her plane to Kansas City and return to the hospital. And I started on my life-changing journey.

The National Panel of American Women had a small office in Kansas City and one paid assistant. As promised, Esther sent a huge number of "how to" documents: how to find good candidates to join, what each category should attempt to relate, hints for the moderator to get a good conversation started, speech writing, and practice questions. Fortunately, we could benefit from the mistakes other cities had made and adopt the good practices they had developed. We were not reinventing the wheel, and Little Rock was just down the road to help us.

I had no idea how all-consuming the role of Panel coordinator was!

Unfortunately, Esther said we had to eschew being a project of the NCCJ. That would have been so much easier for all, but our complete independence of any other organization and its agenda was essential to our premise. We were merely housewives and mothers, although some of us had jobs outside the home, speaking solely for ourselves. The coordinator, without help from any paid staff, received all invitations to appear and then filled a Panel with a member from each category, which often took three to four calls to ascertain who would be free. The coordinator confirmed the invitation, reminded the selected panelists, and then had to show up and be charming. I carried every panelist's speech just in case someone had a flat tire.

Getting the Panel off the ground was a huge undertaking! Each of the original signers sought other members for their category, and I had to meet with each nominee. It was a gut thing assessing personality, speaking ability, and comfort with diversity. People were not exactly vying to join the Panel of American Women. Actually, it was somewhat risky in 1968. The Catholic group recruited a Greek Orthodox member to join them to help make up a category.

I made a lunch date to recruit Maeola Killebrew, one of the few Black women I knew as an acquaintance through Republican politics. Maeola was the daughter of a noted Black Republican leader in Memphis, Lieutenant George Lee, who was pretty powerful with patronage appointments to hand out in the Eisenhower administration. Some other Panel coordinators were a bit suspicious of my Republican Party association. In fact, I was the only Republican coordinator in the country out of the seventy-five Panels that were functioning at that time. And at twenty-eight years old, I was the youngest coordinator. Esther wanted diversity, so none of that bothered her.

Dorothy Snowden 'Happy' Jones (1937-2017)

Dorothy Snowden "Happy" Jones was sitting there. I didn't like Happy. I met her for the first time in the early 1960s when I went to Republican headquarters to volunteer, and she wasn't particularly pleasant. She stuck me in the back of the room alone to stuff envelopes when others were gathered performing a task, laughing, and having a nice time working. I did as assigned for about an hour.

Shortly after that, I encountered Happy at a practically empty downtown movie matinee. There were three of us in the whole theater to see James Joyce's *Ulysses*. It had an intermission, and I would have loved talking about the movie, but I wasn't about to make the first overture. "Snob," I thought to myself.

I was coolly polite; it is said that a southerner is someone who is never unintentionally rude. I chitchatted a few minutes and then said, "Maeola, I've evidently interrupted a meeting; we can reschedule for lunch."

"I've invited myself to join you," Happy said.

"O-o-oh, I don't think you would be interested in this project," I said.

"I'm definitely interested!"

And that was the start of an enduring and close friendship. And it began Happy's extraordinary avocation of human and civil rights activism. What's fascinating about that is her father funded Phyllis Schlafly and started the John Birch Society in the Memphis area. Mr. Snowden was my father-in-law's lake house landlord.

He called me one day out of the blue and said, "Jocelyn, you appear to have a level head on your shoulders. My Happy is going half-cocked into activities I don't approve of, and I need you to help me rein her in. I need to depend on you."

"Oh, I don't know, Mr. Snowden. Happy's pretty headstrong for a woman, but I'll try," I said. Little did he know!

Brave Women Unite

Through personal contacts, we gathered about forty women and commenced an arduous process of educating ourselves. We invited community leaders in the human rights and civil rights arena to come speak with us about local issues. We wanted to be informed if, in the question and answer period, the audience raised questions of current events.

Also, being an object of prejudice didn't make you an expert on the dynamics of prejudice and discrimination. For example, we learned there were three kinds of prejudice: One was symbolic, where angel food cake was white and devil's food cake was black. Individual prejudice was learned negative feelings about others not in your own group. Institutional prejudice was society's institutions adopting those individual prejudices and functioning on them — such as employment discrimination or the telephone company charging a deposit for Black folk that it didn't charge residents in white zip codes. We needed a crash course on Memphis problems that were based in prejudice.

Then each category had issues it wanted its members to discuss. The Jewish category thought mentioning what Israel meant to us would be helpful, if the panelist was comfortable doing it. At the beginning of each Panel presentation, the moderator gave the caveat that being a member of a category did not mean that panelist was speaking for all members of that group. Each panelist spoke only for herself. Members of each category met and helped each other with their speeches.

As coordinator, I went to every category meeting and met with each panelist to go over the speech and its delivery. Providentially, I took speech in high school and represented Central High School for public presentations. I also inherited my father's ease in front of a microphone. I helped each panelist write for listening, which is different from writing for reading. In a speech, the predicate can't be too far away from the subject.

In other words, I was at meetings three to four nights a week, to the chagrin of my husband and family. A number of the panelists worked outside the home, so we had to meet at night. We met for about eight months before we felt confident enough to go to the public. We — I — had no idea how time-consuming this would be.

In February 1969, we decided it was time to show this project to our husbands and a few friends. We met at Monumental Baptist Church and gave our first presentation.

We were met with dead silence!

As coordinator, I served as moderator and had been given hints about creating engagement. "The first question is difficult. Who would like to ask the second question?"

Dead silence! We were crushed! The silence was pregnant.

Out of role, I asked, "What is the matter?" We were dumbfounded; our loved ones were the audience, and they seemed to hate it.

"Talk to us," I begged. The dam burst.

"I don't know what to say."

"I am stunned!"

"Y'all are absolutely compelling."

"What a fabulous idea!"

"Y'all are great!"

"I am so proud of you."

And then they commenced telling their stories of prejudice — as objects of it or as perpetrators.

Whew!

We felt ready for the community. The panelists secured engagements, and some gave us permission to invite the press. The press got it! They understood how powerful this was, even in its simplicity. They said we made education of human rights entertaining. And they got the risky part of it, too. "Speaking out against prejudice takes courage. Silence gives assent, and these ladies are speaking out," was a comment shared by the media.

Invitations poured in, often two or three a week. As coordinator,

I also learned which combination of speakers worked well together. We were a huge success.

The stories were poignant. Inez Boyd shared her problem with child-rearing in the presence of prejudice: Her son asked if Jesus was Black or white.

"We don't really know, darling, but why do you ask?" she said.

Her son answered, "Well, if he's white, he doesn't love me."

Urania Alissandratos told of a KKK cross being put in her parents' yard and set afire.

Anne Shafer, a Catholic, shared that she was accused of praying not to God, but to statues.

Marcia Levy, a Jew, spoke of receiving college letters proclaiming her qualified for entrance, but sorry, the Jewish quota had been filled.

Modeane Thompson, a Black panelist, said her son told her, "Mama, a Negro's gonna get you. They are the bad people."

Jeanne Thompson, a white majority panelist and the wife of a popular Methodist minister, spoke of feeling like Rip Van Winkle, sleeping through a revolution and awakening to understand a whole different world and time.

Happy, as a white majority panelist, spoke of shame that a Black mother burying her child at Arlington Cemetery in Virginia couldn't find a public bathroom to use on her car trip back to Memphis.

These stories really held an audience's attention and spurred conversation.

One day, Happy sat on a plane next to a man who said he was the president of the Shelby County Council of Civic Clubs. She touted the Panel and secured an engagement. Happy knew what his council was. It was the White Citizens Council in disguise. But he thought we were a patriotic group of similar ilk. Our husbands went with us to that engagement. When we walked in with Modeane, our Black panelist that night, you could see jaws drop.

Esther was pleased as punch; she had launched another Panel. But she was concerned that the total organization would be in funding jeopardy when she died. It needed an endowment or support. So she turned to the local Panels for help. She needed us to fork up money to sustain the national office. Not much, but some. A thousand dollars from each Panel would do it. This was 1969, after all.

Oh, Lord, the thought of having to raise funds intimidated me. We didn't have time for bake sales, and our work was far too important to do knit-shit raffles. I presented the problem to the group. Perhaps the easiest way would be to ask ten people for a hundred dollars each. Jeanne Thompson came up afterward and suggested we take her mother to lunch.

Mrs. Scott, Jeanne, and I went to the Asian Palace; after lunch, we all ordered tea. I then told her about how successful a project the Panel was, how the national organization needed help, and that, frankly, we just didn't have time and shouldn't have to cook cupcakes to sell. Daddy had taught me to make my pitch and then shut up; let the other person speak first. So I did. I said my piece and raised my cup of tea to my lips for a sip.

Mrs. Scott said, "Would $1,500 help to start with?"

All my affected sophistication immediately flew out the window! I spewed my tea across the table!

I hugged Mrs. Scott and thanked her. And after she left, I said, "Jeanne, who are you?"

"Well, Mama is a Hyde," she said. The Hydes, a prominent Memphis family, owned a huge wholesale food supplier. The Hyde family now has AutoZone stores worldwide.

In early 1970, our Memphis chapter of the Panel of American Women had planned a training weekend meeting with our Little Rock, Arkansas, and Jackson, Mississippi, chapters. About three weeks prior, our beloved Esther Brown died. The national office coordinator called and asked us to enlarge the event to encompass all the chapters. I held an emergency meeting of the entire Panel, and we agreed to do it.

Previously, no one had had any Panel responsibilities except me. All anyone had ever had to do for the Panel was show up for total group meetings and at presentations when assigned. This was going to be different, and time was of the essence. Everyone rose to the occasion.

I pleaded, "Y'all, we are going to divide up to perform duties, but we don't have the time to assign responsibilities and then hash and rehash the jobs. I don't have time to bird-dog it. If you volunteer and say yes, it just has to get done! I completely trust you to know how to do whatever you've volunteered to do. We need a hotel secured, meals and events planned, agenda created, transportation committee, decoration committee, registration mail-outs and back in, and press coverage. We don't have time for follow-up."

This was to be a "now what" meeting. Our creator was gone. And it worked. No one fell down on the job! Hundreds of women came in from around the country. It was perfect — almost.

Our last-minute, affordable hotel choice didn't have good banquet facilities, so I arranged for my Jewish country club, Ridgeway, to host our final banquet. Many small southern towns had country clubs that included Jews because they needed all the dues-paying white members they could get, but the major southern cities didn't. All were "restricted," so those cities had exclusively Jewish clubs for socializing, golf, and tennis. It didn't have any Black members — there weren't too many Black Jews — but there had been meetings there where Black people were in attendance. They agreed to let us hold the dinner there.

I was staying at the hotel but had run home to get dressed for the event. A terrific evening had been planned. There was a short play that was going to be presented. Family Service of Memphis created *Plays for Living*, and this one depicted the harsh reality of economics for African American families, such as securing loans for businesses and redlining of housing zones. We also were going to show an award-winning documentary, *When Hair Came to Memphis*, depicting the social dynamics when the University of Memphis theater department performed the controversial play *Hair*. Controversial even though they eschewed the nudity.

We had a keynote speaker, Lois Mark Stalvey, a Pennsylvania panelist who wrote a book, *The Education of a WASP*, about how the Panel of American Women changed her life. The press covered her arrival at the airport the day before, and she waxed on about how she, as a white majority American, came to grips with her own racism and how much joy she has experienced with diversity in her life. Her book could have been written by many of us panelists, but she wrote it first and expressed it so well. The newspaper article listed the events of the weekend, including the banquet at Ridgeway.

While getting dressed, I got a call from the angry president of the country club.

"What the hell are you having there tonight? There are bomb threats against the club! You have to cancel it!" he demanded.

The police were called in, and my husband, Richard, was a reserve sheriff's deputy. We threw on our clothes and ran out there, and Richard was armed. The police tried to calm the staff down, assuring us this happened often where racially integrated events were planned. They wanted me to brief them on the attendees expected. Then I remembered the play. There would be a car or two of younger people, dressed in character and not for a banquet!

The dinner was delicious. The decorations consisted of black, white, and brown gloves stuffed in handholding shapes as centerpieces. Everything was going well. The attendees were oblivious to the drama of the police stationed downstairs and my husband next to me packing heat. Jesus! I had seen the play before, but when the frustrated Black kid who couldn't get a job pulled out a pistol, I couldn't remember if he shot it or not.

When he pulled out the gun, I jumped up to say, "Young man, hand me that weapon now," afraid he was going to pull a blank, and the police would run upstairs.

Just as I was about to yell at him, the actor threw the gun down in dramatic disgust, emoting, "No, this is not the way!" I sank to my chair, fully spent!

The rest of the event was uneventful, thank God. In fact, it went swimmingly well, and everyone raved about Memphis hospitality. We agreed to continue as a national organization — and it did for years.

Meanwhile our local Panel grew in number. We were in demand and enjoyed a good reputation. We continued our monthly meetings, one month as a total group to share experiences and have speakers and the other month with our categories. We never stopped training. We engaged Dr. Ted May to assist with group dynamics. His contribution was to help us see our own value: "You are a first. You are southern women actually expressing an opinion in public! Don't underestimate your abilities or influence."

The best part was we began to share other experiences: weddings, Bar Mitzvahs, dinner parties, and we became a partying bunch — Panel parties. And the husbands loved it, too.

US District Court Judge Robert McRae laid down the law and put our local education systems under court order to integrate. My phone was ringing off the hook to go work in the schools. I applied for and received a US Department of Education Emergency School Assistance Program (ESAP) grant to help pave the way for school racial integration. I needed it to pay one of us to run a part-time office and schedule the engagements for me. It also bought us a retreat to do some intensive training.

I received no pay as coordinator, which turned out to be a good thing. One of my senator's staff was on the DOE's case about this government program and was quoted as saying it was a waste of taxpayer money and only lined the pockets of grant administrators. I called Sen. Bill Brock himself, which I could do since I had worked for his election, and protested, explaining how indignant I felt about these accusations when I didn't take one dime. He apologized and asked me to let him know when I would be in Washington so he could take me to lunch in the Senate dining room. His staff person got off the DOE's back.

The Board of Education engaged us to do four concurrent panels and repeat them four times each for an all-day teacher in-service training — sixteen panels in one day. As much as we trained and prepared our little speeches, I learned something important that day. I was sitting next to Pat Shaw, the Black panelist for that session, and I started coughing. It wouldn't stop, and Pat slipped me her glass of water. I thanked her and drank the water, and the coughing ceased. I didn't think anything of it, but later an audience member came up and said, "I noticed that you two drank out of the same glass. Y'all really are friends, aren't you?"

Once I was put in the awkward position of denying our expertise. The Memphis Police Department was under a federal mandate for race relations training in light of claims of police brutality. They said they had engaged the Panel of American Women to address new recruits and for training. I had to say, "Whoa." I had to explain to the Department of Justice that we were just a mild introduction to human relations, not the kind of training they had in mind.

The Memphis (and Shelby County, at the time) library system engaged us to speak at every branch, sometimes twice per locale, once during the day and another time at night. One night was a lesson in stereotyping. On the front row in a South Memphis branch sat a huge man. He was dressed in denim overalls. His belly sat on his thighs almost to his knees. And he had a scowl on his face. We gave our program; he showed no indication of approval. I got to the place where I opened up the program for questions, and his hand darted up.

"Yeah, I have a question," he said.

Oh, Lord, I thought.

"Is it okay if we smoke in here?"

That evening was especially interesting. There were only about five folks in the audience and the four of us. After a few years, we had dropped the moderator as a barrier between the audience and the four panelists. So I suggested that, since there were so few of us, why didn't we all go down to Shoney's for dessert and good conversation. My denim-clad questioner turned out to be a delightful person.

Memphis was beginning to change after Dr. King's assassination. All the organizations knew they needed to integrate their boards. They would lose people. It was okay for a white woman charity to provide formula for newborn Black babies; it was Christian duty. But to serve in the organization with Black women as equal peers was taking Christian duty a step too far. So these organizations now needed folks to serve who would be comfortable in racially integrated settings. Enter the Panel of American Women! I got calls asking if I could get panelists to serve on this board or that commission. It was heady; I felt like a power broker getting our women placed in important positions all over town. And the demand on the Black panelists was overwhelming.

Perhaps my favorite Panel story occurred not on a Panel. I had taken my daughter Cheryl to Ellis Auditorium for ballet. She was about seven. Just when we were leaving, the heavens opened up to an unpredicted torrential rain, and I was unprepared. It was late, and I needed to get her home. I knew I couldn't carry her all the way to my car a few blocks away, so I leaned over and asked her if she would be okay if I let her stand by the door, and I would go get the car to pick her up.

She said, "I think I'm going to be afraid."

A woman standing behind us said, "Ms. Wurzburg, you don't know me, but you and the Panel spoke to my church last year, and if your daughter would let me, I will be happy to stay here with her while you go get the car."

Our retreats were wonderful! What a way to bond. Nothing like going away from town for the weekend with women we had come to know well and really liked. We shared rooms, met in the hospitality suite, and drank! Once after I had gone downstairs to pay the bill, I sneaked into the suite unnoticed. Our women were sitting all over the room, Black and white and Christians and Jews, mostly in clusters on the floor, draped over the sofa and chairs, and laughing — really laughing.

Olivette Fuess, a Catholic panelist, saw me and waded over from across the room. She leaned over and sweetly whispered into my ear, "Na-a-a-ah, integration will never work!"

Chapter Twelve

Concerned Women of Memphis and Shelby County

The Memphis Panel of American Women came into being as a response to the assassination of Dr. Martin Luther King on April 4, 1968. He came to Memphis to aid the sanitation workers with their grievances for the deplorable working conditions they experienced. Their strike in 1968 was for recognition of their right to organize into a union and bargain collectively; AFSCME was their union of choice.

The catalyst of the first strike — the straw that broke the camel's back — was the February 1 accidental death of two sanitation workers, Cole and Walker. While Mr. Cole was sitting in the back of a trash-mashing truck to get out of the rain, lightning struck the truck and activated the crushing mechanism. Mr, Walker jumped in to save his friend, but both men were scooped up and mashed. If that wasn't bad enough, each family was offered $2,500 in restitution. What a loss and what an insult!

The big issue for the city was "check-off," deducting the workers' dues from the paychecks and sending it to the union — similar to the way United Way contributions were deducted and sent. Lore has it that to settle the strike, Abe Plough, of St. Joseph Aspirin and Coppertone suntan lotion fame, agreed to pay the workers' dues that first year.

In 1969, the unionized workers were threatening to strike again, this time over hours, wages, and working conditions and this time in the heat of July in Memphis. A garbage strike — the smell, flies, and humidity — wasn't going to be pretty. A summertime strike was going to be a bitch! Although the first strike won recognition, the workers didn't accomplish much over the real issues facing a city sanitation worker. The union and the city had backed themselves into corners and ceased all negotiations; neither side would come back to the bargaining table.

The union was dreaming up all kinds of crazy strategies to employ. One suggestion was to collect rats and dump them into East Memphis so we who lived out there would understand the workers' poverty-stricken lives. Rev. Mose Pleasure, a community activist married to our panelist Bernice and who had spoken with our Panel during training, said he did not approve of that strategy. There was conversation about rat eradication in Black neighborhoods using a bounty for collecting rats. But he said, "It could only be for twenty-seven days. The gestation period for a rat is twenty-eight days, and if the bounty was for longer than that, the brothers will start raising rats."

The main ploy they were using was having the workers dress in their nastiest sanitation clothes and go mill around the fancy shopping centers. One of the issues being negotiated was uniforms. These men came to our backyards with big empty pails to pick up our garbage. They would place the filled pails on their heads and carry them, in my case down a steep hill, to the street to the truck. A lot of times some garbage was liquid with maggots and it would drift down their bodies and their clothes. It was terrible, a terrible job, no doubt about it.

Hundreds of sanitation workers all showing up in one shopping center in smelly clothes caused all the other customers to leave. And Father's Day was a week away. One Laurelwood merchant, Jim Davis, a guy I knew personally and didn't like (he didn't like me either), had an upscale men's store. He wanted to call out the National Guard, as if we housewives were going to come shopping for Father's Day presents while armed guards walked up and down the shopping center. That was his solution.

Another man I knew was Lester Rosen, the chair of the Memphis Human Relations Committee. He was in communication with some leaders of the Black community and with AFSCME folk trying to work out alternatives to the sanitation workers' demonstrations. Jesse Epps and Bill Lucy were the Memphis union point persons, and Jerry Wurf was the national director of AFSCME. His wife was the national director of Girls Inc. I'm not sure who spoke with whom first, but Lester Rosen called and asked if I, as coordinator of the Panel, would be willing to meet with some Black leadership and union leadership. They had an idea that they wanted to discuss with me.

The meeting was held at Christian Brothers College. Instead of the union coming to East Memphis to demonstrate and to protest their inhumane treatment, they proposed, would I be willing to ask if the Panel of American Women would accept an invitation from the sanitation workers' wives to visit their homes? The purpose was to see what some city employees' living conditions were like. Here were people we paid to do the work that we didn't want to do. With low wages, and none if it rained, they had to live in dire poverty. The theory was that, perhaps, we affluent wives and mothers would be willing to assess whether this was fair, and if we agreed it wasn't, then perhaps we could be influential in talking to the city fathers and the city council.

I told Lester that we couldn't do anything political in the name of the Panel for credibility purposes. We had no other agenda than to help explain prejudice and how it worked to hurt people.

Mr. Rosen and Mr. Epps accepted that, but I did say I would see if I could get some members, as individuals, to accept the invitation. The deal was that if I could find fifteen to twenty women willing to accept the invitation, the union would call off Saturday's demonstration at Laurelwood. We women would meet at the shopping center instead, and a bus would pick us up for a tour of the sanitation facility and the homes of some workers. We would be allowed to ask questions of our hostesses and walk around their houses and yards.

The panelists usually communicated by a telephone tree, a process whereby I would call four people, usually the category chairs, and each of them would call four pre-assigned people, and those four would call another four. It usually worked!

"This isn't a Panel project; invite anyone you want," I said.

The Black panelists understood immediately. They said, "This has got to be a white-only event to have real clout. You guys are on your own."

Since this wasn't a Panel project, Mr. Rosen asked, "Do you have any problem with there being publicity about it that would maybe get a bigger crowd?"

"No, I don't care," I said. Hell, what did I know? I would sure find out!

The union received a two-inch blurb in the *Commercial Appeal* and the *Memphis Press-Scimitar* newspapers in response to their press release. "Instead of the sanitation workers going to East Memphis this coming Saturday before Father's Day, some East Memphis housewives are willing to visit the homes of the sanitation workers."

But it was just enough information for the crazies to call. The phone calls were so nasty I was unprepared. Ugly calls using pejoratives saying I was a n*%#@r lover, and if I was helping the union, then I was a pinko commie. Communist! And here I was enjoying spending every capitalist dollar my husband would let me!

Even an aunt called to tell me I had no business doing this and that I better be careful, that I was being used.

"Yeah," I said. "I know that. That is the point! We are trying to get the sanitation workers out of the shopping center so that one of their biggest sales days of the year won't get ruined."

All this activity started on Wednesday, and the home tour was scheduled for Saturday. It seemed to take on a life of its own. The vitriol was palpable. We immediately got a second unlisted phone line and temporarily suspended the public line.

Saturday, June 14, 1969, was a beautiful day in Memphis, not too hot. I arrived about nine in the morning at the shopping center. There were TV cameras waiting, but the tour was not scheduled to leave until ten o'clock. I was asked to give a statement. What I didn't know was that this was for national TV, not just for the Memphis audience. ABC, CBS, and NBC were there. Some of the panelists started arriving; a bus drove up; some Black leaders I recognized arrived with some union folks and got out of their cars. I was hoping the twenty women who agreed to come would show. And then more women arrived. And then more, and more. More than enough to fill one bus.

Myra Dreifus and Selma Lewis, who founded Funds for Needy School Children, a program to provide breakfast and lunch for children whose parents sent them to school hungry, must have engaged their telephone trees. Their work was not just a food problem. If you're going to serve breakfast, then the school has to open earlier and staff has to be paid. It was a no-brainer; kids needed to start the morning off with a full stomach. They could learn better if their stomachs weren't growling.

I saw the union people confer with the Black leaders. There was a debate whether to limit the number of women to take the tour or to order more buses. Two more buses arrived, and we filled all three. I began to sympathize with our hostesses; it couldn't feel comfortable expecting twenty guests and then being made to feel on display for three busloads of people. But they were willing to serve their cause.

The Black leaders assigned themselves to the buses. The noted Reverend James Lawson led our bus. He was written about in David Halberstam's book, *The Children*, the story of the young adults who took off from college to sit in at lunch counters and rode Freedom Rides to integrate the South. Reverend Lawson integrated Vanderbilt University when he was admitted to its divinity school. He had spent a year in a federal penitentiary for being a conscientious objector, lived in India where he solidified his commitment to nonviolent civil disobedience, befriended Dr. Martin Luther King, and was, in fact, the person who invited Dr. King to come help the sanitation workers in 1968. Reverend Lawson became one of Memphis's most effective leaders. Assisting Reverend Lawson was the Reverend Henry Starks, a man I later became friendly enough with to tease that he was a gentle giant. He was almost 6 feet 10 inches tall, distinguished-looking, and truly a gentle soul. To them, race — racism — was the overriding component of the problem. The working conditions of the sanitation workers were personification of the famous Kerner Commission report of February 1968 that explained how racism worked in America and that we were two societies, one Black, one white.

Memphis never had just one inner-city community of poor minorities; we had pockets of these neighborhoods all over town. None of us were surprised we would see folks living in bad conditions. What surprised us was just how devastated these neighborhoods were for people who work. No sewers, raw sewage between the houses. Single low-wattage light bulbs hanging from ceilings, making reading and doing homework hard. Too many people stuffed into one house.

The yards were full of garbage. How ironic — the homes of the sanitation workers were not being served by the Sanitation Department. And these folks worked for us! How privileged we were that somebody came, even going into our backyard, picked up our garbage, and took it away for us. That's pretty nice living just for being white.

One newspaper photographer following us caught the one house with a TV and rabbit ear antennae. And more than one house had framed pictures of Dr. King and JFK on the walls, as if evidence of extravagance. Some hostesses were asked about their shopping habits. With no cars, they could not get to larger groceries where prices were more competitive, so they were forced to pay higher prices at small neighborhood groceries. One lady said she used the same coffee grounds three or four times. There was evidence of poor economic choices. Bologna, cheap to purchase, is not an economical meat choice. Medium-size eggs may be less economical than large eggs.

The visit to the truck barn where the workers gathered to commence work was disheartening. No uniforms, no showers, and segregated facilities. The white truck drivers had a building in which to gather; the Black workers stood outside. If it rained too hard, the workers were sent home. Time to go to the assigned truck was noted with the ringing of a bell atop a wooden pole. This was typical of the old slave plantation bells as depicted in the movie *Gone With the Wind*. This, too, was an insult.

We passed the word to gather when we got off the bus back at Laurelwood. Among us was a panelist, Sister Cecile Marie, who worked at Siena College across the street from the shopping center. She invited us to convene at the school to debrief the experience. Most women wanted to do that.

We reached consensus that the matter shouldn't be dropped. And besides, the press followed us across the street and sought our reflections. There was overwhelming sentiment that the last thing Memphis needed was a second strike. Riding on our buses, we had heard the union's point of view. The City of Memphis's position had been fully covered by our media: This was merely a dollar issue; race had nothing to do with it.

Perhaps, to be most effective, we ought to be neutral and balanced. We weren't labor-management experts or negotiators, but we could demand that both sides send their negotiators back to the bargaining table to negotiate in good faith. And the place to demand it was at the upcoming city council meeting on Tuesday.

"Demand" became the operative word! Women weren't used to addressing city hall in those days, much less making demands. In this instance, we weren't thinking of the dynamics. While we wanted to be neutral as to the outcome of the negotiations, we were in a dichotomous position. We couldn't help but realize a few things:

1. We didn't need a summertime garbage strike.
2. The union had a legitimate bitch.
3. This was more than a labor-management issue.

Race and racism are in-your-face issues, and there is a nexus between race and poverty. Being poor and white was not the same thing as being poor and Black in Memphis, Tennessee. We saw a level of poverty way below anything most of us had experienced or seen as being white and poor. The experience raised our consciousness that actually there was dire hunger in Memphis, Tennessee!

We collected names and phone numbers and self-selected an executive committee to decide the next step. Participation in the tour didn't obligate anybody to anything. But a show of hands meant folks wanted to know what another step would look like. We told the press, who were pressing us to make a statement, "To be continued."

Anne Shafer, a Catholic panelist; Diana Crump, wife of a descendant of the famed Boss Ed Crump; and Anne Stokes, a Junior Leaguer, agreed to meet at my house later that evening. Somehow, Dr. Ted May, a psychologist, and Father Bill Kephart, an Episcopal priest, inserted themselves into the meeting. The first thing we did was give ourselves a name: The Concerned Women of Memphis and Shelby County.

I called Modeane Thompson and Pat Shaw, Black panelists and now friends, to ask for advice and if we should invite Black participation. Both demurred, saying this still needed to be a white, East Memphis thing. And both were proud of us.

Over the weekend, we met twice more to write the statement to present to the city council. We parsed every word for effectiveness. The result was strong. The statement addressed the three things we realized: No, we didn't take a side in the strike, but we did use the word "demand" in insisting both sides come back to negotiate — immediately. Second, we said we should be ashamed of how our hard-working employees had to live. The economics of this, plus the racism driving the economics, were problematic, and we needed to address the problem. We were going to tell them that we would demand the same of the union.

We asked Diana to be our spokesperson. How cool would it be having a Crump as our leader! Not just the name value, but she was well-spoken and the highest socialite in the group. Her representing us was almost iconic. She and Father Kephart were church friends, and he was so proud of her. He was going to rehearse with her later.

Tuesday afternoon arrived, and the turnout was amazing. Besides the tour takers, more women arrived to fill city hall. It felt electric! We had asked a few council folk we knew to get us on the agenda, and they had us near the top.

When invited to speak, Diana approached the microphone

and introduced herself. And then she read a paragraph, none of which was what the committee had struggled so hard to write. In essence, it said for the city to try and get this settled because a garbage strike in the summer would be unpleasant and for them to keep up the good work in dealing with this. Period!

Dead silence. We, the committee members, were flabbergasted! The women in the room were stunned. They came downtown to support a woman-induced proclamation for sensible behavior. The negotiations to date were way too testosterone-driven, and we women were going to say, "Enough, now get to work." *They heard nothing of the kind.*

The next words we heard were the chairman's call, "Next item."

I jumped up and waved my arms for us to head for the lobby. If I had been looked to for any leadership, *they saw nothing of the kind.* It felt like a total loss. The press followed us out.

The lobby was full, and there was a buzz of incredulity. Anne Stokes and I were near the front door of the building, where I noticed a planter box with a large ledge. I grabbed Anne by the waist and lifted her up to the ledge, telling her to yell, "They didn't even say thank you!"

I yelled, "We will be back next week!"

Thank God, the council was rude. Although we laid an egg, the media's headline was about how dismissive the city leaders were. They wrote about how the council dissed us, not how we blew it.

We regrouped, this time without our dear Diana. We knew what had to have happened. Her husband Charlie, an attorney, community leader, and power structure "innie," evidently put his foot down and rewrote a namby-pamby speech for her.

Things weren't going so well at my house either. The crazies got crazier. Besides the vitriolic phone calls, someone made appointments for salesmen to come to my house every thirty minutes to sell me something. I felt so sorry for them, I bought a vacuum cleaner, new upholstery for the sofa, and an electronic dust filter for the air conditioner. My friend and co-chair Anne Shafer had a ton of sand delivered and dumped in her front yard.

It got serious. We received a card with the Minuteman rifle site on it. More seriously, the children's itinerary was sent to me. It worked. I was scared.

Richard was catching shit from everybody, family and company customers canceling orders. He was displeased. "Shut her up," he was told, and he couldn't. I had no choice; I had to be the next speaker at city hall.

In the interim week, no progress had been made in negotiations. The evening paper cartoon depicted a councilman coming home to a wife silhouetted on the window shade with a rolling pin in her hand. The media knew the previous week was a screw-up, but with the council's rude reaction, we were coming loaded for bear. The council room was full. I was prepared to give the tenor of the speech we originally wrote — and I gave it. What I wasn't prepared for was the Socratic method of questioning the council would engage. That's when I had my out-of-body experience.

I have heard of this happening to people before: an out-of-body experience where you are looking at yourself. The person I was looking at was standing in the city council chamber fielding questions from the council and doing it really very well. She was quick, she was knowledgeable, she was persuasive, and I don't know who the hell that woman was! It felt as if I was floating overhead and watching this twenty-nine-year-old woman named Jocelyn parry with councilmen about poverty, hunger, and racism. And she was doing a darn good job! It was as if "someone" was feeding her intelligent things to say. She reminded the politicians that we had addressed and stuffed their campaign envelopes, and we were now demanding they pay attention to us.

"Oh, now, ladies," said Councilman Wyeth Chandler, "you've seen poor neighborhoods before when you have driven your maid home."

"No, councilmen, we've seen poor neighborhoods when driving through them to get to the homes of our Black friends, who are discriminatorily denied buying a house in East Memphis.

"The bottom line, council, is that Memphis needs to negotiate a labor agreement and avert another strike."

Oh, Lord, here I was. More publicity, more hate mail, more

schism between my husband and me. I dreaded going home.

At last, coming home from vacation was my friend Happy Jones. I told her what she had missed, that the reaction was scary, that I had to get out of the spotlight on this, and that she had to help. She stepped up to the plate and agreed to take over the leadership.

"My name is Jones, Happy Jones, and they aren't going to find me in the phone book," she said.

Happy was terrific as the new leader and spokesperson. Happy was born a Snowden, and she was "higher and earlier" a Memphian than the Crumps.

Before the July 1 deadline, the agreement was reached. The city said we women had nothing to do with it. Jerry Wurf of AFSCME said it wouldn't have happened without us.

Two interesting points of note: For some women in Memphis, taking the tour was their first display of activism and pronouncement of concern about the poor. And Memphis feminist guru Carol Lynn Yellin proclaimed our march on city hall was the beginning of the feminist movement in Memphis.

Later in the 1990s, Happy and I got Woman of Achievement Awards, mine for courage during those times. Courage, hell, I was scared to death.

In 2013, the Concerned Women won the Henry Starks Civil Rights Award from the Memphis Theological Seminary for our role in averting this second threatened garbage strike.

Chapter Thirteen

Comprehensive Employment and Training Act

Six million dollars! It was a heady job, but I got to oversee grant applications to assign $6 million to worthy programs.

As with so many federal programs, the Comprehensive Employment and Training Act required local citizen input for the spending of federal funds awarded to local grantees. Memphis received millions of dollars that the city government sought for employment training programs. I was asked to serve on the citizen advisory board.

These boards had to be racially integrated and diverse economically. We were to decide where and how to spend these millions of dollars. So as a grantee city board, we solicited requests for grants from various local organizations that could conduct employment skills training classes. Competency and efficiency were the watchwords.

I was asked to chair the grant review committee. Hundreds of requests were submitted, and I read every one. But I quickly found out that I may have been the only one who did. We were a volunteer board, and I may have been the only one without a full-time job, so I had the time to read them.

Time was of the essence, so as chair I began to summarize the grants for the board and then offer my recommendations. The staff's job was to take our recommendations, submit our selections to Washington, get the organizations funded, and then bird-dog their performance. The staff wasn't too happy with me;

I recommended a lot of smaller grants for what appeared to be good programs. And I wanted some job programs that pinpointed women as trainees. They would have preferred larger grants to fewer organizations to monitor.

Fred Dorse, the executive in charge, didn't like me creating more work for the staff. We've since become good friends. He married a fellow law school student, Earnestine Hunt, who now serves as one of our city judges, and he owns a taxi company.

A few couples were the winning bidders of a trip his company donated to a local nonprofit. It was a trip to the Helena, Arkansas, King Biscuit Blues Festival. Fred, dressed in a tuxedo, picked us up in his van. One look and we said, "Fred! This will never do. We're going to your house, and you're going to change into jeans."

Now a member of the party and not a chauffeur, he had as much fun as we did. We stopped in a small town in Mississippi for lunch. He was visibly nervous going in, not seeing any other racially integrated tables, and this was in the early 1970s.

"I'll just wait for you guys outside," he said.

But we weren't having any of that. I realized his tuxedo would have been his safe cover, and we made him dress down. But I digress.

At the time, Fred was less than pleased that we wanted to assign a lot of grants to promising projects. Somewhere along the line, I mentioned that this was a heady job.

"Damn, I've learned that she who reads the grant proposals gets to decide where the money goes!" And in this case, I got to give away $6 million.

It was decided that the grant review committee would be redesigned into three separate committees. I decided I had enough fun and resigned.

Chapter Fourteen

Police Community Relations

In 1971, Police Community Relations was what we called "how to stop police brutality." At this point in time, since we have seen Ferguson, Missouri; Staten Island, New York; North Charleston, South Carolina; and the list goes on and on — this is déjà vu. But it is not a sudden moment that police are doing it again. It never stopped in the first place. Do black lives matter?

After a high-speed police chase, seventeen-year-old Elton Hayes, who was a passenger in a friend's pickup during a joyride, was pulled from the truck and beaten to death. Racial tensions erupted with four days of rioting and arson. Nine police officers, eight white and one Black lieutenant, were indicted, four on charges of first-degree murder. Others were suspended with pay. All were found not guilty in 1973.

As the Panel of American Women coordinator, I was asked to serve on the Police Community Relations Committee, which was a function of the State Advisory Committee of the US Commission on Civil Rights (USCCR). Our known interracial experiences made us Panel members in demand.

Committee members were asked to volunteer to ride with police to learn the job. I was anxious to do it for a number of reasons: I wanted to understand the mentality that could cause people with power to attack someone without any. I wanted to know what dynamics were taking place that out of nine people around the pickup truck, no one said, "Whoa!"

And two, why was my husband so enamored with police work? He served many hours a week as a volunteer reservist in the sheriff's department. Reading about the sixty-three-year-old reservist in Oklahoma who reached for his pistol instead of his Taser and killed a kid flooded me with memories.

Out at the Germantown Charity Horse Show watching our daughter ride, Rich saw an acquaintance dressed in a sheriff's uniform. Dr. Shea was an attorney and physician and, we learned, a volunteer reservist in his spare time. The next week Richard applied to be a reservist and was accepted. He already volunteered to deal with kids on probation at Juvenile Court and did some work as a Shriner. Richard was a thirty-two-degree Mason plus. In fact, he was the youngest man in Memphis to achieve that level. He also was a Rotarian. I was proud of his civic activity, but this sheriff's reserve thing had other components to it than civic duty.

Richard collected a few guns, and he taught me how to handle one. He owned the pistol that shot Marshall Field, the famous Chicago store owner. He took me hunting until I gave it up. I only shot quail and doves, and we actually ate what we killed. I was a good shot but not great, and I had to "finish the job" by dismembering the head if the bird wasn't dead. I just didn't want to do that anymore.

Richard held the highest rank in marksmanship. He went to Culver Military Academy and led the class. He taught me skeet and trap shooting, and we shot more than 1,200 rounds some weeks. In fact, we reloaded our own shells with an amazing contraption in the storage room. We took a spent shell casing, placed it on a firing pin, filled it with shot (BBs), and pulled down a lever that recrimped the top. With us shooting every Wednesday, Saturday, and Sunday, four or five games could be costly if we didn't reload ourselves.

Skeet differs from trap shooting in that the clay disks follow the same arc pattern when shot from the high house and the low house. The shooter moves to different locations along a semicircle to shoot the "birds." It simulates dove hunting. In trap shooting, the shooter stands in the same spot and doesn't know what direction the "bird" is going. It simulates quail hunting.

I shot a 20-gauge Remington 1100 automatic shotgun, and yes, I belonged to the National Rifle Association — until it got into the anti-abortion business.

The sheriff's reserves took an inordinate amount of time, but my Panel of American Women activity did, too. And I was happy at first Rich had found a consuming hobby.

Service on the committee was fascinating. I rode with several patrolmen and officers. They had to keep me safe, but we went nowhere that prohibited my accompanying my escort to the scene. One location we were called to was particularly nasty with garbage on the floor and the smell of urine. There was no electricity, and my patrolman was cute pointing out the cockroaches to me with his flashlight.

"Watch out, there's a roach. And there's another roach," flashing on a marijuana butt.

The point of our riding, according to Police Chief Jay Hubbard, was to learn the job these men did. And their riding with us, people who had different relations with the whole community, provided a new point of view.

I learned the job could be boring a lot of the time. But when a call came in, and time was of the essence and the siren was necessary, my adrenaline rose. As a novice, this was exciting. Common to the police officer, I'm sure, but I could tell he was on alert. I got an inkling of what was appealing to Richard.

My escorts were interesting, and I guess they only selected cooperative, willing officers. My being married to a sheriff reservist may have made me more acceptable. I was able to share with the committee a number of points.

I learned there was a mentality of "no one loves us but us." They really felt endogamous; loyalty to each other was essential, hence it was easy to see how one would cover for another.

There is a lot of divorce in police service; the job is stressful on a marriage and for family relations. I don't think there were as many guns available on the street back then as there are today, but it is hard to know your husband could face danger at any moment or that your husband may not come home.

I met some devoted, churchgoing officers, and their marriages seemed more stable. I learned most of the men I met had no interracial relationships other than on the job. Surely that has changed over the decades, but one said to me, "We don't interact with the kind of colored people you do."

I rode with one officer a couple of times. And we really enjoyed talking. We eventually got around to the Elton Hayes case. He confessed he was on the scene. It was like a curtain came down between us. I liked him, and I think he liked me. I don't know why I was so disappointed to learn this, but he was there — after it was over, I think — but he was there. I never rode again.

Chapter Fifteen

State Advisory Committee of the USCCR

My service on the Police Community Relations Committee led to an invitation by Chair Arthur Flemming to join the Tennessee State Advisory Committee (SAC) of the USCCR. Every state had a committee of locals to be the eyes and ears for civil rights concerns for the federal commission. We belonged to a region headquartered in Atlanta under the directorship of Bobby Doctor.

The states adopted projects to study for reporting to the national commission. We had staff to guide us, and most research was in the nature of open hearings to learn from the citizenry. That's how the public became aware of how widespread police brutality was.

We had legitimacy from federal authority, and on occasion the USCCR gave us subpoena power to delve deeper into a subject. Our state's committee decided on two main areas while I was in service: employment discrimination in our higher educational institutions and discriminatory use of Title VI money, federal funds given to state, county, and city entities.

A Title VI example would be federal funding to a county for a sewer system that ended at a Black neighborhood. That was an actual case in Tennessee. We heard over and over about recreational park money buying good amenities for white playgrounds — baseball diamonds, soccer goals, lighting for night use, even swimming pools — but maybe a basketball goal for a dirt court for the parks used by Black kids.

We held a hearing at the Tennessee Valley Authority, our energy giant with a system of dams, coal-powered electrical plants, and even nuclear plants. A Black employee reported someone made a tiny cross out of toothpicks, placed it on her desk, and set fire to it. This was in the 1980s.

We learned that every recipient of federal funds was to have a designated Title VI officer who reported their employment statistics hopefully to show nondiscrimination. We also learned most of Tennessee's colleges and universities didn't even know about Title VI, much less have an officer making reports. Years later, the Tennessee Human Rights Commission became the recipient of these reports.

To the surprise of no one, women academics got less pay, fewer designations as deans and chairs, and less tenure.

Service on the SAC was interesting, and making common cause with like-minded folks across the state and region was fun. I got to meet the revered Arthur Flemming, the first chair of the USCCR, and his successor, Arthur Fletcher, a Black Republican from whom I stole the expression: "I'm a liberal Republican because the line is shorter!"

Chair Mary Frances Berry chose Memphis to hold a hearing on the outburst of church arsons in 1996, since a number of churches had been burned in our surrounding area. I was so excited to get to meet her, a civil rights icon, but she was aloof. I was the SAC chair at the time, so I was to conduct the meeting. She showed her displeasure at me when we called Veronica Coleman, our local US attorney general, to the microphone.

"Ronnie, your mic's not on," I said.

Chair Berry gave an audible hum and I heard her say, "Ronnie?" under her breath. I leaned to the side to whisper my apology and to explain we had gone to law school together, but "Ronnie" was not proper protocol.

Mr. Doctor asked me to represent our region at the final reporting of the church arson research. Not only the happenstance of church burning was studied; the uneven police investigations and the lack of outrage expressed by some political leadership concerning the arson were of concern to us. Almost all the churches were Black.

At the hearing held in Washington, my remarks included comparing these dastardly church burnings to Kristallnacht, the Night of Broken Glass in 1938 when Nazis rampaged Jewish synagogues, businesses, and homes all over Germany. History warns us to take these actions seriously.

In the audience was an intern from the Religious Action Center (RAC) of the Reform Jewish Commission on Social Action (CSA). I was told she came back from the hearing all excited about this southern white woman talking about Kristallnacht at the USCCR hearing.

She audibly exclaimed, "That's the woman!" when I walked into the center the next day for a CSA meeting.

The Tennessee Human Rights Commission, the State Advisory Committee, the CSA — all my activities began to converge. It began to feel like a unity of purpose.

Chapter Sixteen

Tennessee Human Rights Commission

In 1970, a Republican Party co-worker, Winfield Dunn, called to ask my help for his candidacy for Tennessee governor. Winfield was a dentist. He was a perfect gentleman.

"Of course," I said, and suggested I give him a "coffee" at the house to meet some friends. Naturally, I included my new Panel friends, which may have made my house party the only racially integrated party given for him.

He won and served from 1971 to 1975. Shortly after his inauguration, he surprised me with an unsought appointment to the Tennessee Human Development Commission (THDC). Its mission was to encourage equal opportunity in employment. I was to attend a monthly meeting in Nashville, and we planned annual conferences to teach employers the latest fair employment practices. Federally, the Civil Rights Act was passed in 1964, and its anti-discriminatory employment provisions were delineated in Title VII of the law, which was enforceable in all states.

I was excited with this appointment. We learned on the Panel that it could address attitudinal prejudice. Symbolic prejudice — black day, black cloud — was something we needed to raise our consciousness about to see how we teach our kids implicit biases. Real change would be more efficient if we could address institutional prejudice, which probably needed laws and governments to address discrimination since people with attitudinal prejudice ran the institutions.

If the Panel worked on people's attitudes from the bottom up and the NAACP worked on institutions from the top down, perhaps the 'tween would meet. With this appointment, I could work from both ends.

I immediately learned two things:

One, not everyone appointed to this commission gave a damn. It was a patronage appointment commission; thank you for your service in my campaign — and that was what I was.

Two, when I asked our director, Cornelius Jones, whether we had any power to stop an employer's discriminatory practice, the answer was, "We use persuasion."

I didn't use the current vernacular: "How's that working for ya?" But I did ask, "Does that work?"

Mr. Jones was granted an ex-officio seat in Governor Dunn's Cabinet. He was the only Black presence in the room, but I was pleased to know Winfield thought that would be wise.

Jones arranged for me to attend the International Association of Official Human Rights Agencies (IAOHRA) conference in San Francisco. It was a great learning experience. I learned that states such as New York had fair employment practice agencies as far back as 1945, while our federal government didn't create one until 1964. There were nine states left in our Union that didn't have an anti-discrimination law or an agency with enforceable powers; they looked like the Southeastern Conference (SEC) states. Tennessee is in the SEC.

As I recall my ninth-grade civics (which, the American Bar Association bemoans, is no longer taught in some school districts), states have the power to outlaw a lot of things concurrently with federal power. So why would we want a state agency since the feds have one? To redress discrimination, there had to be fifteen employees for the federal law to operate; most states required fewer.

Some states sold their legislation this way: "Who do you want enforcing anti-discrimination law, the Equal Employment Opportunity Commission (EEOC) or a local agency?" The federal Civil Rights Act provided for local enforcement if the state agency's law, staff, and procedures were as good as the EEOC's. These were called "Section 706" agencies. I certainly wanted our Human Development Commission to be one of those. And I said so in one of the workshops.

Wow! Abruptly I was being sought out with offers of help. "If you think you want to write and propose a law that would earn 706 deferral status, it needs to be a good one. Whichever state in the South passes one first, the others might follow."

Fortuitously, Galen Martin and Tom Ebendorf from the Kentucky agency that had enforceable powers, James E. Clyburn from South Carolina's agency that didn't, Carl Glatt from West Virginia, and Peter Robertson from the EEOC all came forward. "We want to help you."

Besides this conference being educational, it also became one of the most fun times I ever had. Happy Jones, then chair of the Memphis Human Relations Commission, was my roommate, and the Reverend James Netters, human relations chair for the City of Memphis, made up the Memphis delegation.

Reverend Netters was a former city councilman, and never was there a kinder soul. Out seeking lunch one day, we walked by a place called Dino's.

"Oh, I think this place is famous, a San Francisco landmark. Want to see if they serve lunch?" I said.

He thought he had heard of it, too, so we walked in. It was a bit dark and not too many people were in there. We were given menus, and then some music struck up. A scantily clad woman came out. We looked at each other, giggled, and walked out sheepishly. It was famous all right! We swore not to tell anybody, so I'm breaking a fifty-five-year-old promise. Sorry, Jim, but it was funny.

Happy and I noticed at one of the conference luncheons a man's name tag denoting the San Francisco agency. I will call him "Nick." We persuaded him to show us a little of the area. He took us to the Trident restaurant in Sausalito and to the Muir Woods. He was a doll.

We got into a conversation about California culture and that the fads that started out there didn't hit the South for years. We thought California was "way out." We had heard about the educational retreat center called Esalen whose mission was to explore change in self and society. In Panel work, we talked about "self-actualization and emotional balance," so Esalen didn't sound that bizarre to us. Nick amused us when he told us that he went to Esalen. He went with his wife and his lover, and they all agreed that they would restrict their relationship strictly among themselves!

Later that evening, the conference had dinner music at the final banquet meeting. He did something I never heard before. While dancing, he said, "I'm tired. You lead." So I did and he could follow.

"How did you learn to do that?"

"My sister taught me to dance and I had to follow."

Happy and I came home determined to use our respective appointments to address illegal discrimination we knew was institutionalized in education, employment, housing, and public accommodations. My mission was to write a law. It would convert the commission to the Tennessee Human Rights Commission and its jurisdiction would cover non-discrimination in employment and public accommodations as a human right. We were going to crawl before we walked.

What I didn't expect was the resistance I received from my fellow commissioners. Hugh McDade had been a commissioner for years. He was an officer of Alcoa Corp., the aluminum company with a plant in Maryville, Tennessee. Alcoa had a national standing in civil rights, but McDade didn't follow the company line. He felt his role on the commission was to protect the "maligned employer" from spurious claims of discrimination.

Another naysayer was an African American conservative named Francis Guess. He was held in high regard with Republicans nationally and locally in Tennessee. Both men voted "no" to my presentation to the commission to seek enforcement powers and against drafting of a bill. Our director, Mr. Jones, helped me secure backing from all the rest.

Of immense help was Herman Ewing, a fellow appointee by Governor Dunn and a fairly recent director of the Memphis Urban League. Herman was from Little Rock and a graduate of Lane

College in Jackson, Tennessee. He became a terrifically effective leader in Memphis in a short period of time and was a dear, dear soul. The Urban League had gained good relations with the business community in Memphis; its approach was more of a "carrot" than the NAACP's "stick." But both organizations cooperated with each other in mutual respect and integrity. I was soon to join and be active in both.

Drafting legislation was easier said than done. I had no experience whatsoever. The first thing I had to do was learn how to read statutes. They don't read like novels! There are words of art such as "may" and "shall," and, applicable to a fair employment practice bill, a "discriminatory practice" and "unlawful practice." I was advised that we wanted an agency with administrative law judge enforcement and appealable to the entire agency of citizen commission members; we should stay out of the courts. Thus, we wanted to name discriminatory practices and only make it "unlawful" to interfere with a discrimination investigation or harass a citizen commissioner.

Enter Dr. Charles Crawford, history professor at Memphis State University. We had a bizarre chance meeting on an elevator. I didn't know him, but he knew about me, my appointment to the commission, and my interest in writing a law. He wouldn't tell me how he knew all this, but he offered assistance.

Now this was 1973, when typing was done on typewriters and a duplicate made with carbon paper. Multiple copies were mimeographed, a sloppy, nasty process whereby a stenciled copy was placed on a cylinder that had been inked to allow the printed word to come through the stencil onto paper being fed into the machine. There were these new copy machines, but copies were a few dollars apiece. I didn't know how to type except by hunting and pecking. Dr. Crawford offered his secretary to help the cause.

I sent my created first draft to a number of experts across the country for review and critique: William Robinson of the Lawyers' Committee for Civil Rights Under Law, Jack Greenberg of the NAACP Legal Defense Fund, the Women's Equity Action League (WEAL), National Organization for Women (NOW), EEOC Chair William H.

Brown III, and others. All in all, it took nine months to perfect it. I often said I could frame and hang all twenty-something pages and label it grounds for divorce!

The women's movement gave me a jolt. They didn't trust a patronage-appointed and majority Black male commission such as the THDC to enforce anti-discrimination laws on behalf of women, so they insisted on adding a provision for the direct filing of a lawsuit into Chancery Court, bypassing the agency enforcement procedures.

Locally, I was led to Alan Black, director of a field office of the NAACP Legal Defense Fund. He and Herman Ewing got Maxine Smith, director of the NAACP local branch, to host a meeting for me and Carl Glatt, the West Virginia agency's director, to present this concept to the Shelby County legislative delegation. Dr. Vasco and Mrs. Smith's beautiful home was a perfect setting to launch my campaign, which I later learned would take years. Meeting them launched the most endearing friendships of my life.

Once a draft is created, a citizen proposer of a bill needs to find a legislative sponsor who sends it to the legislative council, a department of the legislature that spiffs up a bill for entry and checks whether it impacts other laws — either adding to it or amending an existing law. With all the help I had, I submitted a bill exactly how it was to be dropped into the hopper. But the legislative council changed every time I worded an action as a "discriminatory practice" to an "unlawful practice." Wrong! I was forced to retype everything and resubmit as originally intended.

Originally, I sought Republican legislators to sponsor the bill — as a conservative approach to eliminating discrimination. That went nowhere, so I approached Nashville Sen. Avon Williams, the civil rights icon in the legislature.

He wasn't nice. In fact, he didn't rise to meet me or offer me a seat. He just said, "Yes?"

I said, "Senator Williams, I would like for you to review this draft of a bill I have been working on to see if you would be willing to sponsor it."

"So what is it?"

"Well, if it's passed, it would be Tennessee's first enforceable anti-discrimination law in employment and public accommodations."

"Where were you, Mrs. Wurzburg, when I wrote my legislation?"

I paused, then said, "Playing bridge at the country club."

Lord, I thought I saw smoke coming out of his ears! Then he picked up his Dictaphone and said, "Letter please to William Robinson, Lawyers' Committee for Civil Rights Under Law. Dear Bill, please review the enclosed legislation and let me know what you think. Yours truly, Avon Williams."

Then he said, "Mrs. Wurzburg, I will get back to you." I was summarily dismissed.

A week or so later, I received a call from the senator. "Mrs. Wurzburg, why didn't you tell me Mr. Robinson helped you write the bill?"

"Oh, Senator Williams, I was so afraid of you! I wasn't going to say another word!"

"Well, I would be pleased to sponsor your legislation."

Then the hard work began, lobbying it to the legislators and stakeholders. I drove up to Nashville every week to meet with the elected officials and the other lobbyists of interest. I asked to speak at various legislative caucuses and professional organizations. The Tennessee Manufacturing Institute (TMI) was one I was most prideful about succeeding in winning over. The TMI allowed me to speak at its board meeting, and the board voted to support the bill despite the director of the TMI being against it.

One experience was pure embarrassment. I met a remarkable man, Matthew Lynch, who was a strong AFL-CIO organizer and head of the Tennessee State Labor Council. As a stakeholder, he was at the top of the list of folks to whom I had to sell the legislation. He was immediately supportive and offered to help. One day he called and asked if I could come up early the next week; he had told the governor he was helping me with the bill and said the governor had invited him to bring me to a legislative party at the mansion. I was so excited Governor Dunn was helping me, too.

Well, it didn't quite go down that way. When we arrived, there were no seats for us at this seated dinner. Winfield, gracious as always, insisted I stay, and his staff arranged to squeeze in two more places at different tables. That had to be one of the most embarrassing moments of my life — crashing a party like that. And then when it was over, a staffer told me that Mr. Lynch was called away. The governor and his wife, Betty, invited me to stay the night at the mansion, but already aghast at my unintended intrusion, I kissed them both goodbye and caught a ride back to town.

When I called Matt the next day, furious, I learned he had told the governor, "I'm going to bring Mrs. Wurzburg and crash your legislative party."

Then he claimed Winfield said, "You can't crash it because I am inviting you to bring her." And then he probably forgot.

I was awfully naive thinking Tom Hensley, known as the Golden Goose, the liquor lobbyist, invited me to his weekly receptions to mingle with legislators as his approval of my bill. No, he just needed women in attendance. It never occurred to me that my presence at his parties meant I was fair game for lecherous, old rural legislators. These unattractive, obnoxious, not-too-bright, yet arrogant men came on to me. What a sheltered life I had led.

I genuinely thought that the "Mrs." in front of my name was a protective barrier and my dedication to my mission was a badge of respect. My dress was business conservative; my blouses were buttoned up and my skirt didn't "cup under my behind." How dare they? Dumb me, it was all about power. They had something I wanted — their vote — and there was going to be a price for it. I was unbelievably stupid to think they were there to serve the people.

Except for Senator Williams's initial rudeness, I found the Black legislators and Democrats to be perfect gentlemen. This was just after *Roe v. Wade* was decided and before social and religious values had jumped into politics. These conservative jackass delegates who were to be re-elected in perpetuity were the "family values" candidates. Family values, my ass. They were away from their wives; it was all about booze and women! And my being there unescorted by my husband meant I was an eligible woman.

Week after week, I drove up and stayed in hotels at my own expense. I limited my interaction with these legislators to their offices with plenty of staff members around. I thought I was doing a good job. Then the disappointments hit me in the face.

I was in Washington for a Panel meeting when I received a phone call from the governor. I had asked him to make my bill part of his legislative package. He had originally agreed, but now he was reneging.

"Jocelyn, I just can't do it. I'm so sorry to disappoint you, but I have higher priorities."

"But you agreed!"

"I know, I know, but I just can't."

"Will you sign it if it passes?" He could tell I was crushed.

"Yes, I can promise you that."

"May I tell them you said you will sign it if it passes?"

A long pause. "Yes, you can tell them that."

The second disappointment occurred when the bill came up in the committee that allows a bill to be put on the calendar. It had passed other committees that dealt with the content of the bill and even the fiscal notations. This was the most important rite of passage; if it failed here, it was dead. I had attended all the committee meetings, and I was on pins and needles awaiting this to come up.

I was sitting in the rear of the room and next to the head of the TMI. As the bill was called, a representative who never gave me an appointment to explain the bill got out of his chair and walked over to the TMI guy.

"Is this the bill you and McDade want me to kill?" Mr. TMI looked at me, then looked at the representative and nodded affirmatively.

I got up, walked slowly out the door, then ran to the bathroom and sobbed uncontrollably. How I held my tears until I got to privacy, I don't know, but I did. I left the Legislative Plaza, got to my car, and drove straight home to Memphis. I never went back to the legislature again.

In 1975, I did make one more attempt to lobby for the bill. Gov. Ray Blanton, a Democrat, was elected. Senator Williams continued to drop the bill into the hopper every two years. I thought I would give the new governor a briefing to see if he would support it. Blanton granted me an appointment, and it was a strange conversation.

First, he met with me alone, something elected officials rarely did. He wore boots. He was roguish-looking and greasy. He took no notes, and I felt I was talking to a bored, unengaged listener. No questions. He thanked me for coming and said he would give it his utmost consideration.

A week or so later, I got a bizarre phone call from an acquaintance in the administration. "How badly do you want the legislation?"

"What do you mean?"

"Well, it seems the governor took a liking to you and wants to know how much you want this legislation."

"You tell the governor I may someday give it away, but I'll be goddamned if I have to sell it!" I said.

A month later, some poor schmuck called me needing to audit my expense reimbursements from the commission. Since I had no office, I invited him to my home to go over my meticulous records. His presence in my house told him I obviously didn't need to cheat the government.

Then, weeks later, I got a call that my service was no longer needed on the commission. I responded, "My term expires in 1977, and what you see is what you get until then." That was pride speaking. The legislation went nowhere.

The process of learning anti-discrimination law and writing the bill resulted in me probably being one of the most knowledgeable people in Tennessee about Title VII. I got a crazy bee in my bonnet: I wanted to be appointed to the EEOC — the federal EEOC — and my having worked for Howard Baker and Bill Brock for their Senate campaigns entitled me to ask them to propose me to the president. That's another chapter. But I thought a year of law school would give me new vocabulary and look good on a resume. That's also another chapter.

In 1978, I received a wonderful call. It was Senator Williams!

"Mrs. Wurzburg, I am delighted to tell you that your legislation has finally passed the Tennessee Legislature. Discrimination in employment and public accommodations is now outlawed under Tennessee law."

"Oh, Senator, I am so excited to hear this. My only regret is that I wasn't there to hear you debate the legislation," I said.

"Mrs. Wurzburg, there was no debate. I traded it for a trucking weight bill!"

On September 7, 2007, Gov. Phil Bredesen reappointed me to the Tennessee Human Rights Commission. Wow! I got to help enforce a law I had drafted thirty years earlier.

P.S. After years of little commitment by the state to really make the law work, an extremely competent woman, Beverly Watts, was appointed as director. She had previous experience running the Kentucky commission and whipped our commission into shape. Perhaps too well? Under the current conservative regime, there is talk of "sunsetting" the commission.

Chapter Seventeen

EEOC

A crazy bee took up residence in my bonnet. After being appointed to the Tennessee Human Rights Commission and authoring a bill to give it enforceable anti-discrimination powers, I decided in 1974 to seek an appointment to the EEOC, established under Title VII of the 1964 Civil Rights Act. That would entail living in DC part time, enough time to medicate my Potomac fever, and, I deluded myself into thinking, absence might make the heart of my marriage grow fonder.

I took the extreme action of enrolling in law school. I thought a command of a law library and a new vocabulary would give me a leg up seeking this appointment. If I didn't get the job, I could continue legal studies and become a civil rights lawyer.

I had employment discrimination law down pat, federal and state remedies I learned while researching my proposed legislation. The most important thing I learned was the theoretical basis of what discrimination was.

My teacher was Peter Robertson, an attorney with the EEOC who lectured state agencies on Alfred Blumrosen's law review article about how the definition of discrimination has evolved. Blumrosen was a Rutgers Law School professor. I digress to give you a brief rundown.

The problem of no equality is in debate. Is it a problem of being disadvantaged or being discriminated against? The civil rights community differs from the Chamber of Commerce, saying discrimination is a big part of the problem. So what's discrimination?

First the definition was a person acting with evil intent: "Colored" need not apply; men and women job want ads in the newspaper. The remedy to evil intent is to quit!

Then the problem became unequal treatment. Pay a woman the same salary a man is paid for the same job. The pay differential for women now has grown from sixty-two cents to eighty-one cents to a dollar paid to men. Applications listing popular African American names also were being ignored. The remedy for unequal treatment is equal treatment. However, women demand equal pay for work of equal value!

The third evolution of the definition of discrimination needs a bit of explanation. Sometimes you can have equal treatment, but the results are unequal. Sometimes the same application of a qualification in a screening process comes out skewed. In other words, to be fair and non-discriminatory, we need to be aware that we have present effects of past discrimination. The remedy is to perform remedial measures to overcome the present effect of past discrimination.

The case Professor Blumrosen wrote about in his article involved Willie Griggs. An experienced forklift driver, Mr. Griggs was denied a job at Duke Power Company because he didn't have a high school diploma. He and a lot of Black folk didn't have high school diplomas because in North Carolina, African Americans quit school to plant, pick, and chop tobacco plants. Chief Justice Warren Burger agreed with Mr. Griggs that needing a high school diploma was not a bona fide occupational qualification for forklift truck driving and thus was not a reason to deny Mr. Griggs a job. The remedy for equal treatment with unequal results is to act affirmatively to perform remedial measures to ensure your qualifications, universally applied, don't weed out a protected class.

Another example was the Houston Police Department requiring a height of 5 feet 8 inches to apply. That weeds out a lot of Hispanic people who don't grow tall. A test to prove that kind of discrimination may be using statistical data to show disparate effects. And there needs to be a relationship between the job requirement and actually doing the job.

Conservatives today are pushing evil intent to be the proof of discrimination, as if a charging party can prove what's in a respondent's mind.

The fact that I understood this concept put me up there as a good candidate for serving on the EEOC. I went about a campaign to get this appointment from, of all people, President Richard Nixon. Again, my new friend, Professor Crawford, came to my aid. Somehow he knew about my desire to seek this appointment, but he would never tell me how he knew this. Bizarre! Mostly he offered political advice and invaluable secretarial assistance. Charles Crawford became my visiting angel, appearing when I needed him the most.

I first went to my senators, both of whom I had worked for during their elections, and asked them to nominate me. Both were willing. The opening was a year off.

I commenced a strategy of meeting civil rights leaders to let them know I understood remedial measures and that I had great Republican connections despite my commitment to fair employment practices.

Various civil rights leaders received me and most agreed to write letters of recommendation: Eddie N. Williams, president of the Joint Center for Political and Economic Studies; Vernon Jordan, head of the Urban League; Jack Greenberg, director of the NAACP Legal Defense Fund; Jerry Wurf, head of AFSCME, who remembered me from Concerned Women; William Robinson of the Lawyers' Committee for Civil Rights Under Law, who remembered my legislation; Doris Seward, president of the Women's Equity Action League; Stanley Scott of the administration; and the beloved Clarence Mitchell, Washington bureau chief of the NAACP.

I adored Mr. Mitchell. Maxine Smith arranged our meeting. Mr. Mitchell's modest office was on the second floor of a building near Capitol Hill, as opposed to Jesse Jackson housing People United to Save Humanity (PUSH) in an opulent Greek revival building in Chicago. People referred to Clarence Mitchell as the 101st senator for his effective advocacy of civil rights. He did ask me for a favor in return.

"Do you think you could arrange for me to meet Sen. Bill Brock? I've never been able to get through," he said.

The fact that I got his request taken care of that afternoon put me in good stead with Mr. Mitchell. Senator Brock was, in fact, delighted to make a lunch date with Mr. Mitchell. It was a case of his gatekeeper being too insensitive to civil rights to give Mr. Mitchell an audience.

I had an unusual occurrence involving Mr. Mitchell and his wife, Juanita Mitchell, a noted attorney herself. I was asked to give them a ride to the airport from the NAACP convention hotel. Casually I mentioned that Judge Harry Wellford, a Republican candidate for our federal appellate court judgeship, was a really decent man.

Months later, Richard Fields of the local NAACP Legal Defense Fund called me, saying, "Mr. Mitchell wants to reconcile our opinions of Mr. Wellford's nomination. We are opposing it and he says you think he's okay. May I send you our research and his opinions that we think disqualify him?"

I didn't dream that my comment had registered. I said he could, but I would ask Judge Wellford to send me supporting opinions. Ellen Vergos, his clerk, brought me opinions and, strangely enough, both sides submitted a few of the same cases! One saying it didn't support civil rights and the other saying it did! I read cases for days and called Mr. Mitchell. I told him I deferred to Mr. Fields's research but felt complimented that my opinion of the judge's integrity and decency was valued. Harry Wellford was confirmed for the judgeship.

In promoting myself, I got a family friend, Mildred Schwartz, to get me an audience with her cousin Billy Green, who worked in communications at the White House. Besides a White House tour, this was my first official visit and this time to the West Wing. Just going through the security kiosk and walking up the driveway was a thrill.

Senator Baker secured me an appointment with personnel at the Executive Office Building (EOB). My resume was growing with volunteer service for interracial projects. It was mentioned that in the old days an all-volunteer activity portfolio would have been a disqualifier, but my work was impressive. I just explained that I didn't need to work for pay.

I completely made a fool of myself by asking if I could smoke — and then chain-smoking when they rustled up an ashtray. I was a nervous wreck and sabotaged myself.

The opening on the EEOC didn't materialize. The woman holding the seat was going to be appointed chair of a future Nixon-created consumer protection commission. Nixon resigned, and no commission was created. There I was in law school, not really wanting to be a lawyer. But in 1976, my studies were interrupted when President Gerald Ford appointed me to the National Commission on the Observance of International Women's Year. That was a volunteer position, but service was exciting and brought me a whole host of new adventures.

Chapter Eighteen

International Women's Year

The United Nations declared 1976 to 1985 as the Decade for Women and March 8 as International Women's Day. All member states of the UN were to acknowledge and celebrate the designation. In the United States, President Ford created the National Commission on the Observance of International Women's Year. Notables such as Alan Alda and Appeals Court Judge Harry T. Edwards were appointed to a task force that suggested a commission should be formed, and it should host a national women's conference.

President Ford appointed me to that commission on July 3, 1976. I got a phone call on July 2, 1976, from Jeanne M. Holm, President Ford's special assistant for the Office of Women's Programs. And a good choice she was since she was the first brigadier general in the Air Force and then, as major general, the first woman two-star general in any branch of the armed services.

General Holm issued the appointment to the commission (that we called IWY) and invited me to the White House the next morning to be installed. I was beside myself! Then I was crushed when I couldn't get a ticket on any airline. I called Jeanne back and asked if she could call American Airlines and see if she could get me on a plane.

"I don't think I can get you a seat!" she protested with incredulity.

I urged her to try, and she was pretty tickled herself when she called me back to tell me I had a reservation.

I found myself with the other appointees in the Cabinet meeting room next to the Oval Office. I sat myself in the president's chair in the middle of the table's side. We were given a beautiful president's pin, then lined up to meet and be photographed with President Ford in the office.

Standing there, I was anxious. I asked the Secret Service man at the door, "Does everyone feel like this getting ready to walk into the Oval Office?"

"Like what?"

"Like what's a nice Jewish girl like me doing in a place like this?"

"Well, I'm not Jewish or a girl, but I feel excited every time I walk through this door."

When it was my time to shake the president's hand, he asked if I was related to the Wurzburgs in Grand Rapids, Michigan. We knew of the Wurzburgs there. They owned a department store, and a shipment of shopping bags printed, "I just love Wurzburg's" came to our company by mistake. Face to face with the president of the United States in the White House's Oval Office, I stupidly said, "No, sir, but we get their mail!" We both started laughing.

The photo was sent to me with my appointment certificate. Unfortunately, it was dated a week or so later, unfortunate because these presidential documents are dated on "such-and-such day of the month of the so-and-so year of the creation of our nation." So instead of using the July 3, 1976, date and that being the 200th year of the United States of America, it reads the 201st year of the United States. The other would have been a marvelous bicentennial souvenir. But no complaints.

After we each were photographed, the president led us to the Rose Garden, where hundreds awaited us. The president announced the creation of the IWY Commission and that 1977 would be the United States' Year of the Woman.

One woman elbowed me to move over so she could see better. "In case you don't know it, this is a historic moment," she said. Well, it certainly was for me.

Interestingly, all this occurred while the annual NAACP meeting was being held in Memphis; I was on a conference committee. The IWY appointment hit the newspapers, and the evening when I returned from Washington, Clarence Mitchell notified me that I was to be seated on stage of the convention's plenary meeting. I may have been one of a few Republicans in the room of five thousand, and now, with the Republican President Ford appointing me to a national commission, my visible presence at the convention showed the NAACP was bipartisan.

A crazy thing happened while I was sitting up on stage. A table ran the width of the stage with twelve people seated on either side of the dais. I was at the far stage right end. I received a note from Mr. Mitchell.

"Jocelyn, would you please arrange for a reception immediately following this meeting for Andrew Young? Thank you, Clarence."

Lord, I panicked. Throw a party on forty minutes' notice! I slipped off stage and called the hotel where the hospitality suite was. I ordered liquor, soft drinks, ice, and setups. I just decided that if I was stuck with the bill, hell, so be it. Then I called an NAACP member, Jerry Fanion, who owned a barbecue restaurant, and he agreed to send over pans of ribs, slaw, and potato salad. I returned to the stage nonplussed and nonchalantly nodded to Mr. Mitchell. He gave me a big hug of approval afterward.

Again, with the IWY, I found myself in high cotton! At the first meeting I sat with Jean Stapleton, the wonderful actress who played Edith in Rob Reiner's *All in the Family* TV series. She confessed to me she didn't know why she had been appointed.

"Well, Jean, as an actress, you play the role of a woman subjected to her husband to millions of people, but personally, you are a feminist. What a great platform you have!" I said.

"I'll need to mull that one over," she said.

Jean never attended another IWY Commission meeting, but she did come to the National Women's Conference and played a contributing role.

The commission was placed in the State Department, since the observance was in response to the United Nations. The night of the first meeting, a State Department official gave a dinner at her home in Falls Church, Virginia. The food and theme of the evening was Greek in honor of the commission's chair, Judge Betty Athanasakos from Oakland Park, Florida. She had served President Nixon on a number of boards addressing women's rights.

Thanks to my good friend and Panel member Urania Alissandratos, I had been invited annually to the Greek Night Dinner and Dance. She taught me all the Greek dances, so when Greek dance music was played, I became the star at the IWY Commission dinner party. Then, as I left, a staff member whispered to me, "Would you be willing to serve on the commission's executive committee?" I have no doubt whatsoever it was because I could dance the complicated *Sailors' Dance*.

The role of the IWY Commission was to plan and execute the National Women's Conference. It was to be a convocation of delegates from each state and territory who would report on the status of women where they lived. Then we were to develop a plan of action to create full participation of women in American society. We decided each state would hold a statewide conference to assess its status of women, explore ideas for improvement, vote on the IWY proposed positions, and select delegates to attend the national conference to be held November 18-21, 1977, in Houston, Texas.

I am the reason the conference was held in Houston. I tried to get it in Memphis, since the NAACP had a huge convention, but Memphis was ill-equipped in facilities and hotel rooms then. The decision came down to Minneapolis or Houston. I told the commission I didn't own a coat warm enough for Minnesota in November. Houston it was!

One of our jobs was to select the state committees to put on the state conferences. Since we were from various states, the commission member from a particular state was influential in that selection. And if any of us knew of good candidates in the other states, we could propose them for vetting. I became the person who asked each time if there was Jewish representation in each state's proposed group. I had suggested Barbara Zimmer from Indianapolis. When Indiana's group was set for commission approval, I asked if any Jews were on the list. "Ms. Zimmer, whom you suggested."

"No, she's an Episcopalian." They had to go back to the drawing board.

Barbara was interesting and taught me an important lesson. She was her state's League of Women Voters president. We had met on our husbands' business trip to Germany. She said that, with the name Zimmer, she is often thought to be Jewish but has never denied it if someone assumed she was.

"If asked, I'll tell I'm Christian, but I will never correct an incorrect assumption, lest one would think me anti-Semitic," she said.

I advertise in the Gay Yellow Pages for homosexual clients. They have a check-off for "Straight, Not Narrow." From Barbara, I learned never to deny an incorrect assumption I'm a lesbian, unless specifically asked.

When New York's delegation was proposed, I asked the same question, but this time in jest. "Any Jewish women on this list?"

Bella Abzug, who surprised me with not having a good sense of humor — or at least that day — said, "Well, I'm Jewish!"

"Yes, Bella, I know."

Bella and I didn't hit it off.

A huge debate raged whether lesbian rights should be on the agendas of the state and national conferences. I innocently asked, "Are lesbians more or less discriminated against than male homosexuals?" If more so, which I doubted, then the answer was yes. If not, then no. Straights don't stare at women rooming together, traveling together, or hugging one another, but they do more so at men. I had never heard of women gays being harassed or even being the objects of anti-gay violence.

After I expressed that, the staff, mainly Catherine East, approached me about leading the position to leave lesbian rights off the agenda. I asked East to have staff prepare a position paper for my consideration. The IWY staff was concerned that lesbian rights would take the spotlight off the issues all women experience and would make the whole conference feel radical. They feared the press would jump on that and discredit the whole purpose of the national conference.

I read what they had prepared, but it didn't feel good to me. I had not given this much thought, but I knew I wasn't homophobic, and this paper was. The staff wasn't united. Obviously, there were lesbians on staff, and they were more loyal to Bella than their bosses. They leaked the paper to her and said I might be the sponsor of it.

Prior to the next meeting, I told East that I wasn't comfortable with the proposal. She should get another sponsor, or we should work on it some more. At the close of the meeting when the paper had not been introduced, Bella looked over at me and asked accusatorially, "Isn't there additional new business?"

I should have kept my mouth shut, but I knew she knew about it, didn't like it, and didn't like me for even being associated with it. I answered, "I am mulling over an issue for the commission to consider, but I haven't studied it enough to talk about it today." She had come loaded for bear, but I was still hibernating.

Since I put myself on the state conference planning committee and attended the planning sessions, I was involved in our Tennessee state conference, a one-day event in Clarksville. At a committee meeting in Knoxville, the lesbian dilemma came up. We all met in a hotel room for a late-night conversation; we were draped over the bed, sitting on the floor and windowsill.

The word of not including lesbians on the national agenda had filtered down to Tennessee. The advocates for inclusion were there to lobby the committee and especially me. They were able to punch my hurt button. One woman sitting on the floor looked up and said with tears in her eyes, "Please don't leave us outside the Pale. If not here, we have nowhere else to go."

It was obviously Jew to Jew, and it worked. The term "outside the Pale" refers to being left outside the Jewish ghetto at sundown in Warsaw, which was a treacherous situation.

The next Monday, I called East to tell her I was for including lesbian rights as women's rights. Most of the states decided to include the issue in their meetings, so it made the national agenda.

Our IWY Commission worked hard. We secured the location, arranged logistics, and outlined the program. Putting on a convention for thousands isn't easy, but the IWY staff were pros.

And the time frame was short; the national conference would be held in November 1977. The meetings were interesting and fun, and it got me into DC often. I caught a good case of Potomac fever.

Washington is a strange place. I really enjoyed being with a number of the commissioners and decided to have a luncheon. I called Rep. Margaret "Peggy" Heckler from Massachusetts to invite her. I got a call back from a staffer inquiring about the nature of my request of the congresswoman.

"Nothing. I'm just having a ladies' luncheon and want to include her," I said.

"Oh, how lovely, she'll love that! That never happens." But Representative Heckler ended up not being able to come.

At the airport early one morning, as I waited upon my DC flight, I saw a woman, a friend of my mother's, but I couldn't think of her name. And I had homework to finish and really didn't want to strike up a conversation. She didn't seem to see me. I always try to sit in the bulkhead seat, but since it's in economy class, it's a hike back to the bathroom. On my way back there, there was the woman and she saw me.

"Damn," I thought. "If I don't speak, she'll tell Mama, and Mama will give me the devil."

Leaning over, I politely said, "Hi, I'm Rose Dan's daughter Jocelyn. How are you?"

"Well, fine, thank you. I'm Betty Friedan."

"Of course you are; I'm excited to see you. In fact, I'm on the IWY and on the way to a meeting."

"Terrific," she said. "May we talk? I'd like to know how the plans are going."

I invited her up to the empty seat beside me, and we had a good conversation.

Funny how things happen: Often on the same plane with me was Arkansas Sen. Dale Bumpers, and we sat together a few times. Later, his wife, Betty, started a women's anti-nuclear peace organization called Peace Links with a Panel of American Women stalwart from Little Rock, Sarah Murphy. They stayed with me on the way to Nashville once.

Betty did a stunning thing in her presentations. She took a shotgun BB and dropped it into a gallon-size glass jar. She said, "Let's say this ping is the sound of the atomic bomb that was dropped on Hiroshima." Then she dropped a gallon's worth of BBs into the jar. The pings just kept coming and coming. "Now, that is how many atomic weapons we have in the world. What can we mothers do about that?"

Then in fall 1976, our country held an election, and Jimmy Carter beat Gerald Ford. As required of all national political appointees, we had to proffer our resignations to the new president, but we would serve until new appointees replaced us.

During the transition, we continued to meet, and I did a silly thing at a Capitol Hill restaurant. I asked the waiter for an order of hoecakes. "Hoecakes, madam?"

"Yes."

"I don't know what a hoecake is. I need to speak with the chef."

"What? Jimmy Carter is going to be inaugurated in a few weeks, and you don't serve hoecakes?"

A few minutes later the chef appeared, asking me what a hoecake was. For you readers who live above the Mason-Dixon line, or what Memphis attorney and author William Haltom calls the "Sweet Tea Line," a hoecake is like a potato pancake patty but made out of cornmeal. You fry it up and serve it for breakfast, preferably with gravy. It's still famous at the Mount Vernon Inn in a completely different version, served with softshell crab, cured ham, and hollandaise sauce, although George Washington preferred his hoecake covered in butter and honey.

Most of our resignations were accepted, but President Jimmy Carter not only kept Bella Abzug, he made her chair. And he added the likes of Coretta Scott King, Ann Richards, and Gloria Steinem. They did a marvelous job bringing the work to fruition, compiling and publishing the decisions of the state conferences, and running the national conference.

The IWY National Women's Conference was star-studded with feminist icons. There were Betty Friedan, Margaret Mead, and Billie Jean King. Rep. Barbara Jordan of Texas was the keynote speaker, and three first ladies appeared on stage together: Rosalynn Carter, Betty Ford, and Lady Bird Johnson.

The new commissioners honored our work by having us sit on the front row and giving us Green Room privileges. I took advantage of that to meet Coretta Scott King and Gloria Steinem. Mrs. Coretta King was much prettier than her photographs, quiet and demure. Gloria Steinem is petite. Both were so warm and appreciative for the work we had put into the conference.

The agenda was presented in a book, *To Form a More Perfect Union, Justice for American Women*. Items were debated, and the vote was orderly. It was fascinating, however, to see the Utah delegation of Mormon women being told how to vote by men sitting in front of them, raising different color gloved hands indicating their instructions. The end product of the conference was a document, *The Spirit of Houston*.

At a recent Planned Parenthood event celebrating its seventy-fifth anniversary in Memphis, I had a chance to talk with Gloria Steinem, the featured speaker. When I made her aware we both had served on the IWY, she was animated in saying, "It was one of the most important events in America nobody knows about!" She writes about it in her latest book, *My Life on the Road*.

The conference suffered from another extraordinary and unexpected event, one that excited the world — including us. But couldn't it have happened a few days later? Anwar Sadat decided to visit Israel! It was a courageous overture for peace and probably the motivation of his assassination later. The world spotlight turned from us and toward the Middle East. There was so much positive energy arcing around the world; it was an exciting time to be alive.

P.S. Shortly after the IWY conference, President Carter appointed Bella Abzug to the National Advisory Committee on Women in the Department of Labor. When the president proposed to cut some funding for women's programming, Bella objected in her vociferous manner, and he fired her. It's too uppity to speak truth to power, as Myra MacPherson wrote in her April 2, 1998, *Washington Post* article.

As a former IWY commissioner, I had Bella's home phone

number in New York. I called her to express sympathy for how she was treated. After I reminded her who I was and said why I was calling, and that I thought the president's actions were shabby, there was a long pause.

"Of course, I remember you. This is the nicest call. I can't believe you've called me. How kind of you. This whole episode has been hurtful," she said.

Her thanks were profuse. Behind the tough exterior of Bella Abzug was a warm, appreciative person.

Chapter Nineteen

Commission on Social Action of Reform Judaism

In 1968, I learned the Reform Jewish movement had a commission addressing social justice issues, the CSA. I had read a spoof article by Albert Vorspan, *Ten Ways Out for Tired Liberals*, denoting excuses people give for not participating in liberal causes or philosophy. "They should pull themselves up by the bootstrap." Then he goes on to say, "Well, first you got to own a boot."

The commission was an instrumentality of the Central Conference of American Rabbis (CCAR), meaning Reform Jewish rabbis, and the Union of American Hebrew Congregations (UAHC), the Reform Jewish laypeople belonging to Reform Jewish Temples or congregations. UAHC is now Union for Reform Judaism (URJ).

The commission's job is to study social issues and decide whether our movement needs a position on the issue. If that answer is yes, the commission drafts a position paper and then presents it to the CCAR and the UAHC for a floor vote at their biennial conventions. Once a position is passed, local rabbis and lay leadership throughout the United States and Canada can say, for example, that Reform Judaism believes women have reproductive rights to choose what to do with their bodies or Reform Jews believe in a living wage. Rabbis and leaders can sermonize on those topics and can address political power on the issue.

I was rejected. Mr. Vorspan, director of the CSA, told me, "You sound like a social action-nik, but don't call us; we'll call you."

Months after President Ford appointed me to the IWY Commission, the CSA called me to join. I believe they were acting affirmatively to bring aboard a liberal Republican, since the commission was required to be bipartisan. I didn't care how I got on; I was thrilled to be appointed by Rabbi Alexander M. Schindler, 1925-2000, president of the Reform movement. He told me it was a toss-up whether he would become a rabbi or ski instructor.

Again I found myself in high cotton, with extraordinary lay leaders and notable rabbis from all over. The learning process was intense; we would be briefed by the leading experts on current topics and directors of non-governmental organizations (NGOs). Then, debate was stimulating. I was among liberal Jews who could debate liberal and conservative ways to solve a problem. But at least there was agreement on what was a societal problem!

I was with brilliant women and liberal Jewish men. I had not met too many of those. I once made a remark to Rabbi Ira Youdovin of New York, now of Chicago, that I was so excited with the company I was keeping, I was falling in love with these Jewish liberal men in alphabetical order.

"Damn," he said. "You have to go through Vorspan before you get to me!"

He was right about Vorspan. He and Rabbi Schindler were true Renaissance men. Great personalities, fabulous public speakers, terrific joke tellers, fun people! Just to be around them was a treat. I lusted in my heart, big time!

I got noticed at the first meeting. Newly elected Nebraska Sen. Edward Zorinsky was addressing us. From the IWY, I knew of the emerging issue of giving Social Security credit to farm wives. They worked the farm but had no Social Security benefits record in their own name. When I asked Senator Zorinsky his position on this, all heads turned to me. "Who is this woman?" And I bet my southern accent sounded to them like I was one of those farm wives. The senator admitted he had not even heard of or considered such a topic but would get on it right away. Apparently neither had anyone else in the room.

My first biennial UAHC convention was held in San Francisco

in November 1977. Unfortunately for me, it overlapped the IWY conference, and I had to leave Houston a day early. The UAHC convention was all abuzz over the Sadat visit to Israel. While the timing was a detriment to the IWY, we understood the importance; the visit raised the hopes of peace for the world. Shimon Peres flew in to report to the movement the implications of Sadat's courage. But alas, Sadat was assassinated soon afterward. I later got to meet Mrs. Sadat at a UAHC event and immediately one could feel her strength — strength probably influential in her husband's decision to make the peaceful overture.

At a 1978 meeting, the affirmative action issue came up, and I was right on it. The *Bakke v. UC Davis* case was in the forefront of civil rights news at the time. I was asked to present the University of California side in support of affirmative action against its attack by Bakke. The commission often wrote amicus briefs for important court cases.

Jews walked a tight rope regarding affirmative action, always being victimized by and leery of quotas, especially the ones that said, "You're qualified okay, but the Jewish quota has been filled so you can't be admitted to this college." Affirmative action required goals and timetables, but for white folk, that felt like a negative quota to them. Jews wanted to be supportive of affirmative action on behalf of our minority civil rights collaborators but were uncomfortable with assignments based on race or religion. Our Jewish women walked right in, when gender affirmative action was created! The whole civil rights community was zoned in on our debate.

Not sure I won on the merits, but I struck a chord when I suggested no matter which way we came down on this with our thoughtfully nuanced critique, we would not be writing the headlines. "Jews do support ... or don't support affirmative action ..."

I came late to affirmative action. I WAS concerned with an assignment based on race; wasn't that unconstitutional? But I came down on the affirmative side when I realized it was a remedial measure that was necessary if we were ever going to overcome the present effects of past discrimination. The CSA decided to support the university.

The commission decided it would establish a Women and Minority Task Force. Current topics of discussion were assigned to various task forces for information gathering and debate and then presented to the entire commission. While it had a domestic issues task force, the commission decided to carve out a civil rights and women's issues committee and made me the chair of it. The Reform Jewish Sisterhood organization, under the direction of Ellie Schwartz, thought it was the "women's rights" arm of the movement and wasn't really thrilled with this task force — or me.

My first action almost gave Al Vorspan and Ellie Schwartz a heart attack. The 1979 UAHC biennial convention was to be held in Chicago, Illinois. The Sisterhood and the UAHC held concurrent conventions to share renowned plenary speakers and other efficiencies. Now it was 1978, and I asked why we were meeting in Illinois, a state that had not ratified the pending Equal Rights Amendment, giving women a constitutional right of equality. Our task force voted to ask the commission to take the convention out of Chicago. We could hear a collective "Oh, shit!"

We were right, clearly, but moving a convention within months! After all the work had been done. "Even if we wanted to, we will get sued," was the commission's point of view. Naw, they weren't going to sue Jews; we would never come back if they did that.

"Even if we wanted to, the Sisterhood would prevent us from moving; we always meet at the same time," they said.

When the Sisterhood ran this by the local Chicago Temple sisterhoods, they responded, "Hell, yes, move it. We were surprised you would hold this in Illinois in the first place. We've needed your leverage to help get our state to ratify."

The vote to move the convention passed the total commission and went on to the Board of Trustees of the UAHC. The terms for moving were to pick a city with (and use) the same hotels.

Toronto, Ontario, Canada, fit the bill and cooperated with accepting us on such short notice. The weather amused us: When I flew in the night of December 4, 1979, (after my very last law school exam ever that day) there were snowflakes in the air. The next morning, and for the entire time of our convention, the sun was shining and the temperatures ranged from sixties during the day to low fifties at night.

Why I mention the weather is this: It appeared the CCAR had planned its convention in Arizona, also a non-ratifying state. They asked me to come to their board to present a case for moving their conference.

"Shouldn't you catch up with your followers?" I asked.

No! They didn't move and in sunny Scottsdale, Arizona, it rained during every single free time they had. There was no tennis, nor golf, nor hiking. The rabbis on the commission said they would never cross me again!

The commission has a DC presence with a location at Massachusetts Avenue and 21st, the RAC. With UAHC-approved resolutions, we could lobby Congress on behalf of our social action positions. An incredible young, talented rabbi, David Saperstein, was the director of the RAC. With a photographic memory, plus a brilliant mind and superb speaking ability, he was marvelously effective. He inherited NAACP Washington bureau chief Clarence Mitchell's place in being awarded the title "the 101st senator." He became counsel to presidents of both parties, as well as members of Congress. In fact, President Barack Obama appointed him US ambassador-at-large for international religious freedom.

David, while RAC director, went to law school and became the UAHC counsel, as well as a law professor at Georgetown University Law School. The brilliance of David Saperstein and the dynamic leadership of Al Vorspan, who brags he found and hired David, made a knockout team.

The fellow commissioners were fabulous people committed to social justice. I loved the Serottas, whose rabbi son Gerry led my trip to Nicaragua with the New Jewish Agenda. We went to study President Ronald Reagan's claims that the Sandinistas were anti-Semitic — against all five Jews who still lived there, three of whom were in the Sandinista government cabinet.

I adored commission member Betty Golomb. She led the national campaign to help Jews escape the Soviet Union. Her husband owned the Everlast sporting goods and clothing company.

"You know," he said, "it's not right, but I make more money today for the word 'Everlast' stenciled across T-shirts and sweatpants than I ever did employing people to manufacture and sell my products. Something's wrong about that."

John Hirsch and Herb Levy became my good friends. John was a theater set designer and Herb an attorney. Their Rabbi Davidson drove them from New York up to Vermont in order to be the one to marry them. We sort of hung together; they labeled me affectionately a "fag hag" or "fruit fly." The men gave me a great treat: While meeting in New York, they took me to the final production of the male swan's version of *Swan Lake*. Tchaikovsky himself was gay, and this presentation was supposed to be his autobiographical version. We had front-row seats, guaranteeing immersion in the ballet. It was an exquisite experience.

One of my best friends was Israel "Si" Dresner. Si was a rabbi from New Jersey and a passionate liberal. He, too, had a photographic memory, and while watching him debate a point, I noticed him touching the right edge of his glasses. He spoke a mile a minute and with great emotion. One day I asked if he was turning pages when he touched his glasses. "O-o-h, you can tell?"

"What do you have committed to memory?" I asked.

"The Torah in Hebrew, Greek, and English; all electoral votes by states in every presidential election; and all baseball and hockey scores," he said.

He was being modest. One afternoon a few of us were sitting around in front of a bookshelf. A friend, teasing Si, said, "I saw Si looking at this book earlier today. It was a 1930s book about the area, not yet a state, of Israel. Si, tell us, what was the gross national product of Israel in 1938?"

"Come on, don't do this to me," Si said.

"Si, just tell us," the friend said.

"You're obnoxious," Si protested.

"We know you know it."

Si caved. "In shekels, pounds, or dollars?"

Si brought his son to see me in Memphis. He was on a road trip to Mississippi showing his son the various jails he landed in while doing civil rights work in the early 1960s. He shared the funniest story about his father:

The day Si's father went to court in New York to get his US citizenship, he was standing before the judge and acting a bit fidgety. The judge noticed he was checking his watch and asked him sarcastically, "Mr. Dresner, are you sure you have time today to get your citizenship?"

In an accented voice he said, "Vell, I'm so sorry, your Honor, but today is de last game of de series, and de Dodgers are tied and de first pitch is in twenty minutes."

Si said the judge banged his gavel and said, "You're a citizen, go ahead and get out of here."

Harris Gilbert was my idol. He was on the board of Common Cause and People for the American Way. He was retired but became a financial manager for just ten people. He waived the minimum net worth requirement and took me, newly divorced, on as a client. He died way too soon. I've never felt as financially secure as when he was in charge.

The commission worked on current issues and was pretty successful in getting its social justice agenda passed by the Reform Jewish lay leaders, but with one notable exception. As often as we brought the issue up, we were never able to secure approval for voting representation in Congress for the citizens of the District of Columbia. This was Harris Gilbert's chief issue. He felt awful, because the resolution got moved up on the agenda at the Boston convention plenary when he and I decided to sneak out of the conference for an hour to run to the John F. Kennedy Presidential Museum. The resolution failed again. I tried to tell him it wasn't going to pass despite whatever he had planned to say, but he was inconsolable with guilt. North Dakota has two senators and only one congressman, but two guaranteed Black Democratic senators from DC will never fly with Congress.

Evely Shlensky, the first woman chair of the commission, is brilliant and stunningly attractive. She was widowed and later married Ira Youdovin. She, Ira, Bobby, and I were at a meeting in Arlington, Virginia, having a late-night dinner at the hotel bar. It was

May 2, 2011. We noticed streaming words at the bottom of the TV screens announcing a presidential address at eleven o'clock. We asked the bartender to turn on the sound. President Obama announced that the Navy SEALs got Osama bin Laden.

I served for over two decades on the commission before someone noticed my six-year term limit had expired and been ignored. I have recently been reappointed.

Chapter Twenty

Fourteenth Dalai Lama

The CSA's best project is its biennial conference, called the Consultation on Conscience, at which we Reform Jews are briefed on issues of import.

Every forty-five minutes we are briefed on some topic we should give a damn about by a leading expert on the issue.

The last one I attended in May 2017 was the largest ever; more than eight hundred people attended. I think it was the Trump effect!

All the Jewish senators and congressmen sought the podium to tout their causes du jour. I usually presented a speaker. I flirted with Barney Frank before I introduced him, with no reaction whatsoever. Guess I was the only one who didn't know he was gay. Since I was a Republican appointee of President Ford, I was often asked to introduce the token Republican presenter, like Eric Cantor.

Bobby went with me to some of these consultations and had some wonderful experiences. He was tickled when Sen. John McCain, one of the speakers, pretended to remember him from when they both served on the aircraft carrier the USS *Kearsarge*. "Bostick, I've often wondered what happened to you."

Bobby, who served as a secretary in the ship's office, said that while he saw McCain every day, the distance between officers and enlisted men is greater than being Black and white in 1960s Mississippi. Bobby got into trouble when it was discovered he was teaching some officers how to play guitar and bridge. Officers aren't supposed to be able to learn anything from an enlisted man. Anyway, Senator McCain did not often wonder about Bob

Bostick, but it was a nice thing for him to say.

Bobby remembered McCain as a nice guy, really handsome, but of all the officers he served with, McCain was far from the sharpest. Bobby was surprised McCain was senatorial material, much less presidential. His admiral father was head of WESTPAC, and wherever the ship docked, a car with a three-star flag attached would drive up to whisk McCain away.

When we learned that Senator McCain was dealing with a brain tumor and would undergo chemo and radiation, Bobby and I, neither one being virgins to that treatment, wished him well.

There used to be an airline requirement for a bargain fare that the traveler had to spend at least one Saturday between the departure and return flight. So Bobby and I would go to Washington on Friday or Saturday before a consultation started on Sunday and return Tuesday after lobbying our senators and congressmen. We would check out the latest exhibit at The Phillips Collection or the National Gallery of Art, where one of the buildings was designed by I.M. Pei.

Walking one Saturday night in Georgetown, we saw a sign on a light pole that the Dalai Lama was to speak in DC on Wednesday.

"Joselynda, we have to stay over," Bobby said. "I can't miss this. I have been following the Dalai Lama for decades. He's my hero."

"Bobby, we can't afford to change our bargain flight reservation! It will cost a fortune!"

"I got to. I have to be in the same room with him. He's a god."

"Okay, you do it, but we both can't afford to," I said.

Bobby was ecstatic thinking about it.

On Sunday morning, we registered for the consultation. Back up in the room, we were reading the agenda and there it was. Rabbi Alexander Schindler had invited the Dalai Lama to speak on Tuesday. We were beside ourselves! The Dalai Lama was going to speak to our group. Back in those days the consultation drew about 250 people. We would meet in a hearing room in the Dirksen Senate building, a fairly intimate setting.

Bobby had met Rabbi Schindler a few times. Rabbi Saperstein and Al Vorspan have been in our home, so my CSA friends were acquainted with Bobby. At the Monday meeting, Alex greeted Bobby with a big hug and they shared pleasantries. When Rabbi Saperstein went over the agenda, the room erupted in applause at the announcement that the Dalai Lama would be speaking with us. We were told that he was happy to speak with Jews; our movement had expressed disdain over Chinese aggression toward Tibet.

Al Vorspan had previously met with the Dalai Lama with seven other representatives of Jewish organizations. In his humorous book, *Start Worrying: Details to Follow*, Al quotes the Dalai Lama: "Tell me," he said (asking Jews), "What's your secret? How can a people that has been persecuted and exiled and vilified throughout the centuries maintain its religion and its sense of national identity? No other people has done this except you. I want to know your secret to help preserve my people."

Tuesday arrived. People entered the room from the rear from a foyer just off the street and headed for the front of the room down aisles running north and south on either side of the permanent seats, set up like a small auditorium.

Bobby was giddy with excitement. We were seated on the first two seats halfway down on the west side of the room.

The Dalai Lama entered the room from the rear, walked down the west aisle, and stopped at Bobby Bostick! He hugged Bobby. He actually stopped and hugged Bobby as if he knew exactly who in the room wanted to meet him the most.

I had my camera at the ready and snapped the perfect picture of Bobby and the Dalai Lama.

The Dalai Lama, Tenzin Gyatso, is the fourteenth spiritual leader of the Tibetan Buddhist people. He has a high voice and twinkling eyes, and he laughs at his own comments. I hope I am not being disrespectful, but he is a cute man, someone with whom you would like to be friends.

"Joselynda," Bobby said, "I am indeed a lucky man. As a lapsed Methodist, I have been hugged this weekend by the heads of two world religions!"

Chapter Twenty-One

Minority Business Resource Center of the Federal Railroad Administration

In 1976, and surely as a result of being appointed to the IWY Commission, I was honored with an appointment to the Minority Business Resource Center (MBRC) of the Federal Railroad Administration. Congress had passed the Railroad Revitalization and Regulatory Reform Act of 1976, also referred to as the "4-R Act." This was another appointment where my white, southern, liberal Republican, female bona fides fulfilled a lot of affirmative action goals.

The appointment came from Secretary of Transportation William Coleman. Mr. Coleman was famous for being one of the "Band of Brothers" who participated in school desegregation cases before federal courts all over the country leading up to *Brown v. Board of Education*. He argued before the US Supreme Court with Thurgood Marshall and then for years subsequent to that while the country was integrating with all deliberate speed.

The MBRC was supposed to help identify minority businesses that could receive federal contracts for millions of dollars to help rehab the railroads. Six billion dollars would be spent, and Congress had mandated minorities to get a piece of the action. The committee was really pleased with me — until I brought up that women-owned businesses should be included in the mandate. "Oh" was another of those "oh, shit" moments attributable to me.

The committee met for the first time at the Department of Transportation in Washington, and the secretary greeted us at a luncheon. Then we were asked to take a group photo with the secretary. I was placed beside him. He leaned over and asked, "What should I do with your expressway?"

Devotees of Overton Park formed Citizens to Preserve Overton Park, a volunteer grassroots organization that sued to stop the Department of Transportation from bisecting Overton Park with Interstate 40. Charlie Newman was the attorney for the group.

"The animals won't copulate with an interstate running beside the zoo."

"It will ruin the park!"

"If it runs through the city, there will become a right and wrong side of it to live."

Secretary Coleman had inherited the *Citizens to Preserve Overton Park v. Volpe* case from his predecessor.

This wasn't one of my causes, but I was semi-sympathetic. You could drive on I-40 from the Pacific Ocean to the Atlantic and not have to get off the road until you got to Memphis. It was the only unfinished portion, since the case halted all construction. But mainly our Overton Park is to Memphis as a miniature Central Park is to Manhattan. It would have been a shame to usurp so much of it for an expressway.

The MBRC met with Amtrak, Conrail, and the contractors for what they called the Northeast Corridor project; the group was designated to enhance rail transportation from Boston to Washington.

Samuel C. Jackson, a noted African American civil rights activist, was on the committee, and he was a delight. According to his *New York Times* obituary, Sam Jackson, until he resigned the post as the third-ranking Housing and Urban Development official in December 1972, was considered the leading Black policymaker in the Nixon administration and a vocal advocate of open housing. In a meeting with President Nixon in March 1970, he called for "open communities" and open housing as a way to ease school desegregation problems. Mr. Jackson told President Nixon that Blacks were insisting on the freedom to move into any neighborhood and that they also wanted quality education.

Mr. Jackson was active in the NAACP locally and nationally. In 1965, President Lyndon Johnson made him one of the five original presidential appointees to the EEOC.

Early in his career, Mr. Jackson was with the Topeka, Kansas, firm of Charles Scott. The firm represented the plaintiffs in the landmark 1954 case, *Brown v. Board of Education of Topeka*, in which the Supreme Court held that school segregation was unconstitutional. I didn't know that at the time, so I never asked him if he knew my Esther Brown. Six degrees of separation!

He was later the first Black partner in a major Wall Street firm, Stroock & Stroock & Lavan. Sam died of cancer on September 28, 1982, at the age of fifty-three.

Our little shtick between us was to pass one another a note when companies sent their highest-positioned affirmative action officer to tell us what a great job of inclusion they were going to perform.

Note from me: "Sam, is this guy Black or white?"

Return note from Sam: "Damned if I know, but I think he is supposed to be Black."

One fun meeting was held in Philadelphia at Conrail. A huge video screen semicircled a room, and every railroad car in America was depicted by lights moving across the country. They attached an old railroad board of directors' car to the back of an Amtrak train and took us back to DC while the committee conducted business with cocktails.

When Secretary Coleman asked me that question about what to do with the expressway, I was bowled over. "Mr. Coleman! I daydreamed you were going to ask me that question! I'm not believing you're asking me that!"

"Well, what did you say to yourself?"

"Dig it under the park."

"Nah, that's too expensive."

"Build over it! I promise, the animals will 'do it.'"

He glanced at me like that was a bit risqué. "That's too expensive, too."

"Oh, Mr. Coleman, it's a really nice park."

Chapter Twenty-Two

Mallory Knights

In 1975, I wrote a letter to the editor of the *Commercial Appeal* suggesting that we, Memphis, needed a monument dedicated to Dr. Martin Luther King Jr. I thought a good spot would be at Main and Beale — where Black met white. Surely, for the same reason, someone else thought of that corner first and put a monument to Elvis Presley.

But a group of men, members of a charity club called the Mallory Knights, had the same idea and called me supporting it. The Mallory Knights consisted of middle-class and lower-middle-class African American men; their biggest project was distributing food and gift baskets to the poor for Christmas. The men were amiable people, particularly Rev. D.E. Herring, their president. The Knights had been given a room at the Minimum Salary Building to serve as an office. Mr. Harry Strong was the Knights' staff.

Well, I liked the men and they liked me at first; they gave me my first honor for Black and white involvement. I was so flattered, especially since I was one of two honorees and the other was none other than the remarkable Reverend James Lawson.

Anyway, I agreed to help them with a monument project. It took on a life of its own. First, I needed a crash course on art in a public place, which led me to call for an appointment with the National Endowment for the Arts. I had learned a bit of strategy from my ESAP grant for the Panel of American Women: You should always take a staffer from your senator or congressman's office with you. In fact, if the staff person makes the appointment for you, the NEA person then gets to report to their boss: "I met with a staffer of Senator Baker and his constituent ..."

I wanted an "Arts in Public Places" grant to memorialize the work of Dr. Martin Luther King in sculpture. Not a statue, but a sculpture, a piece of fine art. The NEA staff person said, "The NEA doesn't fund memorials."

I responded, "But this is different," and then I shut up. The silence was deafening.

The staff person looked at Baker's administrative assistant, then at me, and said, "You're right."

Federal grant writing is arduous. Lots of statistics to state, forms to fill, endorsers to secure — it's hard work. Previous grant applications took reams of paper, but this NEA staffer handed me one 8½" x 11" piece of paper and said, "Tell us what you want on the few blank lines in question 4."

We got the grant: $25,000 on the condition I raised $25,000.

I adored Lucius Burch, probably Memphis's most respected attorney and an extraordinary citizen. He was one of Dr. King's attorneys back in '68. Lucius was an adventurer, mountain climber, outdoorsman, and a pilot. A story is told on him that he had a minor plane crash. Neither he nor the plane was hurt too badly; about one-third of one propeller was stripped off lengthwise. So Lucius took out his knife, shaved the other propellers to match the broken one, hopped in the plane, and took off.

Lucius was my divorce lawyer. When I met with him, his first comment was, "Thou shall not get a divorce until thou hast someone else to marry."

"Lucius, how do you pull that off while you're still married!" I said.

He just rolled his eyes at me and shook his head.

Lucius had clout — professional and social — and would make the ideal chair of this project. I did the same thing to him that I did at the NEA: I made a pitch and shut up. He obviously knew the "rule" and didn't say a word for the longest time. Neither did I. And obviously he really wanted to do it because he agreed on the condition that a member of the Mallory Knights and I co-chair it with him. And the Knights had to raise $5,000 of the $25,000.

Rev. D.E. Herring joined the team, and the Knights held up their end of the bargain. They went door to door and had "tag" nights where they stood at high-traffic street corners and the main Black radio station, WDIA, told folks where to go to drop off their change. This was a nickel and dime campaign.

But one source of the nickels and dimes was a bit hurtful. Someone I thought a friend, the husband of a panelist, said he would make a pitch to his employees and donate a match. I was excited at the prospect. I received a note with a check. He went out into the warehouse, said he was raising money for the King memorial, passed a paper cup, collected $2.34, and sent me a check for $4.68. Why he wanted to be such a jackass, I don't know.

Lucius got the city and the county governments to donate $7,500 each, and we garnered the remaining $5,000 easily. The big remaining problems were the artist selection process and location.

I received a grant from the Tennessee Commission for the Humanities to pay for the judging process. We had to pay expenses for the national art notables selected by the NEA to come to Memphis armed with slides of sculpture from credible candidates. It was to be a blind selection. Lawrence Anthony, my art professor at Southwestern and a famous sculptor himself, agreed to chair it for us. We asked Francis Gassner, the architect for our newly designed Main Street pedestrian mall, to be on the selection committee since he was going to have to suggest the monument's location to the city council. We knew we wanted it in the Civic Center Plaza, which housed City Hall, the state building, the Shelby County government office, and the Federal Building. We wanted it to be an "in your face" reminder of Dr. King and the reason he came to Memphis.

The committee worked all day, with lunch brought in. Professor Anthony hosted the selection process at the college, and the pictures of art thrown up on the screen were stunning.

Another problem was explaining to the Mallory Knights that none of us would get to design the monument or select the sculptor. Bless their hearts, they brought me a design they created: a representational statue of Dr. King with a crown of stars lit up in multicolor. It wasn't easy explaining abstract art that had the power to speak to you.

The committee awarded Richard Hunt the commission. What a great choice! I first saw his work at the Hirshhorn Museum in Washington. Richard is talented, patient, and he is African American. He is a doll! He not only had to fulfill the commission, he had to ingratiate himself with the Knights and give them a crash course in art appreciation!

Francis Gassner immediately began to work with Mr. Hunt. When Richard shared the first concept drawings with Francis, he secured a spot right at the front door of the performing arts center. The sculpture, called *I Have Been to the Mountaintop,* was placed in the middle of the space between the performing arts center and the FDIC building. It's huge. It rises up like a mountain, perfect for kids to climb on and even slide down. It was made of weathering steel that would rust over time. Francis didn't tell the city council that the monument would bleed for years. It did, and the staining of the concrete was so symbolically potent.

Mr. Hunt went along with the Mallory Knights' scheme to place a hugely oversized plaque directly on the monument itself. Yes, it has Lucius's and my names on it, along with all the officers of the Knights and all their monument committee members. Their volunteer executive director's name appears on it three times. I was horrified and begged Richard not to do it. The sculpture was so magnificent and so powerful, and the plaque was so tacky. He felt they needed and deserved to have the plaque as they designed it.

It was so embarrassing I skipped the unveiling on April 4, 1977, the ninth anniversary of Dr. King's assassination. I went downtown and hid behind an obstacle to watch the ceremony from afar.

When the city fathers put a trolley with tracks down the middle of the mall, the monument was shoved to the east and into the stairwell of the FDIC building. It was almost hidden, and the kids couldn't slide down it.

Memphis Mayor Jim Strickland arranged to relocate the monument to a newly created meditation garden in 2018 in superb commemoration of the fiftieth anniversary of Dr. King's death.

Chapter Twenty-Three

Beale Street National Historic Foundation

Dr. W.C. Handy, credited with capturing and putting to pen the blues, memorialized Beale Street in song. But Beale Street wasn't Beale "Street!" All big streets running east and west in Memphis are called "avenues." North-south streets are called "streets." Smaller ones might be "drives," or "roads," or "lanes." Danny Thomas, the entertainer who created St. Jude Children's Research Hospital, was aghast when he learned that Beale was Beale Avenue. He wrote a song about it and stayed on the case until the city officially changed the name to Beale Street.

Mayor Wyeth Chandler appointed me to the board of the Beale Street National Historic Foundation on December 10, 1977, to help develop the area into an entertainment venue. When Beale was mostly Black and Jewish, it was Black Memphis's music Mecca. Illegal liquor was sold there, and there were houses of ill repute and gambling. The likes of Duke Ellington and Jimmie Lunceford played the nightclubs.

We white kids went down to Beale to the Home of the Blues record store, owned by Ruben Cherry, that once claimed title as America's largest record store. Mr. Cherry once told Bobby, when he went in to buy a Chuck Berry record, that his father wouldn't approve of such music. "Bobby, this music is bad for you, son." I bought my first Elvis record there.

During the days of urban renewal, most of Beale had been shut or torn down. A few old building facades were standing, propped up with huge steel anchors. The area looked like it had been bombed out for a decade. Remaining, however, was A. Schwab, a small department store that included voodoo potions for sale. Mr. Schwab always thought we were related, and I would have been proud to be so.

The mission of the foundation was to bring the fun and excitement of the illegal activities to be legitimate, wholesome, and entertaining. Also, how would we keep it Black enough to be authentic and not too Black to scare off white people? And lastly, being Beale Street, there had to be Black-owned and -operated businesses. For this, we were going to have to act affirmatively.

I was a misfit from the very beginning. I wanted to be a part of it, and I wanted it to be as Black as possible.

"Y'all, if the food is good and the music is happening, I promise people will come. I know we Jews will!" I said.

First, they wanted to chase off the pawnshops. Bobby had unpleasant, intimidating experiences with the shops when he was young and seeking guitars he could afford, but they were part of the Beale Street scene. Surely we wanted to keep one or two of them! Then there was conversation that ingress and egress had to be from the north facing white downtown. If it faced south, then whites wouldn't feel comfortable.

Interestingly enough, the Chamber of Commerce said that, to be successful, Beale only had to get less than 10 percent of the Memphis nightly entertainment money. Aubrey Howard was named director of the commission and Ron Terry, president of First Tennessee Bank, was chair. Ron and I served on an ongoing seminar put on by the Brookings Institute that studied how to make Memphis live up to its potential. In an exercise prioritizing project expenditures, Ron didn't even mention Beale Street. A powerful family who served on the bank's board was developing an office park on the old Ridgeway Country Club property in East Memphis. I chided Ron with where his loyalty lay — downtown or out east?

As a perk of service, members were assigned the task of visiting various projects in other cities to see what they were like and how the cities developed them. Lucky draw, I got Pioneer Square in

Seattle, Washington. A representative of the mayor's office met me at my hotel. I was dressed in heels and hose appropriate for meeting a mayor's rep. She showed up in jeans. Cool. I ran upstairs, changed into my jeans, and off we went.

In Memphis, if you fix up your property, the city raises your taxes. Seattle's theory was that unimproved property needed more attention paid to it — fire and police protection — therefore, if you improved your real estate property, they gave you a tax break.

Pioneer Square is the neighborhood Seattle's original settlers created in 1852. When I saw it, they were just beginning to rehab the buildings and start the redevelopment. It's now a tourist area with restaurants, retail, and gentrified housing. During the planned construction, they were making use of the empty office buildings, where vagrants and the homeless hung out. Seattle made sleeping quarters out of one building, let the homeless stay there, and then hired the homeless to keep the area clean.

My guide said since there wasn't much to see at the time, perhaps I would like to see Pike Place Market. It was like a farmer's market on steroids, but it was mainly a fish and seafood market down at the water. Seattle announced plans to tear it down for new waterfront development. The citizenry was up in arms! NO! My guide said she hoped her boss would leave it standing.

We did a lot of talking about Beale Street, but very little was accomplished. It was eventually turned over to private enterprise, with the city retaining some oversight. Today it thrives with tourists enjoying good music and food. Y'all come.

Chapter Twenty-Four

My Divorce

If you are smart enough to have an uncontested divorce, the climax is when the parties sign the marital dissolution agreement. That's when the spouses can take a deep breath and perhaps reflect on what really went wrong.

Richard turned to me and said, "Well, I can tell you that in twenty-two years, I haven't changed one bit."

"I know, honey, and that's the problem. In twenty-two years, I've changed a whole lot."

While this book could be a thesis on the impact of the feminist and civil rights movements on marriages — and a lot of the women of the Memphis Panel of American Women could weigh in on the topic — it's not.

My life in the early 1980s was in turmoil. I finished law school, studied for the bar, got my first job in twenty-two years, negotiated a divorce settlement, left the house of which I had a part in building every square inch, and moved into a new home. Somehow I kept it together, for the most part. I had to; I was the protagonist after all.

Divorce negotiations can feel mean. "You can use Cheryl as a child tax deduction."

"Richard, Cheryl's twenty; I want Richard Jr.; he's fifteen."

"No, you can have Mindy." The children were pawns of negotiation. We did the wise thing. I let Richard use all three kids, since using them for deductions was more helpful to him, and he gave me cash in the amount I would have saved on my taxes if I had deducted one.

Feeling guilty for being the one to sever the marriage, I didn't ask for all I was entitled to and, at that time, retirement plans were not considered marital property. I did ask to redeem the stock in the company I had been given and sever my business relation as well. A plan was offered that I would be given a certain amount over five years commencing three years hence in 1985.

At the time there was a federal tax provision that if no rate of interest was specified in an installment payment, then the IRS would impute one. In my case, it started running in 1982 when the divorce was final. My attorney didn't catch it. I lost almost 30 percent of my property settlement agreement! The sad thing was, while I had to pay taxes on the imputed interest, guess who got to deduct it off their taxes? The imputed interest the IRS said I earned threw me into the 50 percent tax bracket. All my earnings and all my alimony were taxed at 50 percent. My tax person said, "Don't work too hard!"

After twenty-two years of preparation of joint tax returns, our CPA firm said it was really Richard's CPA, not mine. I sued, pro se, and got my ass whipped.

The hurtful thing was there was a letter in files I found in discovery that was written to Dad explaining I would be charged with imputed interest. In other words, they knew I would get screwed and didn't tell me. Dad must have felt a little guilt himself; he had all the stock redeemed the following year to stop the interest from running and the hemorrhaging of money.

The sad part of all that is that it impacts me today. My financial folks say I'm good until I'm eighty-one. I had no maternal female ascendants who ever lived beyond the age of sixty-one, so I wasn't worried about that. But now on the shady side of seventy-seven, I fear if I live to eighty-one, I'm in trouble. I tell my clients, "Thou shall not spend corpus." That bit of hanky-panky back in 1981 is making me spend corpus.

There is a Jewish expression used in difficult situations: Surely, nothing should be a total loss! All this was a learning experience that has helped me with my clients. An expensive experience, but an experience, nonetheless.

A lot of time went by between New Year's Day 1981, the day I decided this divorce was necessary, and the day we received a final decree in May 1982. It's a weird time for people facing divorce; the decision, "I need a divorce," is often years in the making. It feels as if a boulder is sitting on your shoulder, and you take it off and put it on the ground. So many folks then decide to go to therapy or hear, "Why don't we work on the marriage?"

Once that boulder is off the shoulder, it's too late. My divorce lawyer-mediator experience tells me that by the time people agree to call the therapist, it's too late. If only they had called at the first sign they weren't communicating, but now they aren't a team anymore.

Even more weird is the time between the signing of the agreement and the day you get the divorce. Like Richard and I did, a lot of folks are still sharing the house, taking care of the kids, sharing meals, and going about the daily routine. You're in limbo. Richard and I were always civil, so we could handle this. I don't remember us ever raising our voices to one another; our therapist suggested perhaps we should have.

At a Bar Mitzvah party of panelist Barbara Zitron's son, I danced with someone I had just met, David Bornblum. I had heard of David and his brother Bert; they were wonderfully philanthropic and had established the Department of Judaic Studies at the University of Memphis.

David was an easy dancer to follow, but at one point he "dipped" me. A dip is a dancing move where the man leans the woman backward to the point where her upper torso is parallel to the floor.

"David, better not dip me. I'm heavier than I hope I look."

He came back and asked to dance again. Again he started to dip me, and I protested in time.

I was flattered he kept coming back for more dances, but a bit embarrassed because he actually had a date that night with my neighbor. He asked if I was married, and I told him I would be getting my divorce soon.

David asked me to dance the last dance and, toward the end of the song, he bent me into a dip. Here I was in this man's arms on one foot trying to steady myself, and he leaned over and said in his Polish accent, "Vell, I think you are a beautiful voman, and your husband is crazy to let you go!"

Never had I had any man say anything like that to me before! But all I could think of was the cramp that started in my calf, surged up the back of my thigh, and assaulted my left buttock.

"Thank you very much, but please, please let me up!"

On leaving, David said, "I want you should meet my brother."

"Does he dance as well as you do?"

"Better."

The actual day of my divorce was a hoot! As an attorney, I was able to get the clerk's office to assign my case to Judge Alan E. Highers, the only judge who thought favorably of joint child custody, a status my husband and I decided we would seek. At a specially set hearing, Judge Highers granted my divorce. Minutes later, I was getting a divorce for one of my clients. So while I was in the clerk's office getting the paperwork in order for my client's divorce, a colleague, Hunter Lane, walked in with his big smile. "Jocelyn, how are you?"

Hunter Lane Jr. was a politician, a superb attorney, and a genuine public servant. And he had a terrific sense of humor. He ran for mayor of our city and lost miserably. I told him his defeat was such a disappointment because we were at an election party and everyone in the room had voted for him. Hunter said, "It must've been a very small party."

So to answer his question of how I was, I said, "I don't know."

"What do you mean you don't know?"

"Well, Judge Highers just granted me a divorce!"

Without hesitation Hunter looked down at his watch and looked up at me and said, "I'll race you to the motel!"

Freshly divorced, in this case by minutes, it was the perfect joke at the perfect time.

Bert Bornblum, David's brother, must have been watching the newspaper and called me for a date. No, he could barely dance at all, but he was a wonderfully interesting conversationalist. Since I met Bobby soon after my divorce, and since he worked on Saturday nights, I became David's Saturday night dance partner until he found another dancing girlfriend.

The two men flattered me by asking me to serve on the board of the Bornblum Foundation. Steering the foundation to some projects with which it was unfamiliar was a worthy endeavor.

Also at that Bar Mitzvah party was Bill. Bill called me for a date, but I had to refuse because the divorce wasn't final.

"Well, we can talk, can't we?"

And we did talk about every other week for months. When the divorce was final, Bill called for a date, but I was busy for the night he asked. He said he would call again.

This was strange. Here I was forty-two years of age, and I didn't know the current rules. But I did know we women were still the askees, and men were the askers. Bill had a ladies' man reputation. Women said he had a first-date routine: He would take a date to Justine's, Memphis's finest restaurant, then home to get into his hot tub and then make a move on her. I had my own hot tub and would be up for that program!

Hell, I decided to call him back. "Bill, would you like to be my first post-divorce date or not? Why don't I tell you when I'm free and you pick the time?"

We made a date, and he suggested we go to Justine's. Would you believe my now ex-in-laws were at the next table! My first date and I run into my in-laws. Actually they knew Bill and were gracious to us both.

Bill had an early flight out the next morning and said he would call me from San Francisco the next day. I never heard from him again. I flunked my first date.

People ask me what is the main cause of divorce. I say, "Money or sex." I used to say, "Money, sex, or drugs," but drugs make men impotent and take all the money.

I served for a while on a committee for the URJ dealing with the changing Jewish family. We discovered that most synagogue programming was geared for the nuclear family: Mother, Father, Dick and Jane, Mac and Muff. Statistically, that represented 17 percent of the Reform movement! There were widowed, divorced, empty-nesters, never married, gays and lesbians.

We had a subcommittee to look at divorce recovery and premarital counseling, which we had not addressed at our local Temple. We had a high-ranking person in the New York Catholic hierarchy come to offer us advice. In the documents he shared with us, there was no mention of money or sex. Another divorce attorney on the committee and I were stunned when we asked him about that.

"Oh no, we don't talk about that," he said.

I asked a local Baptist church if I could attend their divorce recovery program as research for my committee. They were delighted for me to attend. When I showed up for the first session and identified myself, the woman I had spoken with on the phone was all a-flutter.

"Oh, Mrs. Wurzburg, I am so glad I found you. I need for you to know that this will be Christian divorce recovery, and I didn't want you to feel I let you come under false pretenses."

I appreciated the consideration and assured her I understood that would be the emphasis. I irreverently referred to this church as "Fort God Two." It may be the second largest megachurch in town. The head minister introduced the minister in charge of "singles," who said that regardless of the "church home" we attended, that night we were at home. Attendees dropped their children off at the nursery but would pick them up in the gymnasium.

"We apologize; we forgot to mention that there is a ten-dollar charge for the four sessions for the snacks and refreshments, but since we didn't tell you earlier, it is voluntary."

It was genuine, but it was the best marketing theme I had ever heard. Psychologists presented lectures, and then we broke out into sessions. One was a religious perspective on divorce recovery; the other was more psychological. They needed an economic one!

There's a lot of loss of status in a divorce. It's terribly awkward with your couple friends. And it feels strange at the Temple. "Oh, Jocelyn, I have meant to call you." The address-o-graph plate for Temple mailings was amended to be "indented, indented, indented Mrs. Richard Wurzburg and back to the margin for the old address" that the post office had to forward. When do you get your own address-o-plate?

Bobby says if you are a happily divorced woman, men don't want you around their wives; if you are unhappily divorced, women don't want you around their husbands.

And sometimes the recently divorced can be their own worst enemy. I received an invitation to a wedding party for a son of a good friend. It was the crowd's first child's wedding. All dressed up and ready to go, I realized not a single old friend had called to offer to take me downtown. I was going to have to drive to the Peabody myself, find a place to park, and walk alone into the hotel. I had my first pity-party meltdown. I was so worked up I got undressed and went to bed. My friend was furious, and I didn't blame her.

I do have a bit of advice: Let your divorced woman friend pay for her own dinner or movie ticket. If you pick up the tab, then she feels awkward about calling you to go out to eat or go to a movie. There's dignity in a Dutch-treat relationship.

And yes, I got the famous phone call — thank God, only one — of a good friend's husband offering to "service me." Men, for your information, that's a pretty repulsive thing to do!

Chapter Twenty-Five

Joselynda, You're a Slut

"Joselynda, you're a slut!" *he* said. "And you have other good qualities, too."

As I have said before, I was such a go-o-o-o-d little girl. A genuine prude, well-behaved, inhibited from any sexual expression, I was a teen of the 1950s. We know the '50s; *he* calls it the great pussy drought of the '50s.

But I went overboard on my prudery; I was a virgin on my wedding night — the whole bit. You couldn't be a bad girl. To "put out" would hurt my reputation, embarrass my family, and bring shame on the whole Temple! You just had to be good. The virgin part went like this: If I slept around, boys would talk. When Mr. Right came along, he would hear about it and would never marry me. Sounded logical to me!

After the 1960s, society was sending different messages. I have a hat that reads "Well-Behaved Women Seldom Make History" and a T-shirt stating "Wild Women Don't Get the Blues." There was a song from somewhere that I heard later whose punch line was: "It's a sadder but wiser girl for me." For the record, I told my kids to "live with 'em before you marry 'em! You wouldn't buy a dress without trying it on."

We know what a slut is: A slut is a girl who does it 'cause she likes it! So despite all that perfect behavior, that wholesomeness, that restraint, Jocie hit her forties, got a divorce, and, *he* says, turned out to be the greatest slut this side of the Mississippi.

The *"he"* is Bobby Bostick, Robert Lee Bostick Jr., my high school crush whom I wasn't allowed to date because he wasn't Jewish. We ran into each other six months after my divorce and have been dating more than thirty-five years. He doesn't like me to say "dating."

"We should say 'going together.' We are more than dating," Bobby said.

We used to dance at Central High School at all the rainy-day sock hops — lunchtime dances in the gym when going outside for recess wasn't possible. We had to take our shoes off to protect the basketball gym floor, hence sock hop.

Bobby was hall monitor and, as yearbook editor, I managed to go down the hall every day to flirt with him. He sent me a postcard from the first of six colleges he attended, the University of Mexico in Mexico City, and I was able to fish it out of an attic box when we remet in 1982. Why I had saved it all those years, I don't know.

The last time I had seen Bobby was at a Vanderbilt Zeta Beta Tau party in fall 1957. Vanderbilt was his second school. He heard from my date that I was coming up, and he and his Delta Kappa Epsilon fraternity brothers crashed the party to dance with me. My date was a freshman and not exactly what we used to call date-bait. He grew up to be a noted attorney in Oregon.

Nobody else asked me to dance until Bobby burst on the scene, yelling, "Where's Jocelyn Dan, the best dancer at Central High School?" Amazingly, I became popular with the Zebes.

Bobby asked my date if I could walk him to the car. He asked for a late date, but I refused, thinking that was rude to the boy who brought me to the dance. Bobby kissed me goodbye and that was the last time I saw him for twenty-five years.

I almost didn't go to the party where we remet. The venue was a luncheon club I belonged to, TWRSFTPOTOTS. That's on the door. It stands for "The Wolf River Society for the Prevention of Taking Oneself Too Seriously."

The Wolf River runs into the Mississippi River. It starts up in West Tennessee east of Memphis, runs a bit north and ends up flowing parallel to the Mississippi for a short distance before entering it at downtown Memphis. When I was a little girl, sewage was dumped into both rivers, and downtown smelled pretty bad in the summer.

The club was created in the 1970s by Lucius Burch, Ann Rickey, Judge Bob Lanier, Robert Gooch, and others who wanted a place to have lunch in an integrated setting. For a long time it was the only place downtown that Blacks and whites could go eat together. The party was in honor of the birthday of Millard Fillmore, one of the labeled "do-nothing presidents," and thus idol of the club.

I had invited Marilyn and JoAnne, we three being recently divorced. JoAnne called at five to tell me she had cut her hand badly, was heading to the emergency room, and needed to cancel. It was storming outside, and Marilyn wasn't anxious to go out. At six thirty, JoAnne called again, saying she had been stitched up and she and Marilyn were coming.

When I got to the club, it was pouring down rain and the only spot I found to park in had a puddle at my door. I debated whether to get out and get all wet. Then I said, "What the hell." If love is a certain percentage timing, it's kismet we remet because I really almost didn't show up.

After a bit of time, I realized I hadn't checked out the music yet. I walked over to the banjo-playing duo, one of whom I knew. They were beginning their last set.

"Who's that playing with Dan Wilkinson?" I asked an acquaintance, who coincidentally booked the players and, I later learned, expected to be spending the evening with Bobby. He said the woman had nine cats in her house and that I probably saved him from cat-scratch fever.

"His name is Bob Bostick," she said. Out loud I exclaimed, and probably too loudly, "Bobby Bostick?"

"Jocelyn Dan?" he said, walking off the stage. He didn't have to say, "Don't leave." We instantly knew neither one of us was going anywhere until we had a chance to talk.

By the end of the set, the gals had gathered a group to go to dinner, and I invited Bobby to join us. At dinner he asked, "Will your father let you go out with me now?"

I said, somewhat indignantly, "I make those decisions for myself."

Only because my father was dead! If he were alive, I probably would have had to say no.

The storm had become a slight drizzle; the streets were wet. I think of that night often when it's dark out and wet because I fondly remember the street and traffic lights reflecting on the pavement. Red, green, yellow, white — colors on a black canvas. I smile on those evenings because I recall the delicious anticipation of driving home and Bobby following me. Oh, being single was going to be fun!

We talked, caught up on the twenty-five-year hiatus, kissed goodnight, and made a date for the next night.

Bobby had a gig every Saturday night. His father owned the Strand Theater in Millington, and Billy Owen and the All-American Band played country music every weekend. It was like a talent show; singers would audition every Tuesday night, and winners got to play on Saturday. There were regulars, and the winners brought their own audience — at five dollars a head. Bobby was the banjo player in the house band.

Our date started at "round midnight." Spooky, but it was the date of my ex-husband's birthday. Bobby calls that night the date of "La Grande Compromise."

He came in with a kiss, and we talked and "necked" a bit. "Necking" for me was done on a couch. I wasn't very good about necking in a car. In fact, my father told me he never wanted me out necking in a car. And when I asked him what if I liked somebody and wanted to kiss him, Daddy said he would always provide a comfortable couch in the safety of our home. I got an amazing amount of necking done on my house's couch, when I was assured it was private. I'm trying to remember now how I accomplished that!

Necking was a lot of kissing, but not touching breasts or the crotch area. That was "petting." I only had my breast touched once by a man before I got engaged to Richard. I was a prude!

We southerners had a scoring system in high school. It was like baseball scoring. First base was a goodnight kiss, second base was necking, third base was petting, and a home run was sexually going "all the way." Ann Landers, the syndicated columnist for the lovelorn, used to say you would not get in trouble if you kept all hands on deck and four feet on the floor.

Bobby and I were necking. In barely over twenty-four hours, he had already nicknamed me. Bobby nicknames everyone, and it's a sign of affection. His nickname for me was rather clever. His wife's name was Joella. Joella and Jocelyn, too close for a misnomer, particularly in passion. I immediately became Joselynda, pronounced in Spanish. This man's no fool.

We were necking, and I pulled back to propose: "Why don't we stretch this out?" reverting to high school.

I said, "We both know we're going to make love, but let's not jump right into bed. We could make this really fun and delicious."

"Like, how long a stretch?"

"Well, we could date and neck. And after a while when we get to know each other better, we can pet and just stretch this out before we have sex," I said.

"How long do you have in mind?" Bobby asked.

"Well, a few months — six months or so," I said.

"I'll compromise with you," he said. "How 'bout fifteen minutes?"

It ended up closer to his time frame than mine. But first there was a silly tête-à-tête between us.

We went into the kitchen to get a drink, and I opened the icebox door. Bobby was standing behind me and wrapped his right arm around my waist, giving me a back hug and peering into the fridge. It was pretty obvious I wasn't a cook. The refrigerator looked more like a bachelor's than a divorced homemaker's. My pride and joy of the contents was a water bottle. All my life we were never allowed to drink directly out of a cold water bottle. That water was shared, for God's sake, with the whole family. But I now lived alone, and it was my water bottle, damn it. I could drink out of it whenever I wanted. It stood beside a bottle of vodka and a bottle of wine. That was about it!

With the icebox door open and Bobby behind me, I turned around and said, "Sit down. We need to talk."

We did, cross-legged with my back to the open refrigerator shelves. "We need to have a conversation about disease!" I said.

When I got my divorce, I had promiscuity in mind! If I wanted a man, he was not going to be safe from me. But damnation, that was in 1982, just when herpes hit the scene. Damn! NOT my body!

So, "We need to have a conversation about disease!"

"I don't have any, and I don't want any!" he said.

Right answer!

Later that night, and later again that night, was when he gave me his supreme compliment: "Joselynda, you're a slut!"

Chapter Twenty-Six

Bobby

Running into your high school crush as a newly divorced person is a prescription for fun. For me it was a hoot! While I really knew nothing about him, there was a slice of our lives that had a common history. We went to the same college prep high school, and I knew he had at least started college, interestingly enough in a foreign country, Mexico, and then at Vanderbilt. We had listened and danced to the same music.

He was a clean-cut kid back then; his pants had a useless little Ivy League buckle in the back, and he didn't have a ducktail hairdo like the rogues wore. He was performing music when I remet him, and I loved music.

Horny as a toad, I planned to have a short-term f*#k buddy — a goy, boy, toy. What I didn't expect was his being a person of substance. He turned out to be a Memphis society renegade, denoting he wasn't shallow, and he didn't remain a member of Mensa because the self-conceit was obnoxious. Robert L. Bostick Jr. was intelligent, funny, entertaining, and ready when I was!

Before the relationship went from dates to dating, I pronounced to Bobby that if we were going to get along he needed to know that I took my civil rights, my women's rights, very seriously. "Don't bait or tease me about these subjects."

He responded, "Oh, Joselynda, everybody knows you're a n*%#@r-loving lesbian."

Bobby went to six colleges before graduating from Ole Miss. He joined DKE at Vanderbilt, which was a party frat in the tradition of *Animal House*. While Bobby was at Vanderbilt, James Lawson integrated the school; when he was at Memphis State University (now the University of Memphis), Maxine Smith and Laurie Sugarmon were integrating it; and at Ole Miss, Bobby went to college with James Meredith.

"Joselynda, I'm perfect for you. I helped integrate every college I went to," he said.

Explaining having Bobby in my life to my children was going to be a challenge. I had put in a call to my fifteen-year-old electrical wizard son to come fix my stereo, but he came by one rainy morning without notice. I met him at the door and said now was not a good time. When I called him later that afternoon, Richard Jr. came in without looking at me directly.

"So do you have any questions about this morning?"

"Well, what do you mean?"

"Obviously, someone was here."

"Yeah, and the car was dry." Richard Jr. doesn't miss much.

"True. But do you want to know whether the person was a man or a woman?"

"What do you mean?"

"Would you like to know if your mother is heterosexual or homosexual?"

"Oh, I hope you are heterosexual!"

"Then you are going to be glad it was a man."

Unexpectedly, he asked, "Is he going to call again?"

"I'm pretty sure he will."

Not quite sure why I handled it that way. It wasn't planned. But I wasn't going to hide my sexuality. Mama was going to be sexual, so I decided the question at the moment was not going to be if, but what kind.

In the next few phone calls from Richard Jr., he wanted to know if I had heard from Bobby. It was important to him. I was glad to be able to tell him we talk every day. Richard Jr.'s definition of slut is not a compliment.

Bobby didn't play music for me for months. I was curious why not, but I figured he was tired when he came over after rehearsal or gigging. When I asked why he hadn't pulled out his banjo at my house, he said he wanted to be sure I liked him first, and not just the music or the music player.

A banjo rally is held every Labor Day weekend in Eureka Springs, Arkansas, and Bobby invited me to go with him in 1983. On exhibit would be beautiful banjos for sale or just show. The instrument is really a drum with strings, but banjos are often made of exquisite wood and fret board inlays. Sometimes they are bejeweled.

"Joselynda, you will enjoy looking at these banjos more if you could pick one up and hear how it sounds," he said.

He taught me a few chords. I had never learned to play music — except I play a competent stereo. That's all it took. Bobby taught me how to frail a five-string banjo. I got good enough to play rhythm with him so he could play lead.

We traveled with our banjos until they got too heavy for us to lug around with our luggage. Airlines once let us put them in the overhead compartments, but when they began to insist we check them as baggage, we had to quit bringing them. Banjos are more fragile than they look and are very expensive; at least ours were. In Europe and in Mexico, we made friends with our music. We were often offered free drinks and once a free room in Playa del Carmen. In La Rochelle, France, and in St. Croix, we were offered gigs. Playing music with Bobby has been pure delight.

We both loved games: Bridge, Boggle, Jotto. Bobby taught me how to play pinball and Ms. Pac-Man. I quickly decided I couldn't compete against him; he could beat me at will, so I positioned us to root for each other and play against the "house." Playing machines at the bars was a fun date. Huey's had music on Sunday nights with no cover charge, so, since neither of us had very much money, we bragged we had more fun on less money than any two people we knew.

Bobby has a great sense of humor and is quick-witted enough to create a pun on the spot. There is a word game called "Stink-Pink" or "Stinky-Pinky" or "Stinkity-Pinkity," depending on how many syllables are in the words. A "Stink-Pink" is a type of pun and is best when it's a quick response to something said. For example, when we were watching a football game one afternoon, there was a Black guy, maybe Rod Bernstine, playing for San Diego. I need to explain to my reader that in Ethiopia there are Black Jews who are called by a pejorative word, "Falashas." If spelled "Bernstein," the name is thought of as a Jewish person's name. So when the TV announcer described a play by Bernstine, Bobby asked, "What do you call a Black football player named Bernstine who plays tight end? A Falasha flanker!"

When our relationship went from dating to going together, Bobby had a request for me. "Joselynda, I need for you to stay sane. Please don't go crazy on me." I would soon learn what he meant by that.

Mr. Robert L. Bostick Sr. and Jr. were somewhat estranged. I had seen the dynamic before: Depression-era fathers jealous of the silver spoons they had put into their sons' mouths. Bobby hid his parents from me until 1984 when we were going to Europe; the trip was a gift to us from my brother. We invited Mr. and Mrs. B to dinner so I could meet them before going abroad with their son. His mother, my mother, and my mother-in-law were cut from the same cloth. His father's opening salvo to me was, "What does a 100-horsepower woman like you see in my son?" I think that was supposed to be a compliment.

Mr. B was a self-made man and from all accounts had a terrific personality. The Bosticks were members of the Memphi Cotton Carnival "Krewe," and were country clubbers, albeit not the most prestigious club. Ms. Abby was president of her garden club. Mr. B knew my father-in-law, Reggie, so as a Wurzburg I was acceptable despite being a Jew. Besides, his best customers were Jews, so it was not a big deal that I was.

Bobby's father was vice president of the Variety Clubs International. Membership is based on being in the arts, mostly film, but also newspaper folk. My daddy belonged to the local "Tent" where Mr. Bostick was "Chief Barker." The perks of membership included liquor by the drink in a county that didn't allow it and previews of upcoming movies every Sunday night. We didn't realize it until the Variety Club came up in a conversation that Bobby and I knew each other as children and that our fathers were acquaintances.

Bobby was on the fast track at Sears and lived in Savannah, Georgia, when his father had a heart attack. Mr. B lured Bobby home with a promise of taking over the businesses he had on the side of his employed position. Bobby's father used to be with National Theatre Supply Co. and sold everything a movie theater needed, including projectors, seats, curtains, carpet, and speakers. Where Mr. Bostick didn't have a customer in a small town, he built a movie house. Bobby had to live in some of those towns and run the movies. Water Valley, Mississippi, was one such place; Ripley, Mississippi, was another.

An Evangelical Church of Christ minister in Ripley befriended Bobby and became a musical partner. He played a mandolin, and his wife played the Martin guitar. When having lunch, the reverend always ordered what Bobby did; Bobby realized the preacher couldn't read, but he could quote Scripture chapter and verse. One day the preacher saw Bobby leaving the movie in tennis clothes. Mistaking them for underwear, he took his jacket off to cover Bobby. The reverend asked Bobby to play with him on his gospel radio show. One day a call-in listener was accepting Jesus, and the reverend told Bobby to run out and buy another fifteen minutes!

The only place to get any food in Ripley after the movie theater closed down was the bowling alley, where they sold Mrs. Drake sandwiches. So Bobby learned to cook, gourmet cook. I became the beneficiary of that. The dinner party Bobby and I gave his parents was the first time Bobby had cooked for them.

Mr. B wanted Bobby to give up music and be a business "go-getter." Bobby wasn't about to do that. Besides he quickly learned that all the properties his father had weren't producing much income. Mr. B was living off retirement and used the properties as an excuse to keep an office to go to. The estrangement was not pleasant, and the two men were at a standoff. I tried to help the men reconcile, but to no avail.

Bobby was still legally married to his wife, Joella, when we remet. They had been separated four years. Since Bobby and Richard got along so well, I was prepared to like Joella when we met, but that didn't last long. When she realized she couldn't snap her fingers and command that Bobby come back to her — not that she wanted him to and not that he would — but when she realized that option was closed to her, she became hostile — anti-Semitic hostile. She would scream nasty messages on my voicemail, "You husband-grabbing Jew-w-w-w!"

Other than civil rights anonymous hate callers, I had no experience with this type of personal hostility. Bobby said to ignore it, but damn. This attending behavior would have confirmed my parents' prohibition against dating non-Jews. I knew Bobby couldn't stop her, but I was on the verge of telling him to get her out of my life or he would have to get out of mine.

To deal with my anger, I turned to my friend Happy, then a therapist. She came out to the house and suggested an exercise for me. She wanted me to get my tennis racquet, and I would kneel on the floor and hit a pillow with it while venting my quelled anger. On the way to the bedroom, racquet in hand, Bobby said, "Now be sure to keep your wrist straight." I loved it; Happy was not amused.

Joella became furious when she learned Bobby and I were going to Europe, and she even came to my condo and trashed my patio. I had to get an injunction to stop her untoward behavior. She had gotten into cocaine badly, running through her considerable inheritance on expensive, cocaine-laced trips to New York.

I got even with her. One of the reasons she and Bobby had not divorced was that she was dealing with an estate and was advised that a joint income tax filing would accrue to her benefit. Since Bobby was making low wages from his father and playing music, the deal was they would file jointly and she would pay the taxes. The trip to Europe was a business gift, and I was to receive a 1099. I asked that the gift be given to Bobby. So Joella paid the taxes on our trip to Europe! I try to be a nice person — until someone f*#ks with me. I insisted Bobby get the divorce, which he did. Joella died soon afterward — from an overdose of gin.

Being a musician and a manager of movie theaters, Bobby has always led a nocturnal lifestyle. As a late-night person myself, we were a good fit. We are both pretty good nighttime drivers, so we often started out on our road trips about midnight. Hoteliers were cooperative about letting us into a room at five or six in the morning and calling that the day of arrival. We often got two nights' stay for the price of one.

One fun thing about Bobby is his ability to do what I call "thinking it out." We all ought to do it, but as a good chess player, he mentally creates scenarios: If you say this, then he will say that, but if you say that, then he will say this. Bobby intelligently goes to further levels than I usually do. Actually, he has helped me with mediation.

I once told him that when couples reveal an affair, they often tell me it's not the sexual betrayal that hurts, but it's the dishonesty that hurts so much. Bobby laughed and suggested I tell them they don't want honesty. Here's honesty:

"Hi, honey, go ahead and have dinner with the kids; I'll be late. I'm going by Suzie Q's for a quickie."

"Okay, dear, have fun."

The husband comes home and the wife says, "Hi, darling, did you have fun? Suzie goes down on you and I don't, do I?"

"Well, yes, but you are a much better cook and a terrific mother!"

That's honesty. They really don't want honesty.

A few years ago, a sleep doctor prescribed a CPAP machine for me. A test revealed I woke up an extraordinarily high number of times an hour in REM, a condition called sleep apnea. A clear plastic hose runs from the air-generating CPAP machine to horizontal and vertical straps that fit over your head and are attached to nostril pods, which are placed on the openings of the nose. Air runs constantly into the nose. One night I told Bobby, "With this hose, I feel like an elephant."

"Joselynda, you're my long-term pachyderm," he said.

There is an amusing story about Mr. Bostick that falls under the category of Memphis just being a big Holly Springs. Mr. B owned the last two parcels of real estate on the east side of South Second Street where it meets G.E. Patterson Avenue. My father-in-law and Leo Bearman Sr. owned contiguous parcels three, four, and five. The five properties shared a sprinkler system.

Reggie and Mr. B had an annual ritual. Every year Mr. B sent Mr. Bearman an invoice for his share of the water bill, and every year Mr. Bearman said the bill was too high. So Reggie and Mr. B had an annual negotiation of the proper water cost to be reimbursed.

Reggie bought Leo out and devised the property to my three children. Mr. Bostick left his parcels to Bobby. So where but Memphis could I get a divorce from the father of my children and end up dating a man who will, with my children, own contiguous real estate and share a sprinkler system?!?

There's a lot to share about our relationship. After five years of dating, I gave him a drawer. After ten years, a closet. I don't remember inviting him to live with me. He kept his former living quarters, but one day I realized we were living together.

One night Mindy and I gave her best friend a pre-wedding lingerie shower. Bobby helped me with the food prep and then sat down on the sofa. "Bobby, this is a women's party; wouldn't you be more comfortable in the other room?"

"No, I'm fine. I never mind being one of the girls." And he didn't budge.

The bride's grandmother and future grandmother-in-law were talking. Since both had hearing problems, they spoke a bit too loudly.

"Who is that man?"

"I believe that's our hostess's live-in lova."

Another thing about our relationship is that it has been 100 percent "Dutch" treat. There's a lot of equality in a Dutch-treat relationship! This equality has been going on for more than thirty-five years.

Bobby loves to share with friends that we were each other's high school crush. "When we remet, we knew it had to be good. From the time our lips first met in 1957 until we consummated our love in 1982, we had a quarter of a century of foreplay!"

Did I say he is a sweet man? I wish all women a sweet man. And a supportive one through the good times and bad. He was there for me when Richard committed suicide, and I was there for him when his dear mother was murdered.

Family

Jocie's grandfather,
Sol Dan.

Jocie's grandmother,
Molly Berger Dan.

Jocie's father, Charles Lewis Dan.

Jocie's mother, Rose Sternberger
Heyman Dan Felsenthal.

Jocie's grandfather,
Jacob Block Heyman.

Jocie's grandmother, Rae
Sternberger Heyman.

From left, Reggie Wurzburg, Matil Wurzburg, Richard Wurzburg, Jocelyn Dan Wurzburg, Rose Dan, and Charles Dan on Richard and Jocie's wedding day, October 29, 1960.

ABOVE: Jocie won the Miss B'nai B'rith contest and competed in the City Beautiful contest in 1958. LEFT: Portrait by Joseph Dickinson in 1973.

ABOVE: From left, Ray and Barbie Dan; Richard Jr., Mindy, Cheryl, and Jocie Wurzburg; Libby, Robbie, and Dr. Mark Lavine at Cheryl's wedding to Michael Rubenstein, not pictured, in 1993. Front, Barry Dan and Charlie Dan. AT RIGHT: Jocie, Libby, and Ray in December 2017. BELOW: Cheryl, Mindy, and Richard Jr. AT BOTTOM RIGHT: Cheryl, Jocie, and Mindy at a horse show. Cheryl and Mindy have been rated No. 1 and No. 2 in the nation for the adult hunter class.

Bobby and Jocie picking five-string banjos.

Jocie ran into her high school crush, Bobby Bostick, playing banjo at the Wolf River Society, a club she belonged to, on December 3, 1982. They went to dinner that night and have been companions ever since.

Music

ABOVE: Oscar Peterson, Ray Brown, and Herb Ellis play at the Blue Note in New York. As president of the Memphis Jazz Society, Jocie talked her way to stage-side seats. RIGHT: Kathy Chiavola's bluegrass group at '300 Feet of Fun' in 1989.

Bela Fleck and Jocie at the Tennessee Banjo Institute.

Dr. Vasco Smith, Jocie, and jazz great Willie Ruff.

Religion

Ray Dan, Mindy Wurzburg, Dr. Mark Lavine, Libby Lavine, Charlie Dan, Barry Dan (the Bar Mitzvah), Bobby Bostick, Jocelyn Wurzburg, cousin and Rabbi Jay Heyman, Cheryl Wurzburg Rubenstein, Michael Rubenstein, and Barbie Dan atop the Hebrew Union College in Jerusalem.

ABOVE: The Dalai Lama and Bobby in Washington, DC. LEFT: Jocie's B'nai Mitzvah ceremony with grandsons Joshua and Noah and Rabbi John Kaplan at the Temple in Brownsville, Tennessee.

Lifetime Friends

Hallie Elliot, Suzanne Lazarov, Faye Marks, Joyce Lazarov, Jocie, Bobbie Shainberg, and Deanna Kaminsky.

Mimi Rice, Jeanne Varnell, Happy Jones, and Jocie dressed as Western outlaws at the Memphis Zoo.

Clockwise from bottom left, Jocie, Brenda, Patty, Beverly, Rosalva, and Regina.

RIGHT: The Cava Girls celebrate, including Tennessee state Sen. Beverly Marrero, Beanie Self, Gina Sugarmon, Regina Newman, state Rep. Jeanne Richardson, Rosalva King, Brenda Ofenheusle, Paula Casey, and Patty Dougherty.

Politics

LEFT: Jocie and Howard Baker at a 1966 election party for Baker, who was in the US Senate from 1967 to 1989. BELOW: Jocie with former senator from New York, former Secretary of State and Democratic presidential candidate Hillary Clinton.

LEFT: Jocie shakes hands with President Gerald Ford, who appointed her to the National Commission on the Observance of International Women's Year, in the Oval Office on July 3, 1976.

Milestones

Billy Mac Jones, president of Memphis State University, congratulates Jocie at her law school graduation in December 1979. Jocie was 39.

ABOVE: Jocie accepts the 2009 Distinguished Alumni Award at Rhodes College, formerly called Southwestern. RIGHT: Jocelyn Dan Wurzburg at her admission to the US Supreme Court.

Panel

LEFT: For the Panel of American Women, conversations about racism are less threatening while wearing gloves. BELOW: Memphis panelists gather in 2006, decades after the Panel began.

Jocie, Frances Hooks, Maxine Smith, and Dorothy 'Happy' Snowden Jones at the National Civil Rights Museum in 2005.

Photo courtesy Memphis Women Magazine

Awards

ABOVE: Jocie is featured on a YWCA billboard. RIGHT: Jocie with Jeanne Varnell and Happy Jones at the YWCA Distinguished Community Leadership Award ceremony.

Jocie; Margaret Behm, commissioner for Access to Justice; Dr. Wilsie S. Bishop, East Tennessee State University president; Shirley Raines, University of Memphis president; Inez Crutchfield, civil rights activist; and Rev. Becca Stevens of Magdalene House, a sexual and domestic violence advocate, are inducted into the Tennessee Women's Hall of Fame. Paula Casey nominated Jocie.

Bobby, Jocie, Richard Jr., and Mindy at the Women's Foundation of Greater Memphis Foundation Legend Award ceremony. The quilt in the background was commissioned as the art award.

Photo courtesy USA TODAY

Jocie and Modeane Thompson, a fellow member of the Memphis Panel of American Women.

Jocie with Paula Casey in 2013 at the Tennessee Human Rights Commission, which created an award in Jocie's honor.

The Women's Foundation of Greater Memphis honors the 2010 Legends honorees. Back row, left to right, Rebecca Webb Wilson and Jocelyn Wurzburg; front row, left to right, JoAnn Ballard and Gayle S. Rose. Not pictured, Lois DeBerry.

Chapter Twenty-Seven

Lawyer Tales

Law School's a Bitch

Federal Judge Woodrow Seals of Houston scolded me when I told him I was so unhappy in law school.

"I only wanted to go for a year to learn how to use a law library and legal language. I was seeking a federal appointment and thought law school would be helpful. I didn't particularly want to practice law," I said.

"You took the space of another student who really did. You better finish and make a good contribution to society," he said.

He was right. And he was an amazing, inspiring man. We were speakers at Lambuth College in Jackson, Tennessee, and shared a ride from Memphis. He had won a laity award for his Christian service to his church and was a well-respected jurist.

He shared he was furious with a case before him involving the school system. A child had a huge growth on the back of his neck, and the parents sought a waiver of the hair length rule so the little boy wouldn't be an object of ridicule. The school board was being obstinate. Woodrow thought they were being cruel.

"I know I shouldn't prejudge a case, but I'm going to throw out every damn dumb rule they have! How can they be so insensitive to this little boy!" he said.

I confessed law school was hard for me. As an audio word-for-word reader and somewhat dyslexic, covering all the material was difficult. I understood it; I just couldn't get it all read. And I later learned there is an underground education system at a law school that a town student misses by running onto campus for classes and back home to take care of home duties. I thought kids were cheating. They all seemed to have past tests. No one told me they were in the library for the asking. Thoroughly kosher!

Civil rights law was going to be my area of interest. You can imagine my chagrin when my constitutional law professor, H. Newcomb Morse (as in the H. Sophie Newcomb Memorial College in New Orleans) pronounced the first day of class, "The Dred Scott decision was a good one because it kept states' rights alive longer." Shit!

I was told if you don't like law school, you might not like the practice of law. Your constant, continuing education is a fact of life. Doctors need to study the new and latest. Attorneys have to study not only the new and latest, but also backwards into case law and even sideways, studying other states' case law to argue your case.

Since civics is no longer part of junior high curricula, as bemoaned by the American Bar Association, lay folks may not know that laws come from three places: the constitutions of the country and the states, statutes passed by Congress and state legislatures, and case law that judges rule when asked to interpret constitutional and statutory cases and issues before a court.

In July 1976, when President Ford appointed me to the IWY Commission, I dropped out of law school to serve. When he did not get re-elected, we appointees all had to resign our commissions, so I went back to finish my law studies.

There were some wonderful women in law school. Bonnie Ragland, Bernice Donald, and Veronica Coleman were such stars and followed school with brilliant careers: Bernice is a Sixth Circuit Court appellate judge, Ronnie was our US attorney, and Bonnie had a terrific private practice, which she gave up to go into a successful business. They were so supportive of us new students and have remained good friends.

Bonnie, Alayne Adams, and a few other University of Memphis law school graduates started the Association for Women Attorneys in my living room while I was a student. The organization is still going strong, I'm proud to say, being supportive to women. Early on, AWA invited this young, intelligent lawyer, the future first lady of Arkansas — Hillary Rodham Clinton — to speak to us to inspire what our feminism could bring to the law.

At the beginning of my final semester, I received a phone call from a professor who will remain nameless. He needed to see me right away. It seems he had been assigned as my advisor, something I never knew, and, on review of my record, he saw I was missing six bar courses. I had to ask, "What's a bar course?"

"You don't know?"

"No, sir, I don't."

It appears that all bar examinations test their nominees on certain subjects, and I was missing six of them. Here I had been taking labor, employment, and anything related to civil rights in anticipation of the law I hoped to practice. It wasn't like taking comprehensive examinations in undergraduate school for my major studies.

I stuffed as many courses as I could and audited others, but we discovered Mother's brain cancer a few weeks after the semester started. I lived at the hospital with her until she died in October 1979. The school was helpful. They let me graduate that December with my owing them two papers to be finished that spring.

There was a statistic that bothered me. Ninety-five percent of students who took the bar exam in Knoxville passed it. Only 65 percent of students who took it in Shelby County passed. Blacks and Jews failed in high proportions. My friends who are Black tell me standardized tests are trying for them. My friends who are Jews weren't used to a 65 percent pass rate. I got my Jewish backside to Knoxville to take the review course and the test there. I didn't like those stats. A contributing factor was the bar course was given in person in Knoxville and on video in Memphis.

The big issue for me was, with missing six bar courses in law school, this was not going to be bar review study; this was going to be first-time exposure! I went up there with study aids called *Gilberts* and *Nutshells*. No doubt, I was in trouble.

Studying for the bar was a potent time of life for me. I stayed for two months in an apartment of a friend's daughter who was going to undergraduate school at the University of Tennessee. I had never lived alone before. I had left my sister's bedroom for my husband's.

I did it very well. I devised a schedule of study I adhered to religiously, and I developed a plan of diet and exercise that I followed. I lost thirty-five pounds.

There was a funny situation. I got sick for about twenty-four hours. I missed the time I allotted to study income tax, a course I did take. I couldn't make up the time, so I just reconciled I would fail that question.

About a month into studying, I got a phone call from the board. I needed a personal interview with an attorney to complete the process. Would I mind it being a Knoxville attorney? But I never got a call from an attorney.

The exam was awful. The first day was a multiple-choice exam called the Multi-State. Most states used it. It was so difficult, most of us walked out shell-shocked. I called the one woman friend I made, and we had to talk each other into going back the next day. We both felt we had flunked it, big time.

I went to bed early to get a good night's sleep, but I couldn't, and I was afraid to take a sleeping pill. So instead of just lying there, I decided to read a little income tax. God was with me, bless her Black heart, the question on tax was exactly what I had read for forty-five minutes the night before. Directly on point. I aced it!

The next two days consisted of essay questions. I took the recommended course of action: Allocate minutes per question, read it carefully, outline my answer, formulate the answer in my head, then proceed to write. It worked.

I treated myself for the final evening to the best restaurant in Knoxville. The next morning I flew to New Hampshire to celebrate my fortieth birthday. Then there was the wait. Awaiting the results of the bar exam was excruciating, but I had a Bar Mitzvah to put on for my son to occupy my mind.

Back home and on pins and needles, I got a call from an

attorney, Fred Ivy, needing to meet me for the interview. Would this Saturday be okay? Sure. It was a strange encounter.

"Ms. Wurzburg, I am afraid I have to ask you something. It's personal. I don't know how to ask this, but I have to," he said.

"Mr. Ivy, don't hesitate. Please ask whatever you need to."

"Ms. Wurzburg, er, er, er," he stammered.

"Yes, sir."

"Ms. Wurzburg, do you promise to uphold the Constitution of the United States and the Constitution of the State of Tennessee?"

This was now 1980 and the Equal Rights Amendment was still pending for ratification by the states. I answered, "Yes, sir, but I'm trying like hell to amend it!"

"Shucks, I'm not going to ask you anything else. Would you like to see what a lady lawyer's office looks like?"

He took me to a friend's office. Nopey Dykes worked in a cubbyhole. I peeked in and said, "Wow, this looks just like a male lawyer's office!"

It was at the Bar Mitzvah party at the house that I learned the results of the bar. Terry Block Deboo, a high school friend also awaiting the results, had a person in Nashville get the results at the *Tennessean* newspaper before it was published in the papers. She walked into the house with a greeting: "You passed."

My First Court Appearance

When the Honorable Charles O. McPherson died, I regret to say I was not in a mourning mode of mind.

In my first week of my first job in twenty-two years with Williams, Benham, and McDaniel, I got a call from a Wurzburg Brothers business friend, Karl Zimmer. Karl's secretary's estranged husband had come to Indianapolis, Indiana; taken their children out of nursery school; and driven them to the Millington naval base, just north of Memphis, where he was stationed. Karl put his secretary on the line; she was hysterical. She had flown down to get the kids, but because she didn't have Tennessee divorce papers, the police wouldn't help her.

My new bosses allowed me to take the case, and we sprang into action to get an emergency setting for a hearing for the upcoming Friday motion docket. I did a self-taught crash course on the issue, and I was ready.

I laid out the facts and, before I could even mention the legal issues, Judge McPherson started grilling the attorney for the respondent, the ex-husband and father. After a feeble attempt of an explanation, the judge reamed the attorney a new one.

I stood up to insert more ammunition, when I felt the front of the seat of my chair touch my calves. I plopped back down in the chair. My boss, Robert Benham, leaned over and whispered, "When the judge is arguing your case for you, sit down and shut up."

The judge ordered the attorney to have his client return those children by air that afternoon. He was obviously angry at the situation, gave his order, and squelched any further comments by saying, "Next case." I packed up and we left.

It felt so good to call my client and tell her the kids were on the way. After our mutual excitement calmed down, she asked if there was any way to get the children's father to pay for the expenses he caused, her roundtrip fare, missed income, Memphis taxis, and my fee. I told her I was prepared to ask, but the judge made it clear that was all that was going to be said at that time. But I would check it out by going back and asking.

I filed another motion, and we were set for the next motion day. Motion days were Friday mornings when attorneys would come to court for specific, mostly pre-trial prayers, lawyer language for requests. And I was requesting reimbursement for funds she expended and a fee for me.

It was an extraordinarily warm, sunny day in January, perfect for being outside. The courtroom was packed. We were there early, so I was first up. I started by explaining that this was the case that was heard last week, and we were here for reimbursement of expenses. Oh, man, the judge turned on me! "Isn't this the case I ordered the father to return the children immediately?"

"Yes, sir, and we are requesting ..."

"Then let her pay for it."

He obviously had a golf date and justice was not going to get a fair hearing that morning! It was a sad career lesson for me that day. Lesson number one ...

My Second Lawyering Lesson, as Taught by Wyeth Chandler

By all accounts, Wyeth Chandler was a piece of work. I first met him as a city councilman, then our mayor, then a judge, and lastly a mediator. Wyeth was handsome in a roguish sort of way, with lots of early-graying wavy hair. I thought his eyes troubling, a bad-boy look lurking behind them. He was the adopted son of a former Memphis mayor, Walter Chandler.

Wyeth was on the city council when the Concerned Women marched on city hall. But after that, Wyeth called and asked me to join him for lunch to discuss our appearance. In my egocentric way, I was conceited enough to think that maybe someone heard us, that I might be able to influence the most conservative member of the council.

Lunch was fun and frustrating. We happened to meet at a restaurant in a building my father-in-law owned. Wyeth wasn't going to be influenced, and he was enjoying baiting me, even using the bastardized "N" word. Southerners of an upper class would use "nigra," so as not to be lumped into the category who would use "n*%#@r."

At the end of lunch, he asked why I was doing this. "Does your husband support you?"

"Oh, he isn't a bigot, but he wishes I wasn't the one doing this. Why do you ask?"

"Oh, usually a woman out in the limelight is missing something at home."

Strange remark, I thought.

The restaurant was between Main Street and Front. I had parked in a lot on Second Street, almost two blocks away. I got into the car, started it, and looked into the rearview mirror to back up when it hit me. He was making a pass at me! Today the kids call it "hitting on me." It was the first time in nine years of marriage anyone had made a pass at me. Well, I was pregnant almost three of those years, and I was only twenty-nine years old then. My first pass! I pulled out on Second and continued south to go to the company. Wurzburg Brothers was on South Fourth, and I felt the need to run straight to Richard.

Rich's reaction was surprising. He laughed. Wyeth and Richard grew up a block apart, and, while not lifelong buddies, they played together as kids. Social customs at the time would separate Jews and non-Jews around dating time, and besides, Richard went away to Culver Military Academy as a teen. Richard thought the whole thing was funny.

I didn't. I went through the steps a hit-upon person did: How dare he? He knew I was married, and in this case to someone he knew. WHAT DID I DO TO INITIATE IT? I learned my wedding ring and my marriage weren't a shield against a man coming on to me. I ought to be able to go places and do things without being considered fair game; I was married, for God's sake. How stupid I was! How naive!

I didn't run into Wyeth again until years later when he was mayor. He was an interesting mayor — labeled the playboy mayor — and sort of bragged about his running around. He was the speaker at some luncheon, and from the audience in the Q&A, I challenged something he said. After the program, he came down from the dais and joined our group. In front of everybody, he said, "We need to discuss this. There are rooms upstairs; come go with me!" In front of everyone! He was outrageous!

"Wyeth, I'm not going to go to a hotel room with you! I can't lay with anyone I can't vote for!"

One of Wyeth's escapades one night had him passed out drunk in a car on a date. The date picked up his police radio and called, "The mayor needs help." The newspaper monitored the police radios, and it became a news story. The expression became a catch phrase, like "Houston, we have a problem," and our local paper cartoonist used it often.

Wyeth settled down and got engaged. A young Black newscaster whom everybody in town loved gave the happy couple a big engagement party, and somehow I got invited. A friend of Wyeth's told me he couldn't go to the party but asked if he could drop something by for me to take to Wyeth. It was wrapped in a slim, cylindrical shape; I knew it had to be a marijuana joint, but wanting to be cool, I agreed to do it. At the party, I congratulated Wyeth, slipped my hand into his sport coat pocket, and whispered, "This is for your honeymoon from so-and-so" and dropped the package.

Months later I saw Wyeth at an event and asked, "Did y'all like so-and-so's wedding gift?"

"What are you talking about?" he said.

"At the engagement party, I slipped a gift from X into your pocket," I said.

I guess as instinct, he put both hands into his pockets and damned if he didn't blanch; he felt a small, cylindrical package. What's the probability that he would have on the very same coat that day, and the package would still be there! The mayor had walked around Memphis for months with a joint in his pocket!

Wyeth quit in the middle of his third mayoral term to be appointed by then-Governor Lamar Alexander to a Circuit Court judgeship. He was a licensed attorney but had not practiced in years. But he had a constituency who adored him and then elected him. He was considered eccentric, bringing his miniature white poodle to court every day and placing it on the desk sometimes.

In 1985, I invited him, as a judge, to meet my mediation teacher at a reception. Wyeth said, "This mediation stuff will never work in Memphis," and tossed the brochure back onto the table. Well, he retired from his judgeship and became Memphis's foremost mediator.

Actually, it wasn't exactly what we purist mediators called mediation. Wyeth did not allow his parties to dialogue. They didn't talk with each other, learn each other's point of view, nor did he allow disputants to co-create a solution. He spoke with both of them separately, evaluated the case for each side, and then told them how to settle. The attorneys loved it! That process closed the files and, if their parties weren't happy, they told them, "Look, he's a former judge and he knows, so it's best to do what he says."

Tragically, Wyeth died too young at seventy-four. He had a heart attack while mowing his lawn and the 911 dispatchers had a jurisdictional conflict over which government was supposed to respond. He died waiting for help.

Well, Wyeth did teach me my second lawyering lesson:

I had a divorce case where the husband didn't have it on the hip yet but was to inherit a lot of money when probate finished. The wife knew she wasn't entitled to any of it, but she and the kids should benefit from the income from it. Husband had Wallace Maroney, a "good ole boy" redneck, representing him. I had sent a settlement offer, but the husband was having none of it.

This was my first trial, and I was a nervous wreck. We were sitting in Judge Robert Lanier's courtroom in the back when it was announced that the previous day's trial was not finished, and we were to be transferred by interchange to Division 3 — right now. Maroney recognized the division, and, while walking out and down the hall, he kept whispering in my ear, "I got you now, Wurzburg, we're going to Chandler's court. I got my judge, Wurzburg, I got you now!"

Judge Chandler came in, we rose, and he said for us to commence. I stood up and read my opening statement off oversized index cards. Maroney recited his off the cuff, and the case began. Somewhere early on, Maroney was contending that the husband had all this debt and couldn't afford alimony, nor much child support. It came out that the husband was only paying interest on the debt, and the debt corpus would always look high, until the divorce was over, and he decided he would pay it when his inheritance kicked in. I questioned this scheme.

Maroney said, "Your Honor, this is some n*%#@r trick to ..."

I jumped to my feet, stomped my foot, and said, "Your Honor, I will not tolerate that language in a court of law, and you shouldn't either!"

Wyeth rolled his eyes, looked at Maroney, and said, "She's right. I would like to see you two in chambers."

As a gentleman should, Maroney held the door, allowing me to go in first. I looked up at Wyeth and whispered, "This is my first trial."

He whispered back, "I'll take care of you, baby."

And he did.

He was reading the file, and we briefed him on what this was all about. He noted that the plaintiff wife used her maiden name and had not adopted her husband's name.

"What's this two different names stuff? Is she one of those feminist dames?"

My heart sank, oh Lord! Then he turned to Maroney and said, "And he wants custody half the time? Is he really going to get up and fix breakfast for these kids? One of these cereal dads?

"You know, these are weirdos; y'all go out in the hall and settle this case right now. Wallace, you tell him I think I'm inclined to give her half of his inheritance if y'all don't settle." On the way out, he winked at me.

We settled. And it got back to me that my client bragged all over town about my stomping my foot in court in protest of bigotry.

I learned that justice is often based on who you know, which leads me to lesson number three.

By the way, this was 1981, about thirteen years after I first met Wyeth. I had gotten more involved in human and civil rights. I was gone from home a lot; the Panel often met at night when the working panelists could meet. And Richard had become less and less supportive.

Things were beginning to be not so good at home. By this time, I had gone to law school, was practicing law, and was in the process of divorce. Maybe Wyeth knew more than I did at the time.

My Third Lesson in the Law

Carol was a shy woman in her late forties. She supported her drunken husband for most of the marriage with bare minimum wages as a telephone operator, when there were actually women who assisted you in making a call. This was in Millington, a small suburban town north of Memphis with an antiquated phone system. She reared the kids singlehandedly.

Carol wasn't well, and she feared her working days were limited.

But she needed the health insurance. Her husband sobered up and no longer had any use for her, as with too many enablers. In derogation of his twelve-step program, he was mean-spirited and hateful to her, and he didn't want to give her a dime. Husband had become an Alcoholics Anonymous (AA) devotee, motorcycling around West Tennessee and speaking at meetings as a success story. I don't know the AA structure, but he became a "biggie" in the hierarchy and was in demand as a motivational speaker.

We showed up for court, this time Chancery Court, and the clerk directed me to go to chambers. Fortunately, my good friend Bonnie Ragland came to court to give me moral support. She and Carol went outside in the hall to wait for me.

Let me digress to tell you about Bonnie. We met in law school; she was two years ahead of me. Until I got there, Bonnie was the oldest kid in law school. She was a natural redhead and freckled in an attractive way. Reared in Kansas as an only child, Bonnie exuded confidence and competence, perhaps instilled by her father, a school superintendent.

Married to Tyrus, owner of Message Factors, an early and successful marketing and consulting firm, Bonnie was in law school for the sole reason of wanting her own career. They had one daughter, who coincidentally showed horses with my girls, but I had never met her before. Bonnie was a young breast cancer survivor, but she never let the disease nor the partial mastectomy define her.

Eventually, Message Factors grew to a point that Ty needed Bonnie's competence in the business, and she gave up her law practice to become a company officer he could trust while he took the business international. Eventually they sold the business, and they now live atop a mountain next to Fontana Lake in west North Carolina. The magnificent house has a 360-degree view, the west one of the Smoky Mountains on the Tennessee and North Carolina border. And in fact, when you awaken in the morning, the mountains are covered in a haze that doesn't dissipate until afternoon, if then. Hence, the Smoky Mountains.

Bonnie and two male fellow students, one Black and one white, went to the national finals of Moot Court and got tagged as the *Mod Squad*, after the makeup of the cast of a popular TV show at the time. A true feminist, Bonnie and I and a few others conceived the formation of the Association for Women Attorneys in the law school's coffee lair. There were still some uncomfortable with women in the law, like the dean.

With Bonnie and client Carol outside, I went into Chancellor George Lewis's chambers, where he and the opposing counsel, Charles W. Pruitt, city court judge of Millington, were already drinking coffee. I met them both for the first time and was informed that the chancellor had been briefed about the case (in an ex parte conversation). And further, the chancellor thought he was going to accept the husband's proposal to settle. Since I hadn't seen a proposal, I asked what the terms were.

"Your Honor, that's not fair to my lady," I said, and launched into why and what would be better.

"Mrs. Wurzburg, I think the husband's terms are reasonable."

"But your Honor, husband's alcoholism was the cause of dissipation of any assets, and she is not well. She will need to cut down on her work and will need supplemental alimony," I said.

"Mrs. Wurzburg, take the husband's offer or you will get less at trial."

Furious, but trying to contain it, I smarted off, but in a low and calm voice: "Your Honor, I am a new lawyer, and I need to go back to my office and consult with my associates on what I do now to protect my client."

He stood up, fuming. "Mrs. Wurzburg, take that offer to your client! Now!"

I was on the verge of crying when I told Bonnie and Carol what had happened. Bonnie turned to us and said we had no choice. Carol had to take the offer.

I reported back to the chancellor that my lady accepted the offer. But her husband reneged and refused to go along with his attorney's proposal.

We went to trial then and there. It was miserable, and so was I. It was necessary to have Carol's adult children testify that their alcoholic father would beat up their mother. I had placed their children as weapons in a war.

Her husband got on the witness stand and launched into his well-rehearsed AA speech — the one evidently so successful on the AA circuit. He admitted all the facts and cried, literally, that the disease had destroyed him and his family and that the road to recovery was hard, but he said he hadn't had a drink in three years. He did not reveal that since he got sober, he had ridden off into sunsets with one adulterous relationship after the other, leaving his ill wife, who had supported the family all this time, to fend for herself. So much for the Step to Recovery that has one make amends to those you hurt.

A problem in divorce law is that when a spouse survives barely hand to mouth during the divorce process, she (most of the time it is a she) has just proven she can make it on that amount of money. Never mind the credit cards are maxed out, she's borrowed all she can from her family and friends, and she can never recover.

As promised, she got less at trial!

I later learned Judge Pruitt was my chancellor's election campaign manager and that my chancellor was in AA. It was said that he infamously kept a list of election contributors in a drawer at the bench, and he would check it when parties approached the bar. Hell, how would I know those things! So, I learned — again — that justice may depend on who you know.

This experience was devastating to my client and to me. And I learned that I didn't want to do this anymore!

Family Law Code Revision Commission

To represent mediation on the committee, I was asked to serve on the Tennessee Family Law Code Revision Commission. This was an instrumentality of the Tennessee Bar Association (TBA); it was a ten-year appointment. Meetings were held monthly in Nashville at the TBA office. Our recommendations went to the legislature or to the Tennessee Supreme Court. Dearly departed Mary Frances Lyle and Janet Richards were the stalwarts on the commission along with the top divorce lawyers from around the state, such as Amy Amundsen and Steve Cobb. Again, I found myself in high cotton.

The most important work we did was to address issues pertaining to children of divorce. First, we did away with the words "custody" and "visitation." Our mantra was that custody was for prisoners, and visitation was for funeral parlors. Who wanted to be a noncustodial visiting parent? The question became when a parent was on duty and off duty.

A parent who had the children more than 50 percent of the time became the primary residential parent. Less so, then that parent became the alternate residential parent.

We tackled the issue of child support. We had guidelines to guesstimate the amount the alternate residential parent paid the primary residential parent — 21 percent of income from all sources for one child, 32 percent for two children, and so forth. Heavy lobbying by the Dads Against Discrimination (DADs) talked the state legislature into looking at the income shares model. It was a computer program that based child support on each parent's income and the amount of time that the children spent with each parent.

If a stay-at-home mom wanted to remain at home post-divorce, she would be imputed to earn $24,000 a year to put into the calculation. Being a stay-at-home mom was always a joint decision between Mom and Dad to begin with, so now to continue being one when expenses would go up — you now have two utility bills, two places to live, and two phone bills — Mom gets penalized badly.

The other bad news for kids of Tennessee divorce is the assessment of what children cost parents. There are numerous assessments out there in statistics land from which to choose. While based on various locales and the standards of living in those locales, there is a subjective element into what children cost. The lifestyle of a child and the cost vary with the income history of the parents, but there is no universal agreement on what that cost should be. Our legislature chose the least expensive assessment for our children and then based each parent's contribution to the kids on that lower figure. Bottom line: Low child support.

Mediation was even more valid when parties in mediation could ascertain just what their kids cost and then supplement the computer-generated child support assessment with alimony to keep that household afloat. At the time, that was expedient because alimony was tax-deductible for the payer; they could have sent over more dollars if a dollar didn't cost one hundred cents. Tax reform of 2017 chaotically did away with deductible alimony: Spousal support will become a hard sell.

Then the DADs started demanding 50-50 percent of time with kids, knowing it would reduce the child support figure, but also knowing the child would be with Dad's new girlfriend or his mother, since he worked much of that time. Enter the lawyers for that battle.

One case particularly bothered me. The difference between the old guidelines on child support and the new one was over $600. That's a hit! The child was first-chair clarinet in the All-State band. This extracurricular activity was pretty expensive. It involved uniforms, travel to competition, and upgrading the instrument. The new guidelines didn't include extracurricular expenses. When the commission brought this up to the legislature, their response was that Mama could go to court and ask for those. What! That costs more than the activity. The mama in my case said flatly the child couldn't continue with the music if Daddy wouldn't help. The big issue is the extracurricular skill may be the ticket to college. It was for this child; hopes of a music scholarship were dashed.

The commission did create the Tennessee Parenting Plan, either one imposed by the court or decided on between the parties. The Tennessee Parenting Plan outlines time spent with the children, holiday sharing, who gets the tax deduction, who carries life insurance and how much. It does put the children front and center when parents need to divorce. Naturally, parents own the decisions they themselves make.

The work was hard, but the results tangible. Janet, Amy, and I bonded during our drives up and back from Nashville. Janet became our "shero" of courage, driving herself to chemo and writing the latest book on Tennessee divorce law before she died.

Mediation and Me

A few divorce trials later, I learned that I did not ever want to experience again a situation where I had to have children — even though willing adults — take a side in support of one parent against the other. I learned that divorce litigation isn't what I spent more than three years of my life in law school to do.

I felt stuck. Here I had this law degree. I was now forty-two years old, divorced, and couldn't afford to do the area of law I went to law school to do. And besides, I couldn't get a job with a labor firm to help teach me real-world labor law. I had never clerked for a firm, feeling it unfair to take a job the kids needed to stay in law school. They worked to survive, and I didn't need to do that. So I came out of law school less prepared than I would have liked.

I had gotten a few job offers, but I could tell from my interviews that they expected I would come in with a portfolio full of Wurzburg Brothers cases. The name got me in the door. I appreciated the job I was offered with Williams, Benham, and McDaniel. I explained I would not be bringing any cases with me. But as luck would have it, a wealthy woman at the horse barn needed a prenup for her remarriage the next week. I had not yet reported for work, but here I was with a case. I'm sure they thought I would be a rainmaker.

In my early work experience, post-law school, domestic relations law was all I had learned. And I definitely didn't want to litigate divorces. Hell, I had just gotten the fight out of my life; I didn't want to litigate anything. So how could I help people, make a living — I now had to do so — and use what I knew?

The law firm realized this wasn't going well for me. When they fired me, I decided to hang out a shingle in "uncontested divorce." If folks had to get a divorce, I was selling a civilized way to do it.

It meant meeting with both parties, which was a no-no at the time. An attorney is not supposed to meet with both parties, and you can't represent two sides of a law issue. An exception was a real estate attorney; they could meet with both sides because they had a joint interest in transferring property to the buyer from the seller. That was a common interest.

Since Tennessee is not a no-fault state, you have to have a plaintiff suing a defendant to break the marital contract. My thought was that surely there was a joint interest in severing a marriage and being able to preserve enough of a relationship to co-parent children cooperatively. Surely this was a sellable service. This was pre-mediation.

I went to Lance Bracy, head of the Board of Professional Responsibility, to discuss the concept of meeting with both parties as long as the defendant understood I was only representing the plaintiff. The defendant was there "pro se" and had to get another opinion before signing any agreement. Lance, unbeknownst to me, had a daughter who went through a miserable divorce that took forever, and he was for anything to ease the process. In fact, he became my best ally when I was trying to get mediation started in Tennessee.

Bonnie Ragland offered to rent me space at her firm in 1982. My theory was right. There was a market for civilized divorce. I actually got cases and mostly by word of mouth.

I wasn't going to get rich practicing this kind of law, but I had alimony as a cushion. Alimony sustained me; working would give me a better standard of living. Earned income and alimony combined would never allow me my pre-divorce lifestyle, but Richard and I had never lived high. We didn't want for anything, but we were not extravagant — except for the horses. After divorce, he took care of all the kids' needs, without the need of any contribution from me.

And then, thank God, this new thing, mediation, came into my life. In 1984, a pamphlet came across my desk. Marilyn McKnight was going to teach a course in divorce mediation in New Orleans. My brother lived there, and I thought, "Hum, a tax-deductible excuse to visit my brother Ray in NOLA. That can't be all bad."

The course was exactly what I was looking for. I was sort of doing it, but the process I was using had a name and a skill set. I was perfect for it and it for me.

I came home excited and ready to tell the bench and bar about this new discovery. Mediation is a process where a third-party facilitator helps people in conflict arrive at a resolution. Some disputes are distributive: Pay some money and you never need to see each other again — automobile accidents, for example. The disputes I dealt with are transactual: The parties want or must have a continuing relationship after the dispute is resolved — divorcing parents. If the parties themselves make the decisions, they'll own it.

Dave Shearon was a help, too. He headed the Commission on Continuing Legal Education and was always exploring alternatives to the harsh effects of litigation and the stress of a law practice. I came back from mediation training wanting to give CLEs on the subject, and he approved anything I wanted to do. I became Memphis's first professional mediator. Some have called me the "Grandmother of Mediation," but I prefer "Queen."

Anke and Ina

In the year 2000, I received an inquiry via email from Anke Hillienhoff for an internship. Email was fairly new to me, and I had been warned about foreign solicitations that caused mischief. I ignored it, but she kept inquiring. Anke was a law student at Munster Law School in Germany seeking mediation information. She was from Blumberg, a town near the Netherlands border. The German government would pay for all her travel, living expenses, and a stipend. All I would have to do was let her come work for me for free. I admit I was intrigued.

I decided to send her my resume, which clearly shows I am a Jew and civil rights activist, and I asked her to share it with her parents. Then she could get back to me. That wasn't a bit subtle. She responded that her parents were more excited than ever for her to come work for me. I am so glad she did.

Anke and I bonded almost immediately. She is incredibly brilliant and gorgeous. I got her a place to stay at a friend's attic apartment and gave her my BMW to drive.

I gave her a day to catch up on sleep and settle in, and then we went about the business of arranging how one spends months in a foreign country. I took her to my bank and introduced her to the manager for her monetary needs.

We secured a cell phone, which was a bit of a bother. My son sent me to a salesperson friend who called me after we left the store. "Ms. Wurzburg, you don't have any credit. Don't you owe anything to anybody? But since I know you, I can sell you this cell phone."

Anke was a quick learner. I let her sit in on mediation sessions and take the notes. She also served as my receptionist, since I always created my own documents. I took her to court and to Nashville to the Family Law Code Revision Commission on which I was serving. Interestingly enough, there were two members who spoke fluent German.

Anke spoke six languages. She had a slight accent, but I got used to it except when she came into my office to tell me I had a "wisitor." She later told me that when she returned to Germany and performed the oral portion of her comprehensive examination, she had to speak in a few foreign languages. The examiners were amused when she used the word "y'all" and spoke English with a southern accent. Anke got an MBA after becoming a lawyer.

On another trip, I took Anke to Washington, DC. I loved showing her the city and giving her a nighttime tour of the monuments. I think Washington is beautiful, not as beautiful as Paris, but close. The big difference is the age difference, not of the tourists, but of our antiquities compared to those in Europe. When I visited Anke in her quaint town of Blumberg, untouched by World War II, its buildings had dates of 1462 and 1307 engraved in stone. Anke's parents owned a camera and photography store and lived quite nicely in quarters above it.

I took Anke to Atlanta to a CSA meeting. Under the category of coincidences, we happened to sit at lunch at a table next to a rabbi friend. He caught her accent and started speaking German to her. And when she asked how he learned such good German, he said he had gone to the University of Munster!

Anke had a fellow student friend who got an internship in San Diego but, strangely, had only seen her mentor one time. We invited Ina Hoppe to come to Memphis to visit, and we adored her, too.

I got both girls into Larry Rice's family law course for free and then later into a mediation course I was teaching. Ina came back to Memphis a few more times, just to visit us and rest.

Bobby and I visited Europe and stayed with the parents of both girls. Neither set of parents spoke English, which made conversation tiring on the daughters translating everything. My love of Broadway helped me with my opening salvo with the Hillienhoffs. *Kiss Me Kate* taught me the word "wunderbar," and all I had to say was, "Anke was wunderbar!" It's amazing, but after a while you almost feel we are speaking with body and facial expression.

Ina and Anke invited us to the Documenta, an extraordinary art exhibit held all over the town of Kassel, Germany, every five years. Ina's folks owned an apartment, and we stayed on the fifth floor with no elevator. We learned to bring down everything we needed on the first pass!

Anke, her husband Philipp and kids, and Ina have met us in various places in Europe when we have visited. Anke loves working as a stay-at-home mom; Ina still travels the world for her job.

Ina called us once saying, "I got this job and the first week they sent me to Japan to negotiate some deal. I've never negotiated anything in my life! Why would they do that? It must have not been too important, and it was a test." Evidently she passed, since that's what she does for a large corporation.

We stay in touch, not enough, but I am so grateful I answered Anke's email. By the way, Anke's parents had a Jew live with them during the war, which includes them among the "righteous."

Mediation Tales

It helps to teach mediation by telling some of my favorite mediation stories. My all-time favorite was an employment case for the EEOC. Attorney for the charging party came into my office with his client and the client's father. He barged past my receptionist and confronted me: "Ms. Wurzburg, I've got to talk to you and talk to you right now. Get me out of this! We are suing on reverse discrimination. There is no such thing as reverse discrimination. He's my church secretary's son. Get me out of this! We will be dismissed on summary judgment."

I thanked the attorney for the heads up and told him to chill. We would work something out. Charging party was a handsome young white man, movie-star quality. Married with children, he was a nice person. But he was a bit slow, hence his father came with him. While slow, he was qualified for his job. His Black supervisor fired him.

Since I practice facilitative mediation, I had all the parties in the same room: house counsel for the company, its HR person, the charging party, his attorney, and his father. The young man was able to share what had happened to him. His Black supervisor and Black co-workers caught on pretty quickly that he was slow. They were sending him out for coffee; one even had him pick up clothes at the cleaners. It was a hostile workplace and, though reverse discrimination is not a cause of action, this charging party was being screwed.

Because the company was sitting there to hear what was going on (yea, facilitative mediation), they gave him his job back, but in a different location, with back pay and his missed contributions to the 401K. None of this could have happened in court.

After concluding the mediation, the young man stood up and said, "One more thing." I thought I would kill him. I dreaded what was fixin' to come out of his mouth. "Please, God, don't let this man f*#k up this agreement," I thought.

The young man asked, "Would it be all right if I come get my uniform for my mother to alter so I will look really good my first day back on the job?"

I held back a tear, likewise the house counsel and HR person.

All's Well That Ends Well

I walked into the lobby of the Germantown Performing Arts Center, and a woman was at the door. She threw her arms around me and said, "Jocelyn, I am so happy to see you. Would you believe that I am here tonight with my husband, my parents, and John, my ex? We are all friends! Bless you for mediation. This wouldn't have been possible without you."

A Desire for Dignity

The complainant was an older Black man who had worked at Company X for thirty-five years and was now claiming discrimination on the basis of race to the EEOC. He came with his wife of thirty-eight years. Seated in the room were the company owner, his counsel, the regional manager from Atlanta, and the local plant manager. Complainant had five grown children, and all were educated. I knew when I asked that a source of pride for older Black parents was having their children go to college.

The complainant took almost an hour going through a litany of situations and events he felt were discriminatory. One was that the local plant manager wanted the employees to meet in his office every morning to pray. "I refuse to do that. These men quit praying and then come out on the floor bragging about running around on their wives. I'm not going to pray with those people."

"The white guys get to have a cell phone with them on the floor. We Black guys aren't allowed. I needed some time off to visit my dying brother, but I wasn't allowed."

"When my gout acts up, I asked for a stool to halfway sit by the machine but was told I couldn't. There's no reason for me not to have a stool there."

"I have trained men to work every machine in the plant. I've trained men to be my supervisor."

In fact, this man in another place and time should have been the plant manager. But he grew up in this company under Jim Crow.

During the conducting of a mediation, we mediators often form an hypothesis about what really is the issue. Then through various techniques and questioning, we test our hypothesis. The one I formed here was that this man, while supporting his family of seven, never got to participate in the civil rights movement. He just couldn't take off. So now he had had enough.

We reached the point in the process where I asked my parties, "If you could wave a magic wand, have all the problems resolved, and could drop this charge, what would you need?" I perform needs-based bargaining.

The man answered matter-of-factly, "Dignity."

"Okay, what does dignity look like?"

"I don't know. I just want dignity."

I asked for a private caucus to flesh out the meaning of dignity. With his wife ill, he needed to be allowed a cell phone. He wanted reinstated vacation time for expired but unused days. He wanted the stool, but just for those machines where use of one was possible and only when he needed it. But at no time did he mention MONEY. Not one dime. I even asked whether he felt he needed compensation. "No."

I took the requests back to management, and he got agreement for every demand. It was I who pointed out to the company owner that this was not about money.

"Y'all didn't come down here without a checkbook. This man emphatically refuses any concept of monetary restitution. You have learned more about your company than you could have imagined, and I have a hunch that if you didn't accept his demands you may have lost your most valuable employee." They nodded. We resolved the case and dismissed the EEOC complaint.

On the way out, I did something mediators shouldn't do. I did suggest to the owner that a thirty-fifth anniversary of employment or a Christmas bonus might be appropriate.

SCOTUS

Maureen Holland is my latest "shero." The Supreme Court of the United States pulled through, giving Maureen a much-deserved victory in the case giving gays the right to marry. She was the attorney for two men legally married in another state who needed their marriage recognized in Tennessee. One was transferred here for the Navy and suffered the indignity and detriment of their marriage not being honored. She is one lawyer who created a right!

Maureen caught my attention at a Gandhi Institute by giving a lecture on being a "holistic lawyer," caring for the whole client and not just winning a case. That means settling or mediating may be in the best interest of an emotionally fragile plaintiff rather than the fight. We had lunch while listening to a friend play guitar. We learned that we both had wanted to take guitar lessons, asked the friend to teach us, and commenced a friendship with a number of common interests. Maureen started an organization called Lawyers as Peacemakers, Lawyers as Problem Solvers.

And now this fabulous victory. Go, girl!

The court also upheld two important concepts. A major component of anti-discrimination law, using disparate impact statistics to show discrimination was taking place in fair housing practices even if no one intended to be prejudiced, could be proof. Proving "evil intent to unlawfully discriminate" is almost impossible. No one can prove what's in someone's mind.

Also, the court upheld the Affordable Care Act (Obamacare), thank God. It was a good week for progressives and a sorry one for conservatives disappointed with Chief Justice John Roberts. With the 2016 election, Obamacare is in jeopardy. Having survived sixty votes to repeal it, Obamacare is now threatened by the new tax law. Why do conservatives want sick, unhealthy children to run around our grandchildren?

Actually, before I retired my law license, I was allowed to argue before the Supreme Court. Not that I was ever competent to do so, but our Association for Women Attorneys arranged to have us "introduced" to the court. Before you can participate in a Supreme Court case, or any court for that matter, some qualified, admitted member of the bar has to introduce you for admission. Locally, it's usually your boss.

It is a very short ceremony: The entire court comes in, is seated, and then we are introduced. The chief justice moves for our acceptance and it passes. Expensive little process — airfare, hotel, and all — but worth it. The courtroom is magnificent, and the best part for me was Thurgood Marshall was sitting there. It was a thrill.

Memphis has a nexus to a number of historic legal precedence cases. For example, *Baker v. Carr* gave "one man, one vote" to us.

I never met Abe Fortas, who argued *Gideon v. Wainwright*, which said poor folks accused of a crime have a right to counsel. But I know his Memphis family. My friend Jimmy Jalenak, the only person I ever heard of turning down an appointment as editor of a law review, and at Yale Law School no less, clerked for the Fortas law firm. In response to the movie *Gabriel's Trumpet*, the story of the Gideon case, Jimmy pointed out that the country lawyer assigned to defend Mr. Gideon on remand might have had to spiff up to argue before the Supreme Court, but Abe Fortas, who argued before the court a lot, would have been a fish out of water in a county courtroom. While appointed to the Supreme Court, Mr. Fortas had to resign over an undisclosed annual retainer fee he received from a Wall Street criminal case.

I am lucky to say I personally know a number of SCOTUS victors.

The Ratner, Sugarmon firm's Bill Caldwell argued for and won the right for civil rights attorneys to get paid from the public entities they had to sue to ensure the rights of protected classes.

Walter Bailey successfully pled before the Supreme Court in *Tennessee v. Garner* that the use of deadly force for a fleeing felon of a property crime was cruel and unusual punishment. I wrote my criminal law paper on this case while it was still in district court.

My professor was Walter's law partner, Otis Higgs, my first Black teacher of my entire education. Otis was also a friend for whom I would ghostwrite his election speeches. I was so flattered; I would meet him at a speaking event and hand him the speech, and he would skim it while being introduced and then deliver it word for word. Afterward, he said the position and the speech was right on with his philosophy.

Fortuitously, in 1981 the first case ever to use my Human Rights Act in a Chancery Court walked through my door. She was a young woman with a sex harassment case against her contractor employer with never less than eight nor more than fifteen employees. Fearing I was too inexperienced to try it, I gave the case to Don Donati. He won it. Don later argued before the Supreme Court the famous retaliation case where an employer cannot retaliate against an employee for filing or testifying about a charge of discrimination.

And then there is the famous Overton Park case. Memphis attorney Charlie Newman argued for the Citizens to Preserve Overton Park in its lawsuit against Secretary of Transportation John

A. Volpe and successfully stopped Interstate 40 from bisecting the park, which sits smack in the middle of Memphis. Our remarkable zoo covers the northwest quadrant of the park and would have been carved out from the rest of it.

For a while, you could traverse the United States on just one highway until you hit the Mississippi River at Memphis. We should have made lemonade out of that lemon with signage saying, "You've got to merge left. The lion sleeps tonight."

I was disappointed my career was never illustrious enough to argue before the Supreme Court and perhaps create a right, but my friend Bonnie said, "You silly thing, you wrote the Tennessee Human Rights law. You gave rights to a lot of people."

Chapter 28

Women Tales

Hillary

Hooray for Hillary! That Hillary. On July 26, 2016, Hillary Diane Rodham Clinton was formally nominated as the Democratic Party's candidate for president! There was really a chance I might see a woman president of the United States in my lifetime. And a strong, highly accomplished one at that.

Not only was she the first woman to achieve the nomination of a major political party, she's eminently qualified to hold the job of president of the United States of America. She would be ready, if elected, please God, on day one.

Young women, old-timers my age feel such a sense of pride. It's hard to explain that the struggle for women's rights just to be considered a part of the human and civil rights movements felt so elusive for so long. And now we had the possibility to have a competent, female president. I don't know what took America ninety-six years after women achieved the vote.

I called Maxine Smith, Memphis's civil rights icon and director of our local NAACP, the night Obama was elected. She was bursting with Black pride; I could hear her tears of joy. Just as members of a minority are embarrassed when a fellow member does something bad, those members feel proud for their folk's accomplishments. That's how I felt for both him and her.

To my good fortune, I have met Hillary Clinton personally three times, not that she would remember, and have been in gatherings with her on two additional occasions. Once in an audience of over 5,000, twice in an audience of 250, and twice in an audience of twenty-five; in each case Hillary had charisma that made me feel she was talking just to me. She held me in the palm of her hand. It doesn't translate over the TV screen, but in person she's dynamite.

The first occasion, she came to a dinner meeting of our Association for Women Attorneys. Not yet the first lady of Arkansas, she entreated us to use our talents for public interest. She had already worked for the Children's Defense Fund and was bringing those concerns to Arkansas. I've had the pleasure of meeting and hearing Marian Wright Edelman, the creator of the Children's Defense Fund, a few times; her advocacy speeches leave you spellbound. Her bullet-speed delivery of potent facts and figures bowls you over. To think that Hillary got to work for such an inspiring person seemed like a new lawyer's dream.

Not particularly attractive back then, Hillary had long, stringy hair, not coiffed in a flattering manner. She wore Coca-Cola-bottle-thick glasses. In a term we used in the 1950s, she was plain-looking. She called herself Hillary Rodham, using her maiden name. While in vogue up north, that made her an object of scorn down south. But the minute she opened her mouth, you knew you were in the presence of an extraordinary, brilliant woman. Her female classmates at college claimed back then they were going to school with a future president. I have an acquaintance who said his daughter called home from Harvard, just having met Barry Obama, proclaiming she was in a class with the first Black president. Sometimes you just know in an instant you are in the presence of greatness.

The other small gathering occurred in 2008. I paid $1,000 I could ill afford to have breakfast with Hillary. By then she had spiffed up with makeup and a makeover hairdo. It's sad women have to do that to be taken seriously, but we do. Hillary lost the 2008 nomination to Obama, and I supported him, but the 2016 nomination felt so good!

Bill Clinton is no slouch either. He may be the best public speaker I have ever heard on TV or in person. Well, maybe he and Obama are a toss-up!

The first time I heard President Clinton and met him, I was sitting on the front row of the United Jewish Appeal's Young Leadership Cabinet conference in Washington, chaired by my daughter and son-in-law. Another time he spoke at the twenty-fifth anniversary of Rabbi David Saperstein's tenure as director of the Religious Action Center of Reform Judaism. David and his wife, Ellen Weiss, at the time producer of *All Things Considered* at National Public Radio (NPR), were personal friends of the Clintons, having hosted them often for Passover Seder. Both times President Clinton spoke without notes, candidly and knowledgeably.

The third time I heard President Clinton speak and got to shake his hand was when he received the National Civil Rights Museum's Freedom Award. Bobby and I were guests of Jeanne Varnell and had front table seats. Again, President Clinton excited the audience with his charisma, oratory, and smarts.

Bobby had the response of the evening: "There isn't a dry pair of panties in the house!"

Even the brightest of people can be complete f*#k-ups — i.e. Clinton with Monica Lewinsky. No defense of terrible behavior, I did try to tell my Yankee friends that President Clinton didn't lie when he said he did not have sex with her. As I shared before, we in Memphis thought there were degrees of intimacy with a line of demarcation between being a good girl and perhaps a bit looser. Kissing and necking kept your reputation intact. Petting and intercourse might get you talked about. Clinton could insist he didn't have sex with that woman since he didn't go "all the way." And she even claimed they didn't have sex, "we just messed around."

One of the excuses I often heard for not being in Hillary's corner is "she stayed with him." Imagine a first lady divorcing her president husband! Give me a break! And why should she relinquish her first lady pulpit from which to support her causes?

November 2016

I can't get out of my funk. I've gained five whole pounds since election night. They say people who eat their problems won't get ulcers, we will just die of diabetes or heart failure, but not bleeding ulcers. I may die sooner than later of a broken heart. The unimaginable happened! Hillary lost! Not the popular vote; she won with more than 2.8 million popular votes over Trump. But she lost the Electoral College vote. I might die from the stress of watching Donald Trump f*#k up our country.

And watching Trump appointments is sinking me deeper into despair. His Jewish son-in-law used his chips to take revenge on Chris Christie, who, as a federal prosecutor, prosecuted his father for crimes. Instead he should have told his father-in-law that the evil Steve Bannon, founder of the "alt right," thinks his child is too good to be in a school with Jewish kids like your grandchildren.

I was devastated to watch the prospect of America's first woman president slip through our fingers. And hurt, not only for me, but for Hillary. She worked so hard and was so qualified. The FBI weighing in as it did, the right wing constantly lying about her, Trump's deplorable campaign, the ridiculous email issue, and the false accusations about Benghazi! Such a conspiracy to trash her! And now we know the Russians contaminated our election!

Not only was she competent to be president, she earned the job! America, what have we done? I'm seventy-seven. Unless you take away my Medicare, as "the right" thinks we ought to do, I might live through this. But what are you doing to my children and grandchildren? Why do I feel it's 1936 and I'm in Germany?

Run, Sister, Run

Hillary isn't the first woman to put herself out there.

Margaret Chase Smith ran in 1964. The novelty of her running gave her attention, but as qualified as she was, it was still received as a novelty. While I never met her, I do know her biographer, Dr. Janann Sherman, former chair of the history department of the University of Memphis, noted author, and champion of women's rights. Janann's own story is inspirational:

Jan married right out of high school, and she and her veteran husband, Charlie, both worked in a factory. She rose to a supervisor level, which was unusual for a woman. A service-related disease attacked Charlie's eyesight, and, needing the money, Jan managed to cover for him, performing both his and her job requirements. Both were fired when the company found out. They took their little funds, bought a trailer, and moved to the Ozarks in Arkansas. The only work available was menial, and Jan realized she needed an education. She enrolled in the College of the Ozarks, where a woman professor recognized Jan was a woman of talent and brains. The professor helped Jan get a full scholarship to Rutgers in New Jersey, where she earned her PhD. Jan turned her thesis into a book, *No Place for a Woman: A Life of Senator Margaret Chase Smith*. Senator Smith gave Jan unfettered access to her papers.

Jan went on to write four other books, including the definitive book on Tennessee's role in ratifying the Nineteenth Amendment to secure the vote for women in 1920. Along with Carol Lynn Yellin, she wrote *The Perfect 36*. Tennessee was the thirty-sixth and last eligible state that could put the vote over the top. Ratification won by one vote in Tennessee. Jan's academic books flow with ease and are as fun to read as novels.

I once met Pat Schroeder at a National Women's Political Caucus meeting. Pat is a doll and filled a room with her presence and engaging personality. It tickled me that she was concerned for the security of Israel, not just as a political position, but because her family vacationed on its beaches every year. Her run for the presidency, still a novelty at the time, was met with derision. When asked how she could handle being a president and a dutiful wife and a mother, she responded, "I have a brain, and I have a vagina — and I know how to use them both."

Most exciting for me was getting to converse with Shirley Chisholm. The first American woman of color to be elected to Congress in 1968 and then re-elected six more terms, she was running for president in 1972 and was campaigning in Memphis. I was invited to a reception given for her by Mr. and Mrs. A. Maceo Walker, parents of my friend and Panel colleague Patricia Walker Shaw. I was thrilled Pat had her mother, Harriette, include me. I was sitting alone on a sofa, and Ms. Chisholm came over and asked if it would be all right if she sat with me. "Oh, yes, ma'am!" A great lady — captivating!

Why I Never Ran for Public Office

One of my feminist organizations had a wine-and-cheese honoring our female elected officials. Great women were on a panel talking about the sacrifice and rewards of public service. One bemoaned that there were not enough women in politics, and surely some of us in the audience should run; in fact, "There's Jocelyn Wurzburg out there; why hasn't Jocie run?"

I think it was state Sen. Beverly Marrero, but she was standing there with Councilwoman and former state Rep. Carol Chumney, state Speaker of the House Lois DeBerry, and state Rep. Jeanne Richardson.

I was flattered I got a shout-out. Someone turned to me and said, "Well, why haven't you run?"

I gave my standard answer: "First, I am a card-carrying member of the ACLU. Second, I inhaled and liked it, and third, I go all the way with my boyfriend without the benefit of marriage."

She laughed, and then I said, looking up at the four women, "Hell, so have all of those women — and one of them even with my boyfriend!"

Angela Davis

Angela Davis came to Memphis to speak at the anniversary of the Mid-South Peace and Justice Center's creation. She impacted my life in such a strange way; she may have been one of the contributing factors to the demise of my marriage!

In 1972, Richard and I were on my first trip to Europe and his first business trip out of the country. Richard headed the company's Artcraft division, a tape and label-printing operation. Firestone Tire Company was our biggest customer; we supplied the identification labels on every tire.

We were attending the drupa, an international printing

convention in Dusseldorf, Germany, held at the city fairgrounds. There were meetings the businessmen attended and displays of gigantic printing machinery. We were guests, along with some of our raw material suppliers, of some German company. At the opening reception, I especially liked meeting Karl and Barbara Zimmer, a couple from Indianapolis whose company supplied label-making material.

I was struck by how every German company official we met spoke such good English, and their explanation was that, to the one, they had left Germany in 1938. I wondered who was left to be a Nazi! My first trip to Europe and this Jewish girl was in Germany?

We were housed on a boat docked on the Rhine River bordering Dusseldorf. The riverboat sleeping accommodations were small but comfortable enough. It was the first time I slept under a steppdecke, a feather-filled quilt encased in sheeting that was a sheet and blanket combined. The rooms had intercom connections, and we were awakened with an announcement that breakfast would be served in thirty minutes and "yule ville enjoy it!"

Richard got ready faster than I did, and while I continued getting ready, I listened to an English US news channel over the intercom. And I heard Angela Davis had been acquitted. She was accused of being culpable in a conspiracy involving the 1970 armed takeover of a Marin County, California, courtroom, in which four people died.

Today, according to historical references, Angela Yvonne Davis, born on January 26, 1944, is described as an author, speaker, scholar, and political activist. She's a retired professor from the University of California–Santa Cruz and a former director of the university's feminist studies department. Back then, she was a 1960s radical who was a Communist Party USA leader with close connections to the Black Panther Party. She worked hard on prisoner rights, co-founding a group called Critical Resistance to abolish the prison industry complex.

I had followed the trial and was ecstatic about the news. So I bounced upstairs to the dining room, found Richard seated with the Zimmers, and pronounced with glee, "Great news! Angela Davis was acquitted!"

Richard blanched. The Zimmers lit up with excitement! "Yea!"

We went downstairs to our cabins to ready ourselves for a shore excursion. Richard was furious with me. How dare I come up with that announcement? "How did you know they would be happy with her acquittal? What if they weren't? Don't you know that could have jeopardized a business relationship?"

"I don't know how I knew it would be okay, honey, but I just did! They just seemed okay!"

That was a loaded statement. If the Zimmers weren't okay with it, then would they not be okay with me? What did that say about me supposing to be in the tolerance business? What did that say about me being a good businessman's wife?

You probably don't doubt it for a minute, but that wasn't the only time I embarrassed my husband. There would be many more times to come.

Patricia Walker Shaw (1939-1985)

Pat Shaw was one of the most amazing women I had ever met, and I loved her. I so loved her. She had an engaging personality and was smart as a whip and funny. God, she was funny.

She was the daughter of the stately Harriette and A. Maceo Walker. Mr. Walker owned Universal Life Insurance Company and Tri-State Bank. Pat used to joke, "It was good Daddy owned a bank because I was darker-complexioned than Fisk University was used to admitting." Pat said you could not get into Fisk unless you were lighter than a craft grocery bag.

She was one of three children. Tony Walker rebelled against his parents' social standing and went countercultural. Pat had a younger sister named Candy, who was the first African American student at St. Mary's Episcopal School. The Walkers paid for a friend to go there as well, so their daughter wouldn't be the only Black child there.

Pat met Harold Shaw at Fisk. They had one child, Harold Jr. Harold was a handsome man, and they were a well-suited couple.

Pat was named president of the insurance company, which

gave her a national reputation, and she was often listed in *Ebony* magazine as a Black person of influence.

Pat and I both loved Broadway musicals, and she was the only friend I knew who liked plays that most people had never heard of, such as *New Faces of 1952*, which launched the careers of Eartha Kitt and Ronny Graham. Anyway, Pat was the only other person in the whole wide world I knew who possessed an album of the play. As minor an issue as that was, it made us realize that, despite our different racial and religious upbringings, we both somehow arrived at *New Faces*.

Pat became a loyal member of the Panel of American Women. She was a great speaker and could capture an audience with her charm and wit. She was especially effective at the service club presentations, such as Rotary, since she was CEO of a business and still faced racial discrimination in the wider society.

At a Panel retreat, Pat participated in a skit our fellow panelist Barbara Zitron wrote to entertain us as the conference finale. Panning the discriminatory Cotton Carnival, which didn't allow Jews or Blacks in their societies, Pat came out as Queen Vagina of the Panel Krewe, feathers, sequins, and all!

Somehow we found ourselves at a slumber party in Washington, DC, at the home of Mattie Carol Hall, one of Memphis's first African American TV newscasters. Carol integrated Stephens College in Missouri and was a model-quality beauty. She was the life of our Panel parties before moving on to LA and DC. Carol arranged a dinner with Ernie Green, one of the Little Rock Nine who integrated Little Rock Central High School in 1957.

Pat got appointed to the board of Memphis Light, Gas, and Water (MLG&W); she was the first African American appointed to that board. She took care of business! She got panelist Joyce Blackmon a job and Joyce, in turn, hired Donna Sue Shannon, another panelist. Joyce rose to vice president, and Donna Sue rose to head of training.

Pat came to me, saying, "Jocelyn, you're on the Human Rights Commission. I need help. There is overt discrimination going on all over LG&W, and I feel there is a more subtle form of it, too. I remember you having told me that today you don't need to show intent to discriminate and that disparate impact was enough to show discrimination is taking place."

We went through every section of MLG&W counting how many whites and how many Blacks were employed. The higher the rank of the job, the fewer Black folk there were. It was just obvious that the place was replete with racial discrimination.

We worked on this for months; at last, Pat made a presentation to the board. She not only gave them the facts, she gave an impassioned plea that MLG&W was discriminatory. It was a public institution, and they could fix it without needing to have lawsuits make them do it. She called me after the meeting and said the board members were absolutely dumbfounded!

She said, "The whole board just stared at me with their mouths dropped open. It was like, 'What's gotten into our dear Pat?'"

She laughed and then used the "N" word. "Lord, they shook their heads as if to say, 'What's gotten into our good "N"?' I loved it!"

Pat was a great panelist. She had a great laugh and was so at ease and comfortable in her own skin. When people asked her questions, she not only gave them answers, anything she said was going to be all right with someone because people really liked her. When she told the audience about the needs of the African American community, they just nodded.

I do remember I got into trouble once with a dear mutual friend on the Panel. Something I said in innocence about her turned out to be a private matter. Pat called me for lunch with the other friend, sat us both down, and said, "Now we're going to get to the bottom of this." She took time off from her job to reconcile this. I apologized and begged forgiveness; the friend and I hugged and kissed, and Pat gave us a three-way hug.

Pat, Jeanne, Happy, and I had a women's trip down at Jeanne's cabin on a lake in Mississippi. The first night we held lobster races with our meal before steaming them. The next afternoon we got wasted down at the dock and sunbathed seminude. We pretty much had the lake to ourselves, but the sillier we got, the less we remembered we were an unusual gathering in Mississippi.

We entertained ourselves creating scenarios of what to say if the Game and Fish commissioner motored up. Pat told us it was a club she started, and we could pledge it if we promised to live by its premise. HTSFIAMI. I pledged allegiance and bought us all T-shirts. HTSFIAMI is still my screensaver today. It stands for "How to say f*#k it and mean it."

They kicked me out of Pat's funeral. She died at age forty-six. I was hysterical. I was in the far back of the church, and I was sobbing uncontrollably. The usherette came and asked me to step outside. I promised to try to control myself and begged to return. Judy Wimmer, another panelist, saw me, asked the person beside me to switch places, and held me in her arms.

The minister, the Reverend Alvin Jackson, told us that toward the end Pat gave him a note. By then she could not speak. Her note expressed her frustration but was typically all business. "I need a plan I can see." That became my byword.

Pat had cancer of both jaws. And that's a mean form of cancer. She had been treated for a root canal, but that wasn't the issue. Chemo was rough on her. On a visit, I was in her bedroom while she was getting dressed. Pat and I both struggled with weight. We had to laugh; Pat was thinner than she had ever been and looked figure-wise the best she ever had.

"Pat, damn, girl, you look fabulous!" I said.

We both said, "Shit!" at the same time.

I didn't see her after that day. But I took her a gift. She no longer had her *New Faces* album, and I still did, so I made her a tape of it.

Shulamit Aloni

A courageous woman, Shulamit Aloni, died Friday, January 24, 2014. I don't know if it was before or after sundown Friday, but Jews believe God takes the good on Shabbat. Shulamit's voice was the conscience of Israel. "Every human being, including the enemy, has rights." She was referring to the Palestinians who she protested were living under occupation with no civil rights. She spoke truth to power and not just in Israel. She died at eighty-five.

I got to meet her, but I need to give you the background.

In May 1982, right before my divorce court date, my marvelous friends Urania and Andy Alissandratos invited me to go to Greece with them and their two daughters, Theresa and Julia. All the Alissandratos women were extraordinary. Mama taught small business administration and helped run her husband's Canada Dry and Pepsi distributorship. Urania was on our Panel of American Women and shared about a burning cross placed in her family's yard because they were Greek Orthodox. Both girls ended up on Wall Street, but for Julia that came only after she did a stint teaching one of her mastered twenty-eight Slavic languages. She lived in Russia for a few years.

The girls had two brothers; one became a dentist, the other a chancellor. No English was spoken in the home, so the kids were sent to kindergarten to perfect their English. Andy was elected to the city council as a Republican and was pretty much a beloved figure in Memphis. He was the first drink distributor to hire a Black salesman, despite customer protests. I used to ghostwrite campaign speeches for him as I did for a Black Democrat. I had both men saying the same things, and each said I wrote as if I had read their minds.

The trip was an opportunity of a lifetime, going to Greece to visit family of my friends who spoke Greek. They planned to go on to Monaco, where they had family, and I decided to go on to Israel.

Earlier that spring, Richard and I had received an invitation to go to Israel in November with the Jewish Federation. I told them that Richard probably wouldn't be able to go, but I would be interested, not knowing I would be going in June and they not knowing we were getting a divorce. I did call and leave word to relinquish my place when I decided to go to Israel from Greece.

A day before my departure, Israel invaded Lebanon in retaliation for incursions and lobbing bombs into Israel. My travel agent assured me I would be safe but suggested I demur because Israeli sons and daughters were dying, and it was not a very joyous time to go. I took his advice and switched my trip to go to Egypt alone instead — already packed for Israel, and with no pre-trip briefing or study. My wardrobe was inappropriate for the country. It was 100 percent guided, but certainly an adventure.

So freshly divorced, I went on this trip to the Middle East, Greece, and Egypt. I had only been abroad once, but I knew foreign travel would become important to me. Such an enriching experience.

As soon as I got home, I called the federation. I told them I didn't get to go to Israel because of the war and would like to accept the invitation for the November trip. "Well-I-I-I, we have to rescind your invitation. Jocelyn, you're divorced, and you're not the prospect you used to be." The raison d'être of these trips was to inspire people to give lots of money to Israel through the Jewish Federation.

This remark hit me between the eyes. "Are you kidding? I'm the Zionist in the Wurzburg family! You don't know what I got in my divorce! You don't know if I will make a big legal score and give you a third of my third! You don't know if I have anyone out there waiting on me who is richer than Richard!" That fell on deaf ears. And the truth was that none of those were true except about me being the Zionist. Those of us born during World War II grew up knowing that there just had to be a place that wouldn't deny us Jews entrance if we needed it.

A few days later, my brother called me and asked: "How was it? Didn't you just love Israel?" I explained the situation and that I didn't get to go.

"Then you can go this fall with us." Ray lived in New Orleans and had accompanied politicos to Israel on two previous trips for the federation. "Memphis and New Orleans are taking this fall trip together. It will be great."

I told him what had happened when I called to accept the trip. "I'm putting you on hold." Five minutes later, he came back. "You're going to Israel in November, and so is Faye." I asked how he managed it. He said, "I told them there were 25,000 reasons Jocelyn was going to get to go."

At a meeting of the CSA before my trip, I told the president of the UAHC, Alex Schindler, I was going to Israel. Your first trip to Israel is a big deal for Jews. Even the most nonobservant is changed by the experience. Alex said he wanted me to meet his friend Shulamit

Aloni. She was with an organization called Peace Now, and she was a member of the Knesset at the time. He gave me her direct phone number, and I promised to call her.

El Al airline was on strike, so we flew Swiss Air. We arrived at Ben Gurion Airport and deplaned via an old-fashioned roll-up staircase. My first sight departing the plane was all the El Al planes parked around the tarmac. Blue and white planes everywhere! I was a bit surprised at my first thought of Israel. "Those are my airplanes!"

After an intensive security check, which we were told was mild since we were part of a Jewish Federation trip, we were taken by bus straight to Tel Aviv and to our hotel for a much-needed nap. I looked out the window of my room and saw we were right on the beach. My nap was on hold; I ran downstairs without unpacking to walk on the sand, a rare treat for me living so far from the sea.

The next morning we were treated to a renowned Israeli breakfast. We had been instructed to pack a small bag for a few nights at a kibbutz in the north and that the rest of our baggage would be awaiting us in Jerusalem. We were going up to Beaufort Castle, medieval ruins from which the latest attack on Israel was staged. We actually saw shell casings.

But it dawned on me that I had left Ms. Aloni's phone number in the big suitcase, and I wanted to give her advance notice to join me for a drink. I asked the Israeli leader of our bus if he could get me her number and help me make a call to her. I noticed he hesitated, but he said he would try.

We toured the castle grounds, high atop a steep hill, and were inspired by the description of how the brave Israeli soldiers marched through the night, climbed the hill from behind, attacked, and defeated the Lebanese, probably with the Syrians, who had been shelling the kibbutz down at Metula, the northernmost city of Israel. Then we toured it. Seeing the cage-like cribs stacked atop each other down in the bomb shelter struck us with a potent dose of realism about what it was like living in an area where all the neighbors hate you.

Soberly, we walked back to the bus. Rabbi Rafael Grossman caught up with me and asked if he could sit with me.

"Sure, I'm flattered," I said.

Rabbi Grossman was the longtime rabbi of Baron Hirsch Synagogue in Memphis, the Orthodox synagogue all of my father's family attended. My father's mother's Berger family had five generations buried in its cemetery.

We got underway when the rabbi said, "Now, Jocelyn, what's this about your wanting to get in touch with Shulamit Aloni?"

"She's a friend of Alex Schindler's, and he thought I would enjoy meeting her. What concerns you?"

"She is single-handedly tearing down the state of Israel!" he said heatedly.

"Rabbi, wow. I thought it would be nice to meet her, but now that I know how powerful she is, it's imperative that I do!"

Ms. Aloni and I met at the bar of the Jerusalem Hilton. It was not that she was particularly attractive, although a handsome woman, but she had a commanding presence. You just knew as she entered a room that someone of importance had come in. After we exchanged pleasantries, Rabbi Grossman walked over and immediately lit into her. She held her own, but I was horrified. I finally stopped it.

"Rabbi, we are having a private conversation and you are intruding, uninvited," I said.

Ms. Aloni was gracious and truly understood I had not set her up. Since meeting her, I still contribute to Peace Now — and J Street. For the rest of the trip, I felt like the bastard child at the family reunion.

Israel lost a true patriot when Shulamit Aloni died. Being pro-peace is pro-Israel.

Anita Hill

Last night I watched the HBO movie *Confirmation*. It was a dramatization of the confirmation process for Clarence Thomas being seated on the US Supreme Court. I was fascinated by the hearings publicly aired. The movie was more sympathetic to Vice President Joe Biden, then a senator, than I felt at the time. And it gave Sen. Arlen Specter of Pennsylvania a pass; he treated Anita Hill with vitriol.

Anita Hill was sought out to inquire whether the rumors of Thomas being a sexual harasser were true. She was a reluctant witness and was only persuaded to out him because being a Supreme Court justice was such an important appointment. Anita Hill was a professor of law and understood that better than most.

The hearings were important far beyond whether Thomas got confirmed. They opened up the entire conversation of what sexual harassment is. Like rape, sexual harassment is often pronounced to be an issue of power, not sex. I get that, but it IS about SEX. It's having the power for a man to stick his dick into a woman's vagina — whether she wants that to happen or not. Yes, women can be harassers, and same-sex harassment happens, too.

Sexual harassment is so insidious. A woman seeks progress, promotion, position, acknowledgment, affirmation, or ascension, and someone has the power to help that happen. And when they throw in a quid pro quo that has nothing to do with the qualifications for success, it's insidious. So if you demonstrate how insulted you really feel, you're a tight-ass prig, not a fun member of the team, and then a permanent reminder of what a sexist pig the harasser is. You're not gonna get what you want — or deserve — and the sexist pig has no skin off his back. So how do you say and mean NO without showing your total indignation that stops your steps toward success in their tracks? This disgusting pig gets to be a boss?

Grasping the dilemma, how do you try to deal with it? And all in an instant! It's a conflict that requires an immediate solution; it's shocking, and you don't have time to give considered thought for an "appropriate" reaction. Maybe with humor? Maybe with returned flirtation? How do you say, "Hey, man, I need and want to work with you, but what you have just suggested ain't gonna happen!"

Senator Specter went on to denigrate Professor Hill for accepting a promotion — going with Thomas to the EEOC. I understood why she would and what she was thinking: "Well, I've made my stand, and he knows I'm a good girl. I really want this upward position in my career. Surely the shenanigans will stop." It may be self-delusion, but that's why, Senator Specter, a harassment victim hangs in there.

What was so interesting was watching the country divide itself between those who believed her and those who believed him. For fun, I would ask women — everyone I ran up against — okay, who do you believe? Him or her? It didn't make any difference whether the woman believed him or her. Her addendum was "because when it happened to me, I did such and such." I was batting a thousand.

The confirmation hearings drew and quartered Professor Hill. She was humiliated! The movie ended with her being affirmed by the thousands of letters she received from women expressing their thanks for her standing up for them. I was lucky. I got to meet her at an Academy of Family Mediators conference and thank her in person.

In 2017, women stepped forward in droves to tell their stories. Unfortunately, there are too many "me, too's."

Ann Rickey

I've become Ann Heiskell Rickey. I gave a political meet and greet for Gordon Ball, a Democratic attorney from Knoxville daring to run against Lamar Alexander, once a governor, once a secretary of education under President George "Poppy" Bush with the mission to dismantle the Department of Education, and now a US senator. I worked for Lamar's campaign for governor. I give a lot of these parties, and so did Ann Rickey.

Ann was an interesting woman. Strong, ultra-liberal, extremely partisan, Ann was a force of nature. We would meet at the Wolf River Society, discuss current events, diss the local pols, and recommend a good book. Ann held court there every day pontificating how awful Republicans are.

I was still a Republican, albeit a liberal one, because (I stole the quip) the line was shorter — but since I was civil rights-y, Ann tolerated me.

Ann was married to a prominent attorney, Al Rickey. I am sure he was a good lawyer, but the prominence was probably a result of Ann's clout. We all thought him a prince to put up with Ann.

Ann has a beautiful, movie-star daughter. Literally! Lamar Rickey is Lara Parker, who was a TV actress in a long-running soap opera, *Dark Shadows*. Lara was a Rhodes College graduate as well.

One afternoon Ann and I were giving a political party for Russell Sugarmon. Russell's Black, and we asked five of the leading Black caterers in Memphis to donate a dish for the Sunday brunch. They were delighted to participate.

Ann's home was perfect for entertaining, a big house on a golf course in the middle of East Memphis. She built an aviary attached to the house, a beautiful glass-walled room with a high, vaulted ceiling and plants that touched it. The plants grew in dirt beds that lined the floor. Tiny birds flew across the room from branch to branch. Sometimes they flew through the house, but they never seemed to "drop" in any room except the aviary.

Ann loved plants, and one night she had a few of us walk in her garden. It was an early spring night, pleasantly warm and before the mosquitoes had arrived.

Usually gruff, Ann was so mellow that night. Well, we were treated to a few puffs of pot, so none of us were feeling stressed. Ann lectured on the purpose of each plant we passed, claiming every plant has a definite purpose besides being beautiful. She came to one and gave us each a leaf. The leaf was fat, almost as a succulent "hens and chickens" plant, but it was from a deciduous bush. Ann gently rubbed the leaf between her finger and thumb, breaking apart the inside of the leaf, but not the outside membrane. Then she cut a tiny slit at the base of the leaf and blew into it, making it fill like a balloon. "This is the sole purpose of this bush. It makes balloons." I had never seen this gentle side of Ann.

So there was Ann; the late Mary Robinson, Memphis's first woman stockbroker; the late Percy Brown, a Black politico; and I, blowing leaf balloons. We had started Hi-Centennial Art Company to celebrate the USA's bicentennial. We created T-shirts to sell on the Washington Mall on July 4, 1976. The vendors secured those coveted slots almost a year in advance, and we didn't have a chance at securing a license to sell anything.

One of the shirts was a stoned George Washington standing among his hemp plants; that shirt came with a booklet making the case he smoked marijuana. I came into the business after that idea had been developed, and it sounded to me like an idea that seems fabulous when you're high but doesn't stand the test of time the next morning.

The other shirt pictured the famous three Revolutionary drum and fife players, only they were walking away. It was titled "Bye, Bicentennial." I thought that was the really clever one. I happened to be invited to the White House on July 3, 1976, and took one of those shirts as a gift to Susan Ford, President Ford's daughter. She got it and wrote a note; she was pleased. But I digress.

I showed up at eleven thirty in the morning as instructed to help Ann organize and receive the contributed food. I peeked into the dining room and the table was clear. Ann was drinking coffee in the kitchen and offered me some. I thanked her and accepted a cup. At about eleven forty she said, "Well-l-l-l, I guess we need to polish some trays."

Back then I was a hostess who had my party table set two days ahead with a sheet thrown over it to avoid dust. Ann hadn't even pulled out her serving dishes?

She calmly started pulling out trays; I stood at the sink polishing silver. She put out placemats, and the food started arriving at about ten minutes to noon along with the guests. So help me, we placed the food right on the shiny serving pieces just as the folks headed for the dining room. My initial panic turned to admiration that someone could be so cool that she could be expecting seventy-five people for brunch and start putting things together fifteen minutes before it began.

So recently I had a political party. My co-host, Kemba, was in charge of food. My usual offer is a clean house and a complete bar. I met Kemba on a Sunday, and she offered to allow me to meet the candidate she was working for, Gordon Ball. Somehow I heard myself offer to gather a few folks at my house on Thursday.

Bless her heart — we say that a lot down south, usually to make light of an annoying mannerism — Kemba called or emailed four to five times a day trying to organize the event. She sent menus and guest lists, and she asked, "Are you sure you don't need for me to come help you set up?"

She wanted to come at three o'clock for an event at four thirty. I heard myself say, "Honey, come on over about a quarter to four."

I got home at three thirty. Now I admit the house was cleaned by the cleaning crew that afternoon. And I started setting up a bar — getting out a folding table, liquor, beer, setups, wine, ice buckets, napkins, glasses, serving trays, lemons, and limes — the whole bit. Kemba arrived and was a wreck because she thought we couldn't get it ready in time. We did, and with time to spare.

I admit: In my old age, I've become Ann Rickey.

Gwen Ifill (1955-2016)

When Gwen Ifill died, watching her colleagues on TV struggle not to cry while eulogizing her almost brought me to tears. I was a real fan. She was a journalist extraordinaire, print and television, and a no-nonsense interviewer. I cheered when she was given the coveted role of moderator of PBS's *Washington Week*. Then she and Judy Woodruff became co-anchors of the old *MacNeil/Lehrer NewsHour*. Even from the screen, I felt she was talking to me. She had such a natural presence.

I may have been the beneficiary of her largesse. It was fall 1997. Memphis annually hosts the Southern Heritage Classic, a big football weekend featuring Tennessee State University and Jackson State University. Both colleges were traditionally Black schools pre-integration, and their alums have created a weekend of seminars and parties surrounding the big game.

Joyce Blackmon, a friend and Panel member, convened a business seminar and, to be supportive, I attended. And besides, I was anxious to go because Gwen Ifill was a speaker. I believe I was the only white person in the room.

After Ms. Ifill spoke, someone came over to me and issued an invitation, "Ms. Ifill would like a word with you." WOW!

I don't remember the question, but it was inconsequential — confirmation of a restaurant recommendation or something like that. I told her what a fan I was, and she hugged me. And that was it.

Walking back to my seat, I wondered, "I think she noted my being the only white person in the room and just wanted me to feel welcomed and wanted."

Her loss is great to news junkies like me. Rest in peace, Gwen.

When Mimi Moved to Memphis

Mimi Rice moved to Memphis in 1977 with her husband, Richard, when he was appointed head of the theater department of Memphis State University. She sought me out because she heard I might have a way to get her into the upcoming International Women's Year USA observance, also called the National Women's Conference, in Houston. I did.

Shortly before the conference was to be held, I received my registration packet along with six passes I could distribute at my discretion. So when Mimi, an early feminist, came along, I was able to accommodate her with a pass. She became an instant friend and paid me back with some fascinating experiences; for me, this was the beginning of a loving friendship.

Mimi was an actress and artist. She came from a fascinating family named Smith from Gouverneur, New York. Every member was talented — mostly in music. Her father, like mine, was a newspaperman. It was a family of some wealth, and while her first marriage was to a wealthy man, she later opted to explore a simpler lifestyle as the wife of a professor and actress in the theater world.

Mimi's previous marriage was to a man from a fancy family from St. Louis. That husband was an alcoholic, and they divorced before he died of cirrhosis at age thirty.

They had a son, Ross, whom the fancy grandparents ignored, which was sad because Ross has a genius IQ, is a musical phenom, is a gentle, soulful man, and needed help when it was time to go to college.

Mimi married Rich, who adopted Ross, and she reared Rich's two sons from a previous marriage.

Mimi, Richard, and another family, Dave and Marg Radens and their kids, lived together as an extended family in an old stagecoach inn, Mount Lookout House, built in the 1700s in Contoocook, New Hampshire, population 1,440. They converted the forty-room inn into a twenty-room home. Mimi and Marg had been reared with means, and this lifestyle was without modern conveniences. In their arrangement, one adult could take a yearlong sabbatical at a time, supported by the other three. All four adults were rearing the six children, and the kids had to mind all four adults.

Mimi and Rich once sailed the Intracoastal Waterway from Maine to Florida. Mimi shared the story of being on duty on a foggy night when they almost had a wreck. Seeing red and green lights, maritime symbols of directions for entering and exiting a port (red, right or starboard, returning) she almost guided the boat onto land when the lights turned out to be inside a bar on shore. Both of her brothers were boat builders.

Mimi was a natural for the Panel, and, with our grant, we were able to engage her as the project manager. That job came with a whole host of new friends. Mimi taught us new ways to have fun. One day she had Happy, Jeanne, and me meet her at the zoo, where there was a photography studio equipped with costumes of all types to play dress-up. Mimi had us wear old Western female outlaw garb like Belle Starr or Etta Place would have worn. So for a dollar per picture, we spent an hour having the time of our lives.

One summer Mimi invited me and Richard Jr. up to the inn in New Hampshire. Mimi's son and Richard Jr. were twelve years old and classmates at Lausanne Collegiate School. The plan was for the four of us to drive up to New Hampshire in Mimi's antique orange Volkswagen van. With a bright yellow canoe perched on top, we looked like a bowl of fruit driving down the highway. The starter motor was a bit of a bother; we sometimes had to use a huge screwdriver to connect to wires to make the engine start. Her husband Richard drove my car. Richard Jr. and I would drive home through Detroit to visit my sister.

We camped out the first night, something I had never done before. I slept in a tent with the two boys, and Mimi and her husband slept in the bus. I became the boys' age, giggling and laughing at nothing. Mimi peeked into the tent to remind us that, without walls, we could be heard all over the campground.

As I mentioned earlier, the trip didn't go as I had planned. My husband Richard didn't approve of the trip. He made Richard Jr. call him collect every time we stopped the car for gas or food. After four days, I flew my homesick son home from Washington, DC. Later I had to smile when he told stories of camping out and canoeing in a lake.

The best gift Mimi gave me was suggesting that this trip would be an ideal time to quit smoking. "We will wake up to fresh air and camp coffee. There will be no first phone call of the day requiring anything of you, causing you to light up."

My smoking habit had gotten out of hand. Four packages a day! I had become a chain smoker. Sometimes I had two lit in the ashtray. Heavy smoking in the bus would have been unpleasant, so I took up Mimi's challenge. I quit smoking on June 6, 1979, at 1:35 p.m. That was when I had my last cigarette.

Mimi had me doing little things I had never done before: I rode atop a hay wagon, sat in the back of an open truck, picked vegetables for dinner out of a garden, flushed a commode with a bucket of water we drew out of a lake, body-surfed in the ocean, and slept on a horsehair mattress on the floor — things I had never experienced in my spoiled, sheltered J.A.P. life.

I was treated with patience when I said the only thing I knew how to fix for a party she and the Radens family were hosting was chopped liver. Mimi had a friend who had a hand crank to mince the chicken livers. So I found myself fixing chopped liver in the kitchen of a hotel built in the 1700s. I was delighted to peek into an entirely different lifestyle, and New Hampshire became my "power place," where I felt free from convention.

One night we drove to Lake Ozonia in upstate New York, near St. Regis Falls and the Canadian border, to meet up with Mimi's siblings. Mimi's grandmother built the Smith family Adirondack camp in 1915. It was the Fourth of July, and it snowed! The cabin was under renovation from a fire, and my assigned bedroom had no walls and was furnished with only a mattress on the floor. The bathroom had no running water, so I bathed with two paper cups of water, one soapy and the other clear, and a washrag.

A foreshadowing of events to come was the evening Mimi's brother Tim put a longneck banjo into my lap while I was sitting on a sofa. He stood behind me, fretting the neck while I strummed the strings. Never would I have ever dreamed I would someday learn to play a banjo.

Rich and Mimi moved to St. Petersburg, Florida, where he took a job running the theater department of Eckerd College. She still acts and commenced a practice in the Feldenkrais movement for acting and for people with disabilities.

Mimi invited me down to celebrate my divorce a few days after it was final. They lived in a comfortable home with a pool, and they would send me to the backyard to pick grapefruit off their tree for breakfast.

Mimi drove me back to Memphis. I was tickled to show her my post-divorce condo and new lifestyle. I was blessed to have her there because a few days after we returned I was in a terrible automobile accident in which I killed a child, and Mimi was able to help me through it.

Mimi and Richard Rice later invited Bobby and me to London, where they were house managers for the Eckerd College Spring Semester in London program. Always boaters, they took us on a canal boat trip through the British countryside. We also went to the theater and museums. Mimi took me to hear a luncheon concert at the famous church in London, St Martin-in-the-Fields.

Ross Rice now lives in Nashville, teaching and working as a session musician in the studios. We like to bunk him when he has a gig in Memphis. I attribute to Ross my first time ever to play music with anyone. Well, that's a stretch; he and a friend came to visit me at the condo, and they brought in guitars and a bongo drum for me to play with them. I had never done that before, but by God, by the end of the evening I got into it. I actually kept a rhythm they approved of with winks, smiles, and nods. What a gift Ross gave me!

Both Mimi and Richard Rice still act, sail, and travel a lot. We have a standing invitation to visit the restored Smith camp in New York, and I hope to go. This time I will be able to play music with this talented, extraordinary family who has given me many gifts.

Chapter Twenty-Nine

Male Tales

Sen. Howard Baker

Oh, Lordy, Howard Baker died June 26, 2014. Not only was I sad I lost a friend, but the last hope for restoring sanity to the Republican Party died. He was a major statesman and politician. When he last spoke at Rotary and I asked a question about the Republican big tent shrinking, he urged patience.

"The pendulum swings back and forth, and this current conservative swing will swing back," he said.

Unfortunately that was a decade ago — pre-Tea Party. So many of us begged: Where are the Howard Bakers, the Chuck Mathiases, the Jacob Javitses? Who is going to blow a referee's whistle and yell: "Timeout!" "Foul!" "Play fair!" Especially to Donald Trump!

I met Howard in 1966, when I went to hear him speak at a meet and greet at a private home, an open house. He was darling. His opening salvo was, "I may be little, but I'm loud."

Upon leaving, I signed the sign-in sheet. I was being observed. "Oh, great!" I heard a woman say. "I'm Peg Shultz, and I am a neighbor of yours. I was wondering who built that house. Did you like him?" I did, and the next thing I knew I was a precinct captain for Howard Baker's senatorial run.

The Republicans had a well-oiled organization, which was impressive since it was fairly new. The Republican Party in Shelby County was an all-Black party until 1960, when white Republicans held a coup, taking the party away from Lieutenant George Lee, a Boss Crump-appointed leader, to stave off East Tennessee Republicans from competing with Crump. In essence: "I'll give you a party down here in Memphis — it will be all Black — but I'll give you a party. Now leave me alone."

My job was to conduct a door-to-door survey and ascertain every potential Republican voter in the precinct. Every house in the area was listed on an index card and then sorted as Republicans or Democrats. I even took elephant-shaped cookies to newly moved-in neighbors.

A few of us couples gave a meet and greet for Howard and for Dan Kuykendall, who also was running for Congress. Little did I know at the time that later I would be involved in civic work, civil rights, and projects for which I would apply for federal grants, and these elected officials would be indispensable.

Once the voters were ascertained, I was to stand at the polls and check off my listed names as each voter arrived. At noon, three thirty, and five thirty, I ran home and called volunteers who were waiting by their phones with our prospective voters listed according to assigned numbers. At noon, I would call a volunteer and say eight, eleven, fifteen, sixteen, nineteen, and so on. Then the volunteer made a call to remind the prospective voters to go vote or to ask if they needed a ride to the polls. Then I ran back to the polling place and waited for the voters to show up. If they didn't, I would repeat the process.

Time magazine wrote about our precinct work. I set up a playpen with stuffed elephants so parents could deposit their babies while they went to vote. We had a fabulously high turnout of our voters. No paid poll workers, no paid ballots, just grassroots organizing. Howard won handily, which was an accomplishment in the solidly white Democratic part of the state.

And Howard was appreciative. I would see him at events, and he always acknowledged me. He helped me when I asked. On three occasions, I sought federal grants, and he sent his administrative assistant with me for the interviews.

Howard also recommended me for law school. That was probably the deciding factor in getting me accepted!

In 1974, I decided I wanted a federal appointment to a seat on the EEOC, and I met with Howard to discuss it. One of the commissioners was on a fast track to head a new Consumer Protection Commission if Congress passed the Consumer Protection Act, and I wanted her job. As the drafter of the proposed anti-discrimination law for Tennessee, I thought I was qualified. Howard asked me if I wanted the job if the seat was vacant or if I wanted it when the commissioner's term was up.

"I want it," I said.

"Okay," he said.

When Howard ran for president in 1980, I went to New Hampshire to work for a few days. It was a bizarre experience. I was sent up a few flights of stairs to work a phone bank. I was alone up there, but I did it for a day and a half. Mid-morning of the second day, I went down and made a suggestion.

I had been serving on the CSA since 1976. I thought that many social action committees of the Temples in New Hampshire might love to get political visits. They were New Hampshirites, after all.

"I think I could make a few calls and see if we can get Howard to speak at some of the synagogues. Would that be helpful?" I asked.

"You can do that?" this guy asked incredulously.

"Well, I could try," I said.

It got done. Later, I decided that I could take Russell Sugarmon and Happy Jones to New Hampshire and make a showing in a primary. It was unbelievable retail politics!

All volunteers were asked to attend all events on the third day when Howard was in town to speak. He saw me standing in the back on his way out of one event and gave me the warmest smile. The big issue for him was that he was low-key. He was charged with having no fire in his belly for his run. After his address at one restaurant, a staffer from DC said loudly, "No fire in the belly? Hell, he was smoking from the navel."

In the political turmoil of 2017, it was Howard Baker's name that was frequently evoked. His role in the Watergate hearings became legendary. "What did the president know and when did he know it?" It shouldn't have, but it did take courage to put country over party.

Joseph

Joseph Dickinson was, in chronological order, my mother's friend and bridge partner, my portrait painter, my friend, and my symphony partner. He was probably one of the most extraordinary men I've ever known. While he painted your portrait, he told you stories, amazing stories about his life — and he told them so well.

For example, while he was painting me, he told me about the time he lived in New York. He moved into an apartment with Wally Cox, who became an actor-comedian but at the time was a jewelry maker, a goldsmith. Joseph said when he rented the apartment, Wally told him not to be alarmed if he heard someone climbing up the fire escape, that there was a young actor who would occasionally sleep at the apartment. Young Marlon wasn't able to get a job and occasionally needed a place to crash.

"Marlon was an extraordinary-looking man and, I was told, quite a good actor, but this intrusion became old after a bit. I just casually mentioned to my friend Tennessee Williams that there was a handsome young man who would be a wonderful candidate for Biff in his new play. I thought at least if he had a job he would quit sneaking into the apartment. But no, he didn't. In fact, it got worse. He would sit in the bathtub for much too long a period of time and plead, 'Stella, Stella.' I believe, Jocelyn, he has a sister the same name as yours."

Joseph said that he found himself on the new book-signing circuit in New York. He was frequently asked to bring Maginel to the party, if he didn't mind.

"Maginel," he said, "was a very endearing older woman."

One evening when he buzzed the intercom, she asked Joseph if he would mind coming up for just a minute.

"Joseph, what do you think about these new pillows I bought for the sofa?"

"Why, Maginel, I think they're very handsome."

"Oh, I'm so glad you like them. Frank dislikes them immensely."

And on another occasion, Maginel asked Joseph, "Would you mind coming up? I'd like for you to look at my new draperies."

"Maginel, they're absolutely beautiful. I think they just set the room off perfectly."

"Oh, Joseph, I'm delighted you think so; Frank thinks they are hideous. He doesn't like them at all."

Joseph thought, "Damn, who is this Frank? I hope it's not some irate husband."

After a while in New York, Joseph's money began to run out and he mentioned to his friends, "I need a job. I don't know how I'm going to be able to stay up here for the rest of the year."

His friends said, "Why don't you try to get on with the new Guggenheim opening?"

"How in the world would I get into the Guggenheim? I don't have any pull to even get an interview."

"Well," his friend said, "why don't you ask Maginel to say something to her brother — Frank Lloyd Wright?"

Joseph got the job. He told me that prior to the opening in New York, the Guggenheim was going to send some of its collection to Europe for an exhibition honoring the NYC grand opening. The selection process was interesting, he said. The curator, Baroness Hilla von Rebay, would have the staff make selections from the collection and lean them up against the wall, starting at the top of the architectural spiral. She and the staff would walk down and stop in front of each piece of work, and she would say, "No, no, yes, no, yes, no, no." The next day the staff put out some previously selected "nos," and they became "yeses."

When the crates from the crating logistics company arrived, it appeared that the measurement specifications were not made for the inside of the crates, but for the outside dimensions. None of the measurements worked. The baroness and the staff immediately stuffed the crates with whatever would fit. The European exhibition met with rave reviews.

Joseph was Joseph Dickinson from Brownsville, Tennessee, a small town about sixty miles northeast from Memphis. Somehow the town produced some extraordinary people. Billy Walker was the librarian for the Metropolitan Museum of Art in New York; the conductor of the St. Louis Symphony was a product of Brownsville;

and Joseph was an artist and a composer. He could compose music sitting up in bed without a piano, and he was an extraordinary storyteller. Joseph was from an old family in Brownsville, landed gentry if you will, and was wonderfully popular with the women in town but somewhat a threat to the men. My mother adored him; my stepfather wasn't particularly interested in cultivating Joseph as a friend.

Joseph reminds me now of Joe Wilson, the former member of the State Department who wrote an op-ed published in the *New York Times* saying that he did not find evidence of "yellow cake" uranium in Niger being sold to Iraq, as the Bush administration had claimed as proof that Saddam Hussein was making weapons of mass destruction.

I recently watched *Fair Game*, the movie about Joe Wilson's wife, Valerie Plame, being outed by Vice President Dick Cheney's office to try to discredit her husband's article, to see why Joe Wilson came to mind when I thought of Joseph Dickinson. Sean Penn played Joe Wilson brilliantly in the movie, but I realize that it was a full shock of hair, gray and black, parted in the middle, that makes the connection for me. Joseph was a taller, leaner, less kempt, less handsome man.

Joseph loved to tell stories about old Brownsville and old Nashville. I'm not sure I know exactly who the Caldwell family was in Nashville, but my father had a book in his library, *Caldwell and Company*. The Caldwells were old-moneyed Nashville aristocracy. Joseph told the story of having lunch with Mrs. Caldwell at the country club when she called the waiter over to admonish him about the little cellophane packages on the table.

"What are these?" she asked.

"Why, madam, they are saltine crackers."

"But," she said, "they are still in their wrappers."

"Yes, madam, the better to keep them fresh for you."

"Simon," she said, "if I had wanted to prepare lunch, I would have remained at home!"

One of Joseph's Brownsville stories described relationships between the races. He told me about an old Brownsville grand dame who was getting up in age and out of the house less. She was talking with her maid about the upcoming wedding of a friend's grandchild. The maid asked, "Are we going to be entertaining for the Ramsey child?"

"No," she answered. "I don't believe so."

"Well, I hear all the important folk in town will be entertaining for the girl."

"Well, I'm not," she said. "I used to be very important, but I'm all petered out."

I adored Joseph. He introduced me to Betty and Benton Fisher in Washington, DC. One night he asked Betty if he could bring me as his dinner partner to a supper she was having in her beautiful Georgetown home. The home was fascinating; the kitchen and the cozy dining room were downstairs subterranean — almost a basement in this period house.

Betty had me sit with a Mr. Biddle. He and his wife were adorable. Both seemed a bit reserved, but in a pleasant way, and both were a bit chubby. They arrived to dinner a little late, still dressed in their square-dancing costumes.

I enjoyed my conversation with Mr. Biddle. He inquired how long I was to be in Washington. I told him that I was leaving the next morning for Philadelphia for a meeting with Conrail, the freight train network, as a member of the Minority Business Resource Center of the Federal Railroad Administration.

Mr. Biddle said it was a shame that he had not met me a little earlier; he would've been happy to open up the house for me. Joseph later told me that my dinner partner was part of the Biddle-Duke family, and the Philadelphia house would mean the old Biddle estate. I recognized the Biddle name from a movie Walt Disney made about this family.

Benton and Betty gave beautiful dinner parties, and I was so pleased they took a liking to me. Whenever I came to Washington for one of my committees, they would have dinner parties to include me. Benton's family was from Jackson, Tennessee, and they visited in my home en route to and from huge family reunions each Fourth of July. Joseph's best gift to me, besides a portrait of me and one of my mother, was the friendship he enabled me to have with Betty Fisher.

I must say that the portrait of Mother, though of great sentimental value, was not the prettiest portrayal of her. She looked a bit tougher than I used to think of her. When I mentioned that to Joseph, he said, "You didn't play bridge against her like I did."

Joseph and I went to the symphony when he was in Memphis. Joseph lived most of the time in New Orleans when I first met him, and he would come to Brownsville to help take care of his mother and paint commissioned portraits. One night at the symphony, he was furious. Our conductor, Alan Balter, came out dressed as Mozart for a birthday tribute to the composer. Joseph was disturbed, claiming that Maestro Balter had placed himself between the audience and the music. He was not amused.

Once when I was visiting in New Orleans, Joseph invited me to his home, a typical Vieux Carre structure on Dumaine Street where the door at the street opened into a courtyard and then one climbed upstairs to the apartment. I was tickled to be inside a French Quarter house.

I think Joseph felt I was much too enamored with him. In fact, I did love him. After tea, he took me to a pool hall, saying he wanted me to meet a special friend, a young African American man who seemed flamboyantly gay. I already knew Joseph was gay.

Joseph became extremely ill. "Mr. Dickinson is the first AIDS patient I've ever seen," his nurse told me.

As a veteran, Joseph had privileges at the Veterans Administration hospital, but they were more afraid of him than nurses today would be. They treated him with what appeared to be a terrible lack of compassion.

I wasn't very good about it, either. I visited him twice and was afraid I wasn't very helpful. The staff wrapped me up in protective garb and told me not to touch Joseph and certainly not to kiss him goodbye. I was much less the friend I wanted to be, but this disease was new to everybody, and I have to admit I was afraid to get too close. In the movie by Larry Kramer, *The Normal Heart*, the health care delivery system's actions toward gay patients were an abomination. Everyone was scared, and I'm not very proud of my last moments with my good friend Joseph.

I asked Judy Peiser of the Center for Southern Folklore to tape some of Joseph's stories, and he agreed to "perform." Self-conscious at first, he got into it. He delighted Judy as well. I sent a copy of the tape telling his Maginel story to the Guggenheim for their archives, but they never responded — even that they received them. I still have those tapes.

The portrait Joseph painted of me is beautiful. Mother commissioned it in 1973. She was a bit dismayed when I insisted on being painted in a pantsuit, and I posed the entire time with a pencil in my hand. A pencil holder was in the background on a desk I was standing and leaning against. I had long red hair that Joseph liked, and he granted my wish to paint me thinner. I was surprised when he presented me with the finished piece. He used a frame with a flat surface extending a few inches beyond the silver-painted, raised border. On that surface he continued painting to the edge, so it looked like the piece went beyond the frame. He took out the pencil and the pencil holder.

"Jocelyn, I replaced the pencil holder with a clock and, for you, I have the hands at the eleventh hour."

Joseph was the first noted AIDS death in Memphis in 1985.

Two Alberts

I have been totally, madly, head-over-heels, girlie giddy in love with two different men named Albert. Unfortunately for me, both men were totally, madly, head-over-heels in love with their wives.

Albert Vorspan, vice president of the UAHC and in charge of the CSA, was, next to my father, the best public speaker I have ever heard. Vasco Albert Smith and his wife, Maxine, were undisputedly Memphis's most important civil rights activists. Vasco may have appreciated music even more than my father. If my loves had been requited, psychologists would have had a field day diagnosing me as a father-figure f*#ker!

Al Vorspan, like Daddy, was wonderfully witty and could tell a good joke. Our thing was to trade jokes whenever we were at UAHC or CSA meetings. They were slightly risqué and often Jewish. He authored books: *My Rabbi Doesn't Make House Calls*; *I'm OK, You're a Pain in the Neck*; and my favorite title, *Start Worrying: Details to Follow*. His mission was to convert people to understanding social justice, not shame folk into it.

Al says his best achievement was bringing Rabbi David Saperstein in as director of the Religious Action Center, our Reform Jewish presence in Washington, DC. I think his greatest achievement was making our movement the moral voice for social justice for Jews the world over.

Al's wonderful, artistically talented wife, Shirley, has Alzheimer's disease, and in his nineties he has been her primary caregiver.

Vasco Smith, a dentist, and his wife, Maxine, director of the local NAACP chapter and a member of the national board, were both elected to public office. Maxine won her seat on the school board while in the hospital recovering from open-heart surgery. Vasco was elected to the Shelby County Commission, the legislative body for the county.

Both were fierce, unrelenting fighters for civil rights. But that wasn't the plan. Maxine, a graduate of Middlebury College with a master's in French, wanted to come back to Memphis to teach a little French and play a lot of bridge. She was the only bridge player I have ever seen who could bid and play a hand without sorting her cards by suit. To teach, she needed a teacher's certificate, but Memphis State University refused her entrance because it was still segregated. That launched the Smiths' civil rights careers.

Maxine always did her homework and was a very persuasive speaker and skilled negotiator for the NAACP. There was a lot of talk about changing the name to the National Association for the Advancement of Black People; I thought, just change it to Colored Peoples, plural, since they fought for the rights of other minorities as well. It was cleverly organized so that all movie theaters and restaurants in Memphis would desegregate on the same day. I was in awe and admit to a girl crush on Maxine.

As fans of Dr. and Mrs. Smith, various caterers in Memphis kept

Maxine's freezer stocked with goodies so they could host a last-minute meeting or a visiting dignitary — such as Thurgood Marshall. Black folk below the Mason-Dixon line maintained a registry of hosts for traveling dignitaries since the hotels were segregated. Talk about jokes, the Smiths said Thurgood Marshall had a fabulous sense of humor and was a pure delight to be around.

With only a few days' notice, Alan Black of the NAACP Legal Defense Fund asked Maxine to allow me to present my legislation for non-discrimination in employment and public accommodations to the Shelby County delegation to the Tennessee Legislature. She put on a beautiful event. That's when I met Vasco for the first time and actually got to be with Maxine other than being spellbound in one of her audiences. Lucky me, we became friends.

And what hosts they were! Thanksgiving at their exquisite home was a lavish seated dinner for forty or so. One holiday, they accepted Richard's and my invitation to drinks at our house and brought Vernon and Shirley Jordan.

My daughter Cheryl, ten at the time, asked Dr. Smith if she could ask him a political question. "Commissioner Smith, we need an equestrian center at Shelby Farms and I would like for you to vote 'yes,' please, sir."

"Cheryl, I would love to help, but it is very important that I help my people first by building a new public hospital. I hope you understand that's what I have to do. When that is done, then we will talk."

He put her down so gently while giving her a lesson on setting priorities. Actually, both projects were voted on in the same year, and he voted "yes" for the horse show arena.

The Smiths were fun when they took a break from "being on the case." Vasco was a jazz aficionado extraordinaire. His jazz music collection was vast and comprehensive, and he loved to tutor new devotees. We started the Jazz Society of Memphis, and a perk of membership was that Vasco taught jazz lessons along with some of the music faculty of the University of Memphis, including Gene Rush, pianist, and Tim Goodwin, bassist. Whatever a photographic memory is to the eye, Vasco had it for his ear.

While I was in law school, I "clerked" for Vasco and introduced him to Title VI of the Civil Rights Act, a rarely used tool to root out discrimination in county government. All federal money coming to the county (or any recipient) had to be spent in a non-discriminatory manner. For instance, Vasco complained to the Federal Aviation Administration that the snack rooms at the Memphis airport were racially segregated and unequal, which, if not addressed, would risk continuing federal funding for the airport.

Vasco got through the commission set-asides for minority participation in all county-funded projects. In research, we learned that one subcontractor actually got a minority contract by claiming: "My wife is part Indian, and my grandmother was one-eighth hebrew" (with a little "h").

Vasco teased, "One-eighth was enough to make me Black everywhere, doesn't that make this SOB a little bit Jewish?"

Dr. Smith, very much a politician, kept a sign in his dental clinic: "Don't talk politics in here unless you are registered to vote." One day when I was working with Howard Baker for one of his re-election campaigns, we were at a rally near Vasco's office. I asked him if he and Joy (Dirksen, his first wife) would like to meet Vasco Smith. Impressed I could arrange that on short notice, Howard was greeted with praise: "I've just got a second, but I want to tell you, Senator, you were entirely right on your position on the Panama Canal. It was a brave stand, and you've got my vote because of it!"

I was asked to say a few words at Vasco's funeral; they wanted his love of jazz in the eulogy. Thank goodness, I remembered and sent word to the funeral planners that he wanted "Come Sunday" from Duke Ellington's *Sacred Concert* sung at his funeral. I told how proud Vasco was of the Black jazz musicians, the learned ones like Jimmie Lunceford and the geniuses who couldn't even read music, like vibraphonist Milt Jackson.

I don't know what possessed me, except it was true, and I did run it by a friend of his and Maxine's for approval before inclusion at the end: "Apropos of absolutely nothing, I want to declare Dr. Vasco Albert Smith to be, not only an equal opportunity, but an affirmative action flirt! Fat, thin, short, tall, young, old, Black, white, Asian, you have never been flirted with, nor made to feel as good about yourself, as when you have been flirted with by Vasco Smith. If there is any other woman in the sanctuary who feels as I do, would you please signify by saying 'Amen.'" Practically every woman in the church resounded "Amen."

Jesse Jackson

All my paths that have crossed Jesse Jackson's have been unpleasant. I first met Jesse Jackson in 1971 when Memphis established a local chapter of People United to Save Humanity (PUSH). In my zeal for all things civil rights, I joined. Larry Shaw, brother-in-law of my beloved friend Pat Shaw, hosted a reception to meet Reverend Jackson.

Someone asked me if I would like to meet him. "Sure!" He was a colleague of Dr. King, was on the Lorraine Motel balcony when Dr. King was killed, and was important to the movement. His oratory was legend. I wanted to meet him; that's why I came to the party. I was led into the kitchen where he and someone else were seated at a small dinette table for two.

"Reverend, I would like for you to meet Jocelyn Wurzburg." Reverend Jackson looked my way. It was more of an up-and-down inspection, as if I was a heifer up for auction! He said nothing, looked back at his companion, and continued their conversation. I backed out through the door, incredulously humiliated.

My second encounter was at a mass meeting of sanitation workers filling the North Hall of Ellis Auditorium. It was an April 4 commemorative event for the anniversary of the assassination of Dr. King. Some Memphians call April 4 "Holy Day." I was a speaker on the program and was immediately after Reverend Jackson. I sat beside him on the podium; no words were exchanged. The whole thing was a seminal event. He rose to speak to thunderous applause. He delivered his speech flawlessly. But I felt uneasy. Jackson did his "I am somebody" call and response, and he held the group in the palm of his hand. But I had a flash: It felt Hitlerian. It was almost a "Sieg Heil!" At the end of his speech and to more applause, he left the stage and took most of the audience with him. Never, never follow Jesse Jackson as a presenter!

The third meeting was dreadful. In 1984, Reverend Jackson held a national convention of his Rainbow PUSH organization in Memphis. He asked the UAHC for a representative to speak on affirmative action.

There had been a bit of bother when Jackson had recently referred to New York City as "Hymietown." "Hymie" is a derogative term for Jew. And then a prominent conservative Jewish leader had recently denounced affirmative action. I think the invitation to the UAHC was a peace offering.

The UAHC asked me to speak. Our position on affirmative action was identical to the NAACP's; we were for enforceable, inclusive goals and timetables. Neither of us wanted quotas. The Jewish experience with quotas wasn't good: it meant no matter how qualified the candidate was for the job, college placement, or promotion, if the Jewish quota was filled, the candidate was SOL. For some Black folk, quotas felt like the only way for them to get in. This was a case of "better be careful what you wish for because you might get it."

I was on a panel of about ten; I was the only woman and one of three whites. I made reference to our mutual insensitive remarks and affirmed our long-lasting coalition could withstand our faux pas. My presentation was well-received. I spoke about the ridiculous situation that UCLA had tens of thousands of students and just a few hundred African Americans. The audience was welcoming and generous with their approval.

Then Reverend Jackson stood up to reply to my remarks. "Ms. Wurzburg is right! But what she doesn't understand is that it is hard for Black people to commit suicide jumping out of the basement window." The audience turned toward me with an audible growl. Gr-r-r-r.

William Robinson, a noted civil rights attorney and, at the time, director of the Lawyers Committee for Civil Rights Under the Law, was sitting next to me. I knew him from his helping me draft the Tennessee Human Rights Act. I leaned over and asked, "What did I say wrong?"

"Nothing, Jocelyn. The audience liked you, and he can't stand it."

As it happened, Jesse Jackson had asked to come apologize to the CSA, of which I had been a member since 1976, for his "Hymietown" remark. Rabbis Alex Schindler and David Saperstein accepted his offer. I had briefed David about the unpleasant encounter. I guess as an affirmation of me, he and Alex brought Reverend Jackson over to me personally.

"Reverend, I think you know Jocelyn Wurzburg, don't you?"

"Oh, yes, we've been friends for years," he said.

James Meredith, J.D., and Rev. Jeremiah Wright

James Meredith was honored with an "I Am A Man" award at the April 4th Foundation banquet in 2015. The April 4th Foundation was founded by the Reverend Johnson Saulsberry, who seeks to keep Dr. Martin Luther King's dream alive. He hosts civil rights seminars for teens and leads pilgrimages to Atlanta, Georgia; Selma, Alabama; and other southern locales to help kids feel the emotions behind the historical facts. I have lectured to the students, received an award from the foundation, and co-chaired the 2011 banquet.

My chairmanship didn't go so well. The position was more or less honorary. I was chair of the dinner the night Rev. Jeremiah Wright was the keynoter. A controversial figure, he became of note as President and Mrs. Obama's minister in Chicago. His church was involved in social action in the Chicago area. As Republicans attempted to discredit President Obama by all means possible, they released snippets of Wright's more controversial sermons.

In one, where he was on a roll critical of US policies, he said that rather than ask God to bless America, God should damn America. I understand that a man who lived under de jure and de facto racial discrimination all his life might not want God to bless America in all circumstances and may not think everything America has done is sacrosanct. I'm privileged enough so that to hear someone damning America would make me cringe, at least a little bit. I curse like a sailor, but rarely do I use "G-d damn." But I, too, have damned ridiculous actions by my beloved country. And Reverend Wright was a Vietnam veteran, so he has standing to be critical of American policies.

I have had dear friends in the civil rights movement purposefully come into an event after the Pledge of Allegiance has been recited rather than cause a scene by not standing. I refuse to say "under God" when reciting the pledge, as my personal affirmation that church should be separated from state.

But my issue with Reverend Wright is that his vociferous rhetoric in supporting the Palestine cause — as I do some for some things — crossed a line that felt anti-Semitic to the Jewish world. When President Obama needed to distance himself from remarks condemning America's actions in Iraq, Wright said, "Them Jews in his administration won't let him talk to me."

Wright doesn't like the American Israel Public Affairs Committee (AIPAC), but neither do I. AIPAC will support any political candidate so long as they support Israel, even if they are against everything else liberal Jews stand for. The office seeker can be anti-choice, not believe the climate is changing, and think health care is a privilege for the deserved, not a right; but if they are unequivocally pro-Israel, they get a nod.

I called my friend Rabbi David Saperstein for advice. I told him I was not in the loop when Reverend Wright was selected, but I was a named chair of the event. Personally, I found Wright fascinating and was curious to meet him, but I didn't want to betray my Jewish community in its concern that a Black leader of Reverend Wright's stature would spout anti-Semitic sentiments. It's one thing to question Israel's positions in settlement expansion — again, as I do — but another thing to be anti-Jewish about it.

I was advised to avoid being pictured with Reverend Wright if possible, and that if I was pictured with him, my local Jewish community would criticize me unmercifully. It would be hard not to be pictured with him. I wouldn't hurt Reverend Saulsberry's feelings by skipping the event, but I certainly didn't want criticism to hurt the foundation. I decided that I had to take my chances and show up.

God made the decision. I had been feeling queasy all morning, and I attributed it to being nervous about Reverend Wright. By later that afternoon, I was vomiting and going from both ends! I had a case of food poisoning and lifted my head off the pillow only to run to the john.

The 2015 banquet was star-filled. While James Meredith was the award winner, the hit of the evening was keynoter Bobby Seale, the famous founder of the Black Panthers in the 1960s. "Militant, hell, I was an architecture student when I got involved," Seale said.

My mediation teacher, Steve Erickson, said he had a Bobby Seale poster hanging on his Columbia University dorm wall, so he was truly delighted I got an autographed book for him.

James Meredith's presence brought back fun memories of tales told about him. He integrated Ole Miss in 1962 with the help of armed National Guard members. The National Civil Rights Museum in Memphis has fascinating tape recordings between President John F. Kennedy and Mississippi Gov. Ross Barnett, who tried to prevent integration of the school.

My Bobby was at Ole Miss then and occasionally ran into Meredith. Meredith spoke in Chicago, and it seems he got a lot of criticism when he looked out into the audience and said, "One of these days one of you 'burr heads' will be mayor of this town." No one appreciated the term, especially the Blacks in the audience, and it got picked up in the media and disseminated.

He and Bobby were talking, sharing that both had been in the service and were at Ole Miss as older students, when someone walked up and chided, "Hey, Meredith, even the n*%#@rs are pissed at you."

Sympathetically, Bobby said, "Man, it's got to be tough!"

Meredith responded, "You have no idea."

Maxine Smith told me this tale about Meredith:

"We begged Meredith not to take his freedom walk from Memphis to Oxford, Mississippi. We had a full plate at the time and just couldn't be supportive at the moment. So he decided to go it alone. And damned if he didn't get shot in the ass with buckshot! So we are all congregated in his hospital room. I don't remember who all was there; surely Ben Hooks, A.W. Willis, maybe Vernon Jordan. We're at the end of his bed talking about what do we do now, and he said, 'Excuse me, but I'm the one lying here shot. I would like to be included in the conversation.' We said, 'Hush up, Meredith, we told you not to take that damn walk!'"

Both James Meredith and my grandfather, Jacob Block Heyman, were born in Kosciusko, Mississippi. Google says Meredith got his start in civil rights when he rode a train home from Chicago to Mississippi and, when the train arrived in Memphis, he was made to give up his seat to a white man and go back to the crowded Black section of the train. He had to stand all the rest of the way home and vowed then to fight for equal rights.

That was likely the train called The City of New Orleans that runs from Chicago to New Orleans. A group of us kids from Little Rock, Arkansas, and Memphis took the train to Chicago and back for a high school yearbook convention. Going up, the train was segregated. But as I got on the train in Chicago to return home, the railcar was racially integrated, and there were sporadic, single available seats. Ms. Siegman, our advisor and chaperone, went to the conductor and said, "Now I have some young southern girls traveling today — you know what I mean — and I would like for them to be able to sit *together* — you know what I mean?" He did, and he made some Black passengers get up and sit with other Black folk so we young southern girls wouldn't have to sit next to anyone Black. I wouldn't have minded sitting next to someone who was Black, and all this brouhaha was an embarrassment. That memory stuck.

Father Theodore Hesburgh (1917-2015)
The EEOC Kitchen Cabinet

Father Theodore Hesburgh, a strong advocate for civil rights, was appointed as a charter member of the USCCR in 1957 and served as its chair in 1969. President Nixon forced him to resign in 1972 over arguments about enforcing civil rights law. Father Hesburgh served as president of the University of Notre Dame for thirty-five years, retiring from that position in 1987. I met him in a strange way in 1975; we served on the "kitchen cabinet" of EEOC Chair John H. Powell Jr.

John Powell graduated with honors from Howard University, Harvard Law, and New York University. He was counsel for the EEOC when President Nixon appointed him chair in 1973.

I was on the Tennessee Human Rights Commission when I met him and was still trying to lobby the Tennessee legislature to pass my bill. At any rate, I received an invitation to come to DC and serve on this "cabinet" of citizens to advise the chair.

The first and only meeting we had was bizarre. Right after the creation of the group and before we ever had a meeting, the chairman got into trouble with the administration, then of President Ford. The press jumped on him with both feet.

"During his brief tenure," according to his *New York Times* obituary, "the commission became embroiled in conflicts over his power as chairman and was criticized for its growing backlog of unresolved cases." The dispute over Powell's chairmanship involved fellow commissioners who asserted that he had overstepped his powers.

Father Hesburgh was on this committee, as was an impressive woman named Eleanor Holmes Norton. I had heard of both of them before. Eleanor was a civil rights and feminist icon. She was a Yale law graduate and assistant director of the ACLU, and President Carter appointed her as the first female chair of the EEOC in 1977.

The chairman was in emotional disarray. He admitted he was a bit heavy-handed in his leadership, but the job had to get done. The press was lying and harassing him. We suggested he ignore them and just do his job. He was obsessed with them, ranting on the unfairness of it all. In fact, he was pacing the floor and twiddling a pencil in his hand. It felt like Humphrey Bogart playing Lieutenant Commander Philip Francis Queeg in *The Caine Mutiny*.

Eleanor and I eyed each other, thinking the same thing. Father Hesburgh was trying to calm the chairman with sensitivity and logic. It wasn't working.

A secretary came in and announced that it had started snowing and icing over outside. Chairman Powell concluded the meeting and then called his driver, Mr. Randall, to take Father Hesburgh and me back to our hotel and take Eleanor home.

Eleanor was elected in 1990 to be the District of Columbia's non-voting delegate (representative) to Congress and has served ever since. And a fine spokesperson she has been.

John Powell didn't get better. Once he called my house at about two o'clock in the morning. He didn't say hello; he just lit into a diatribe against his detractors and the press and then hung up. That was the last interaction we had.

Chapter Thirty

Cancers-R-Us

Cancer runs in my family: My grandmother, mother, maternal aunt, maternal cousin, and me. My daughter Mindy just finished full-court-press chemo. The biopsy was clean but, thank God, they decided to take out the lump, and one lymph node was cancerous. Only one of us female family members has been tested for the "Jewish" gene, prevalent in Jewish women for cancer, and it was negative so I didn't take the test.

I learned with Mama that dying isn't just falling asleep and not waking up. When the body begins to shut down, a patient can shake violently, and a drug called Dilantin can stop a seizure pretty quickly. So when Mama began to shake furiously, we ran for the resident on duty. He refused to give the shot because the chart said to do it only after so many hours. In an accented voice, he said, "I'm not going to be put in the middle of a lawsuit."

I called her physician at midnight for him to give permission for the shot — and then climbed down the stairwell between two floors and screamed my frustration at the medical system.

I thought evil thoughts: The price of one aircraft carrier and we could cure cancer. And what percentage of the gross national product involves cancer, so they really don't want to solve it?

At a Torah lunch and learn, I was awaiting "the" phone call — whether my latest biopsy was positive or negative. A friend at the table was upset over the meager amount of greens the restaurant called a salad and the charge for it. Here I was waiting to hear if I had cancer, and she was upset about a salad. I admit, similarly situated without the cancer looming over me, I'd be pissed, too. The call came. I stepped out of the room to take it, and the news wasn't good. So what do you do? I went back in, sat down, and finished the class.

The breast cancer turned out to be invasive, but only Stage 1. Only a lumpectomy was required, and then I had a process called mammosite: If your cancer was at least one-half inch below the surface of the breast and you were over forty-five years of age, you could be eligible for mammosite. In mammosite, a balloon is inserted into the cavity created from the cancer removal. It has a tube that sticks out of the breast and into which your radiologist can insert tiny radioactive beads to radiate you on the inside instead of radiation burning you from the outside.

The doctor and staff set everything into motion, exited the secure room, and started the procedure remotely. There was a speaker system so we could talk. It only took about ten minutes.

The good thing is that I went twice a day for five days instead of every day for six weeks. I went to the clinic, got zapped, went to work, came back, got zapped again, and went home. Painless.

I was assigned a "mentor," and she scared me by saying the removal of the balloon on the last day was miserable. So I dreaded it all week; I shared my fear with the doctor and, lying there, I told him to please be gentle and try not to make it hurt so badly.

He said, "Are you talking about this little thing?" and dangled the balloon over me to see.

The bad news is they have ceased to use mammosite. It leaves a big lump inside the breast, making it difficult to see around with future mammographies and ultrasounds. A breast MRI was required, and that is as unpleasant a medical procedure as there is.

Next I had a melanoma, found by a nurse practitioner. I love my nurse practitioner! I use her as my homeroom health care deliverer. My physician went boutique on me, so I asked him what he thought of me using his nurse Cindy as my primary contact. He thought it was a great idea, and in a pre-op exam for my hip replacement, Cindy found the melanoma. Thank you, Cindy.

Then Bobby, my honey, had a lump on his chest. It hurt, and

everyone knows cancer doesn't hurt, so we didn't run to a doctor. But when he visited his cardiologist, the doctor felt the lump and sent him out to Baptist mammography to see my radiologist. She knew immediately it was breast cancer.

Bobby said it was cosmic payback time.

"For all the women I groped when I was a kid, I got paid back. Three women were pulling and squeezing my male breast into a mammography machine! Sheer torture!" he said.

Bobby had a partial mastectomy, and it was Stage 3 cancer. Four of nineteen lymph nodes were cancerous. He had surgery, chemo, and radiation, which burned him to a crisp! Our oncologist said we were his first his-and-her breast cancer couple. Bobby was offered reconstructive surgery to fill in the divot on his chest and make a nipple.

"Good God, no! Go under the knife for cosmetic surgery? There is a pizza parlor up in Frayser that slices a pepperoni the perfect size I can just paste on me."

My left breast had six biopsies taken, and I was left with a scar in the shape of a "Z." Bobby started calling me "Zorro tit."

After his surgery, I said, "If I'm Zorro, buster, you're zero!"

Sometimes you gotta laugh to keep from crying.

Chapter Thirty-One

Death and Dying

Broadway and opera didn't do me any favors to prepare me for the loss of loved ones. Anna and the prince sing while the king of Siam slowly drops his arm over the side of the bed. Puccini's Mimi sings on her way out in *La Boheme*. Until the *Wild Bunch* movie came out, even violent deaths never spurted blood. The movies don't show the violent tremors.

When it comes to the reality of death, I'm afraid I'm an expert. I have dealt with far too many death experiences. Thank God, not the death of my child; I don't think I could survive that. But I killed someone else's.

Two of my grandparents were gone before I had consciousness of them. I remember that Pops, Jacob Block Heyman Sr., Mama's dad, was pleasant. He lived with my Aunt Mildred, with whom I spent a lot of time, but I didn't feel him to be a large presence in the house.

I do have one particular memory of him: He had an automobile with a globe of the earth in the center of the steering wheel. I think it was an Oldsmobile. On V-E Day (May 8, 1945) or V-J Day (August 14, 1945) — I don't remember which night it was — everybody jumped into their cars and drove to town just to honk horns and cheer out the windows. Being five years old and little, I was seated in the front middle seat, and all I could see was the blue globe with stars. Pops died soon after that.

Grandma, Daddy's mother, always seemed old to me. A mother of eight, she lived her later years with my Aunt Dorothy. She and

Pops lived into their eighties and died of what we thought in those days was simply old age.

The day I'm writing this, we buried Robin Dan Hooper, the first of the Memphis Dan cousins to die. Without written directives, her children had to make the "awful decision." She was sixty-six years old. Rabbi Micah quoted me saying, "Robin rolled with the punches better than any woman I ever knew." She was strong and genial at the same time. Robin was a "Georgia Tann baby." The infamous Ms. Tann sold babies, whom she convinced young, unmarried women to give up, to important clients across the country. If she had an impatient client, she was known to tell a young mother her baby had died when in fact it hadn't. Much has been written about Georgia Tann's stolen babies.

Robin's father's death was a true tragedy. In 1958, the wife of Edward Reeves, sheriff of Shelby County, screamed for help and the across-the-street neighbor was Melwyn Dan, my father's youngest brother. Without hesitation, he jumped into the Reeves family's pool to save the sheriff. But the sheriff wasn't drowning. He was electrocuted, and so was Melwyn the second he jumped in.

The court case was famous in Tennessee and is still taught in law review classes. Because an element of proof of negligence is foreseeability, the family could not collect damages for the faulty equipment from the neighbor's insurance company. It is foreseeable that people drown in pools but not that they get electrocuted. Bad decision, and it left the family penniless. No college for Robin or her sister.

When I was at Melwyn and Millie's home for Shiva, the observance of respect for the deceased and supposed comfort for the family, a relative of the Reeves family came through the door and quoted John 15:13: "Greater love hath no man than this, that a man lay down his life for his friends." Melwyn's wife ran from the room in hysterics. I knew the man meant to be comforting, but Aunt Millie wasn't going to be comforted at that moment with Scripture.

Uncle Melwyn's death was the first time I ever saw my daddy cry.

As mentioned earlier, Mother's death in 1979 was the result of cancer. It was in the lungs and metastasized in the brain. She told the doctors that she would reach for something "over there and it would be over here." Lying in the hospital, she would insert irrelevant words into a sentence. Then she asked, "Do I have cancer?" Hearing the answer, she practically shut down and spoke very little after that. She knew she was going to die.

Her death was before folks had living wills and directives. The hospital experience created a feeling of total helplessness. We would anxiously await the doctors, and then they would tell us very little. We would follow them out of the hospital room and walk them down the hall trying to glean any information we could. Would she make it? Was she suffering? How long did she have? Then one day they would say, "Let's sit down and talk." Until then it was useless to try to engage in conversation about end-of-life issues.

My brother, Ray, flew up from New Orleans often, and my sister, Libby, flew down from Detroit. We functioned well as a family, and Mama knew we were with her. I was in my last semester of law school and participating in the school's legal clinic downtown. So I lived at the hospital and bused to town and back a few hours a day. I skipped classes at the law school and couldn't do the two papers due. They were lenient, allowing me to graduate timely and turn in the papers late.

The family all agreed not to perform heroics to prolong Mama's life. But even with the decision made, letting go was so hard. I saw a nurse change the intravenous bag, and after she left, I noticed air bubbles in the line! I ran down the hall after the nurse, saying, "Help, help, there are air bubbles!" She ran back with me and fixed it. That situation would have hastened the end for Mama days earlier, and my first instinct was to save her.

Robert Felsenthal was my stepfather; I met him for the first time when Mama brought him to visit me in the hospital when I was having my first child. A lovable man, he greeted everyone with the words "My friend!" He didn't have to die when he did. It was decided he would move to Kirby Pines, an independent living facility that had graduated living sections to assisted living, when necessary, and then nursing home services. Robert had balance problems, so the sole reason we wanted him to move over there was so he would have an emergency pull cord. And damn if he didn't fall the first month he was there. He fell at about three o'clock in the morning and didn't want to disturb anybody, so he waited until about six to pull the cord. That was just enough time for his brain area to start swelling.

The anatomy of a head injury is interesting. Robert was in a coma state. They could drain the gathered fluid, and then he was Robert again. And then the swelling commenced again, and he would go back into a coma state. After one draining, he was able to call his beloved sister for what turned out to be their last conversation. He just didn't want to be a bother.

My father's death was traumatic. While I was on my delayed honeymoon in June 1961, Daddy attempted suicide, but he lingered a few days. Mother's reaction was to get sick, as she often did under stress, so when I flew in from Las Vegas, I found Daddy in one hospital room and Mama in an adjoining room. It was Wednesday after he had swallowed poison the night before. Given that there was no flight out of Vegas Tuesday night, there seemed no sense calling and telling me until early Wednesday morning. Plane reservations had been made; I just needed to pack and get to the airport.

There was a response of agitation when I said, "Daddy, I'm here."

At one point, all the Dans were gathered in Mama's room, and Mama was telling the group from her sickbed that Daddy hadn't been easy on her. I curtly responded, "Mama, right now this is not about you!" I got "attagirl" glances from Daddy's family and pats on the back of approval, but I regretted the words as soon as I said them. They never really liked Mama and our not going to shul with the family, and I betrayed her in front of them.

I hate it, but it was my brother who found Daddy. As stated earlier, Daddy was sick, couldn't do his job, and was heavily insured. He felt he was a burden to his family and worth more dead than alive.

I left the hospital on Friday morning to go home, take a bath, and change clothes. They called me to come back quickly; he was going. He was gone by the time I got there, minutes later.

I've had more than one nurse tell me that sometimes they felt their patient would time his or her own death for when the family would leave the bedside, even if it was for a very short time. Reggie Wurzburg insisted the entire family get out of the house and go out for dinner for the Fourth of July. He died before they returned.

Suicide f*#ks up everybody. Everyone close batters themselves with questions: What could they have done? What could they have said? I often wished I had told Daddy I was pregnant. I wasn't, but what if I had told him I was? Maybe he wouldn't have done it. That's how desperate I was to conjure up a way I could have stopped him.

Valmid was a drug I was taking at the time for sleep. It was an acceptable drug compatible with my getting over mononucleosis, something about not being digestible by the liver. But who reads the lengthy pamphlets that come with the bottle? My awful nightmares about Daddy continued almost a year — he would be in a cage at the zoo, for example. I often awoke screaming. My poor, patient husband had only been married a few months, and his twenty-year-old bride cried every night for her daddy. Finally I discussed this with a doctor, and we discovered a side effect of Valmid was that it was a hallucinogen. It was no wonder I couldn't heal. God, I still miss my father.

Daddy's death by suicide impacted my new marriage so negatively. Richard and I vowed we would never do such a thing to each other. And never do to our children what Daddy did to us.

When Richard did, I was shattered.

A Child on the Road

Of all the ways to deal with death and dying, I thought none were worse than dealing with suicide. But even more unbearable would be the loss of a child. Then I hit a girl on the highway and killed another mother's child.

It was a terrible automobile accident on Interstate 40 between West Memphis, Arkansas, and the Memphis bridge over the Mississippi River. There was a horrible thunder and lightning storm, and these long white legs — that was all I saw — ran across the expressway. The car's low beams clearly showed they were human legs with bare feet. This happened at about eleven o'clock at night.

A new attorney friend had told me he would be in Hot Springs, Arkansas, taking a deposition at the same time I planned to visit my cousin on Lake Hamilton, so I arranged to hitch a ride home with him. I had gotten my divorce the previous week, and a trip to the lake was a great idea.

We stopped in Little Rock for dinner, and when we got back into the car to come home, I realized he was too tipsy to drive. I insisted I take the wheel. A gentle rain became torrential around Hughes, Arkansas. There was no time for stopping, nor avoiding what or whoever I hit; I hoped to God it was a deer, but I knew it wasn't. Suddenly, something was there.

Immediately, I pulled the car to the roadside, jumped out, and started running back in the storm. Somehow the highway patrol was right there! The troopers must have been following behind us or were already parked on the side of the road. This happened in front of a motel. Perhaps there was a café there, I don't know, but they literally caught me by the waist running back toward the accident.

"I gotta help! I gotta help!" I yelled.

They said no, there was nothing I could do, that it was a young girl. She had died instantly. They led me to their car; all the while it was storming, and I was trying to pull myself back from hysterics.

It was unbelievable. I kept insisting I needed to go help her or at least go see her, but they wouldn't let me go. They said they didn't even have her identified yet, since she had run across the highway in shorts and a halter top.

By then my friend had reached the patrol car. They took my name and number and told him to take me home right away. I guess they took his information, too, since it was his car. This was within minutes. We were actually back in his car and on the road within fifteen minutes. This was hours after we had dinner so, thank goodness, he was sober enough to drive while I sobbed.

Mimi, with whom I had just been visiting in Florida, was staying at my condo in my absence. I ran into the house yelling for her. The lawyer wanted to stay and be helpful, but I begged Mimi to get him to go. I wasn't blaming him for my being the driver, but I didn't know him well enough to seek comfort from him. He later called often, but the history between us was so brief and so unpleasant, I just had to let it go.

There was a short article in the paper the next morning, identifying me as Jocelyn Wurzburg, civil rights activist, but not identifying the child. My girlfriends flooded the house the next day. Two were therapists and started on me immediately. My brother flew up from New Orleans that afternoon. My jazz teacher called with a list of music to play including "Come Ye Thou Disconsolate."

The girl was in the motel with a boy; he came out of the motel looking for her since she had run out into the storm. So the police found out who she was later that night, but they didn't call me.

A few days later, an insurance investigator came to interview me. He had the name of the child and her mother's contact information but entreated me not to call her mother or make any contact whatsoever. As a new lawyer, I knew he was right, but as a mother, I called her as soon as he left the house.

Can you imagine, there's a process whereby doing the right, compassionate thing is the wrong thing to do!

An astonishing thing happened. The girl's mother answered the call. I identified myself as the person who had hit her child. There was a short pause, and I braced myself for anger. I was willing to let her vent her fury.

I was astounded when she said, "I feel so sorry for you. I can only imagine your pain."

Her daughter was a runaway, drug-addicted sixteen-year-old. The mother had not seen or heard from her child in about eighteen months. I told her I was instructed not to call her, but I just had to let her know that her child could not have suffered. It was instant.

I never heard another legal word about the accident or loss. She was there, and then she wasn't.

Bobby's Mother Was Murdered

Bobby and I were on a road trip late at night. We had been to the lower East Coast and made a stop in Nashville on the way home from North Carolina. We went to the Station Inn for music, had a midnight dinner at Fridays, and pulled into my garage about five o'clock in the morning. The phone was ringing when we got into the house. That wasn't a good sign.

One of the men in Bobby's band had volunteered to call every half hour until he reached us. "Bobby, your mother died. She was murdered last evening at the house."

Good God almighty, why would this happen to Ms. Abby, such a dear soul?

Bobby was instantly grief-stricken . He and his mother were quite close, spending many an afternoon together to discuss books they were reading. He took a moment to gather himself and then drove over to his father's house.

The ritual was that Mr. B would call his wife to tell her he was on the way home from downtown. She would put ice in an Old Fashioned glass, and it would melt just the right amount to add their Old Charter 12 bourbon. She would unlock the back door and await his arrival. The murder must have happened just prior to Mr. B pulling up. In fact, the perpetrators must have run out the front door as he came into the back. There was still ice in the glass.

The house was a mess; particularly her bedroom had been completely ransacked. They were looking for money, and Ms. Abby evidently refused to tell them where she had some. The money was found later.

The police thought the perpetrators may have been tree-trimmers who had observed her routine. That fit a similar MO in another state.

Mr. B had left a message on my machine: "Bobby, they got ole Abby!" After Bobby got home, Mr. B started calling Bobby with orders. He was to go to the funeral home and make arrangements with a cousin. Bobby was exhausted and hadn't taken time to be alone and cry yet. He went to lie down, and Mr. B called again. I ran interference, begging him to allow Bobby some time to grieve.

I didn't go to the funeral, remaining at Mr. B's house to get it in order for callers.

Ironically, a few weeks later, Mr. B was down at the South

Second Street office and was accosted by young men with guns. They threw him onto the sidewalk and threatened to kill him. He was sharp enough to say, "Boys, you don't want to do that. I'm going to give you the keys to my car. There is a case of liquor in the trunk. You guys take the car and go have a good time. You don't have to hurt me." The thieves did as he said, leaving the few thousand dollars Mr. B had in his pockets.

A year later, the police thought they had found the murderers in jail in another state for a similar crime. They asked Mr. B if he wanted to press charges to have them sent to Memphis since Ms. Abby's murder was the prior one. Bobby talked to the police and to his father and convinced them to let the other state do its thing. He didn't have the stomach for it and felt his father couldn't survive the process of a trial.

Mr. B married his secretary, who had worked for him for sixty-five years. And then she continued working for Bobby after Mr. Bostick died. In her late eighties, she died driving downtown to work. Mr. B had left her the house and all the contents.

Mrs. Ryan's daughter, Louise, had an estate sale when her mother died. Bobby had to buy his yearbooks from the estate sellers. Puddin Breeding, a longtime neighbor of the Bosticks and a good friend of Bobby's, bought Ms. Abby's roll-top desk. She brought over to Bobby the $2,000 she found in a hidden drawer.

Too Many Funerals

A lot of funerals to attend these days! I guess it's that time of my life. It hurts to lose family and friends, and I have lots of regrets for not making that last phone call or visit.

Some funerals have been beautiful experiences. Eunice had an imam and a rabbi join her Presbyterian woman minister to conduct the service. She died as she lived. Jocelyn Rudner (I was named for her mother) asked for no eulogy; she only wanted music played. Lately, children and grandchildren have been delivering moving eulogies.

I was asked to say something at the funeral of Carol Lynn

Yellin, my feminist mentor and idol and, as mentioned previously, co-author of *The Perfect 36*, the book relating how Tennessee secured voting rights for American women. There was no other eligible state left to give women the right to vote; it was Tennessee or failure. Carol Lynn was an editor for *Reader's Digest*, and she condensed the Bible for the magazine. Women played a better role in her version.

I loved Carol Lynn and feared I might cry delivering my remarks. Since I live across the street from the parsonage of Independent Presbyterian Church, I asked the minister what I could do to keep from crying. He said, "Try to say something humorous early on; that would help center you." It worked.

It worked again when I delivered the eulogy for my longtime cohort in crime, my dear "Happy," Dorothy Snowden Jones.

And then there was Puddin's father's funeral. Bobby was a pallbearer, sitting up front. I was in the rear with John Buhler, a DKE fraternity brother of his. For some reason, the preacher got off on a sheep theme.

"We should be like sheep going home with the shepherd. A sheep is a loving animal. A sheep is a trusting animal. A sheep can be led home by a loving guide. One can see love in the eyes of a sheep. We have a live crèche every year at Christmas. Besides the humans portraying Joseph and Mary, the animals are live. We have a member of the church who volunteers every year to tend to that sheep. He loves that sheep, and you can tell that sheep loves him."

Well-l-l-l, that sheep business hit John and me at the exact same time. We both swear we heard a stifled chuckle from the front. Oh, God, it was so hard to laugh silently. Later, when we could, we asked Puddin, "What's with the sheep?"

Unfortunately, her mother died within the year. Puddin specifically instructed the minister that she wanted no references to sheep, and damn if he didn't start in on sheep. Puddin glared at him. Dear Puddin died recently. More sheep!

The only thing I demand for my funeral is no "woman of valor" shit! It describes the perfect wife or ideal Jewish woman. I failed on all accounts.

Chapter Thirty-Two

Assassination of JFK

Every year I dread November 22, the anniversary of the assassination of John Fitzgerald Kennedy, our thirty-fifth president. I dread the day because we lost a star. But I also dread each year rethinking about my guilt and utter stupidity for the immediate words that came out of my mouth.

TV pundits have made the case that this is one of those moments in life when we remember exactly where we were. I was in a dentist's chair. My friend Dr. Sidney Friedman and his father were the premier dentists in Memphis. He came in and said someone had taken a shot at the president.

I can't blame it on the Novocaine or the gas he gave me to get the Novocaine. It was just a dumbass remark: "Well, I guess that's one way the Republicans can get rid of him."

At that time in 1963, I was still involved in local conservative politics. I had swallowed the propaganda and really took at face value that state autonomy, free enterprise, and personal responsibility were what it took for America to function properly. And I had already read Ayn Rand and fancied myself a Dagny Taggart. I was just twenty-three and had not outgrown her yet. And besides, I had married into a family in which my father-in-law boasted he was never a Roosevelt voter.

But I was a closeted fan of JFK, or at least of his oratorical skills and subtle humor. I thought him brilliant at a mic and loved watching his press conferences. I took a pinpoint photo of him downtown at a political rally that I thought I should attend — to get informed as a new voter. He was an exciting personality.

I later got to meet Sen. Edward Kennedy on two occasions. Whatever it was the Kennedys had, Teddy had it, too. He read his speeches from loose-leaf notebooks typed in large print, a sentence or so per page in plastic, and he read them with his face down into the notebook. But then he would look up for eye contact, and you felt his words were meant for you. We had a brief conversation once at a cocktail party about his new diet when he was looking his most trim. I once shared a sauna with his biographer, who fancied himself as cool as Teddy. But the biographer writes good books.

Sidney, the dentist, would go out and catch up on the news. A few minutes later we learned JFK was actually hit by a bullet. I couldn't take back my trite comment of earlier, and I was genuinely disturbed. Within half an hour, we learned President Kennedy was dead, killed by an assassin.

I bet everyone engaged in any activity at the moment when we learned he was killed had a similar feeling. Whatever we were doing, we felt disrespectful for doing it. No, I didn't cry — then. I didn't actually know him. Was crying appropriate? He was a notable, a celebrity, our president, but not a friend.

I left the dentist's office and went to Judy's for a bridge game. We talked about it. "Should we play?" Well, again, we didn't know him. We dealt a hand, played it, and dealt again. Then we four looked at each other and decided this didn't feel right. We quit.

I went home and was glued to the TV for the next few days through the funeral. The riderless horse, Jackie's grace and bravery, and little John's salute. I cried.

Chapter Thirty-Three

Pearl Harbor

Admiral Gene R. La Rocque, a "peace as an alternative" military man, spoke at one of our retreats of the CSA. He was a leading proponent of nuclear disarmament; he was criticized for having jumped ship.

Admiral La Rocque (born June 29, 1918) founded the Center for Defense Information and had spent seven years on the Joint Chiefs of Staff. When the attack on Pearl Harbor was carried out in 1941, he was serving on the USS *Macdonough*. He retired in 1972, disillusioned over the Vietnam War. La Rocque founded a weekly public affairs television program, *America's Defense Monitor*, in the 1980s.

In 1974, La Rocque stated that in his experience, ships that carried nuclear weapons did not offload them in foreign ports. The statement directly conflicted with the Department of Defense's "neither confirm nor deny" policy regarding such weapons and sparked controversy in Japan, which has had a non-nuclear policy since World War II.

The admiral's wife is Jewish, and she came with him for the speaking engagement. They told an interesting story. They had recently attended a Pearl Harbor reunion. Mrs. La Rocque shared that she had commented to her husband that many of the attendees had Jewish-sounding last names. The reunion felt disproportionately Jewish.

"There's a logical reason for that," the admiral said.

The service, he regretted to tell us, was so anti-Semitic that all the Jewish sailors were always given the weekend duties and were not given a chance to go to recreational places on the weekend. Most of them were out on ships when the Japanese launched their attack that fateful Sunday!

Chapter Thirty-Four

Things I've Held

It goes without saying that the most exciting thing I have ever held is my baby's baby. To hold your grandchild, freshly arrived, is a thrill. And it is a feeling shared by all grandmothers, I'm sure.

But I have held other things that gave me goose bumps:

Gandhi

Arun Gandhi is a grandson of Mahatma Gandhi. Arun grew up in South Africa when his grandfather lived there and practiced law. Then he followed Gandhi to India to live.

Arun and his wife, Sunanda, were amiable. He came to Memphis to start a peace institute, which he funded by selling off precious letters from his correspondence with his grandfather. They lived in a modest house on a street behind the Boy Scout headquarters.

Serving on his institute's board was difficult. He didn't want a governing board as incorporated; he wanted a rubber stamp to approve his sparse expenditures from donated funds to his 501 (c) (3). At board meetings, he, as director, would make one copy of all reports, and we were supposed to pass it around to read.

"Multiple copies for each board member would kill too many trees," he would tell us. Many of us had to quit, fearing the liability.

Arun would go to India every year. On his last trip, he packed and shipped home some of his grandfather's library and stored the documents and books under his bed. Seeking adequate storage, some of the board and Arun visited the libraries at Christian Brothers University, Rhodes College, our public library, and the one being designed at the National Civil Rights Museum. Only the National Civil Rights Museum would be climate-controlled and have closed-circuit TV, but it wasn't ready. None of the other museums wanted the collection. Security was too expensive. Security was required because academicians actually tore pages out of rare books. Who knew?

Therefore, these rare books, as well as Arun's remaining letters, stayed under the bed. The house was lined with photos of Mahatma and other mementos of the family. When burglars broke in, they took Arun and Sunanda's TV, radio, cameras, and small appliances and left the priceless items.

Arun allowed me to peruse the books. All had Sanskrit markings in the margins. Two books, *Treasure Island* and *Cry, the Beloved Country*, were autographed as gifts to Gandhi from Robert Louis Stevenson and Alan Paton. Holding those books was pretty heady.

Marty Stuart

Another almost priceless thing I held was country music star Marty Stuart's guitar. Only it did have an evaluation of $750,000.

Marty was once married to one of Johnny Cash's daughters and became a devoted friend of Johnny's. Johnny had a guitar that once belonged to Hank Williams. It was an early pre-war, meaning before World War II, Martin D-45. C.F. Martin & Company only made about ninety of them, and the first was made in 1933 for Gene Autry. Embedded in the spruce top was a mother-of-pearl rectangle inlay, about one inch by one-half inch, with "HANK" engraved on it. Johnny replaced it with another mother-of-pearl rectangle with "CASH" engraved. He traded it for Marty's Merle Travis guitar. Marty spent the night with Bobby and me, and he let me play it.

In 2007, the Tennessee State Museum exhibited Marty's collection. We ran into Marty at the Station Inn in Nashville and told him we were going to see his exhibit the next day. He arranged for Renee White, the exhibit curator, to give us an escorted tour. His guitar was on view in a glass case. The museum notation stated the guitar's history and that it was evaluated at three quarters of a million dollars. And to think I held it! Gulp!

Critters

The Rotary Club visited the zoo, and the arachnologist put a large, live, black, fuzzy tarantula in my hand. And I freak at spiders in the house.

I held a sea anemone in my hand during my one and only deep sea dive. It was during a "Resort Course" off Cooper Island on one of my all-women sailing trips to the British Virgin Islands (BVI), about which my Bobby says I'm none of the above.

Under the surface of the ocean is another dimension. The instructions were brief, but enough to allow me to go. Escorted by the instructor, and sucking more air than the rest of the group, I descended thirty feet to a shipwreck on the bottom of the sea. Spoons and forks were embedded in rocks, and fish swam around me. I was unpopular with the group because the leader made us surface when my air was running low. Great adventure — once was enough, but I did continue to snorkel.

My best snorkel trip ever was on the Atlantic side of Anegada Island. It appears that guides assess I am the least competent of whatever tour group I'm in; they want to hang with me, I guess to protect me. This particular guide was known in the BVI for sailing solo and nude. To watch him come into port, lower the mainsail, and drop anchor was to see a sailing marvel. For our all-female crew, watching him come into port au naturel was seeing a marvel of another kind. He puts on clothes when going ashore.

A beautiful Black native with a British accent, Roger was a likable man. He led us women to snorkel in one of the best locales in the world. The underwater scenery was exquisite: coral reefs alive, magnificently colored fish, sea plants. Roger shooed a large barracuda away from me as if communicating with it with a flick of his hand, and when he felt it was safe to leave me, he dived to the bottom to bring me a huge conch shell.

Torah

The most important thing I've ever held is a Torah, the first five books of the Old Testament written in Hebrew on parchment. The Torah is a scroll; it is sacred, it is precious, and it is heavy.

On January 20, 2018, I became Bat Mitzvah — twice. Qualification for being a Bar (boy) or Bat (girl) Mitzvah is reading at least three verses from the Torah. About a thousand years ago, vowels were added to assist in pronunciation of the language. But not in a Torah! Fearing I was too old to memorize my verses, I took lessons for over a year to learn to read it. It's easier than French.

That morning I participated in a B'nai Mitzvah for fifteen adult learners at my Temple in Memphis. I adored being tutored by Rabbi Feivel Strauss, but I really took the course to enhance my Hebrew for my second Bat Mitzvah of the day.

That afternoon, my two grandsons and I read from a Torah our Sternberger family brought to Brownsville, Tennessee, about sixty miles northeast of Memphis, in the 1840s. Our stepfamily brought their Felsenthal Torah over about the same time, and the two families helped establish Temple Adas Israel prior to the Civil War. Descendants of the Temple founders around the country now support the congregation for the three Jews who still live there. It's a nationwide problem what to do with Temples and their precious Torah scrolls now that their congregations are dwindling.

Rabbi John Kaplan tutored us and conducted the sweetest service. We did the coolest thing: Instead of the traditional walk around the congregation with the Torah, we invited anyone who had never seen one before to come to the bema to see what an open Torah looked like.

The boys and I did pretty well. We celebrated with ice cream and bubbly at a tastefully appointed pre-war home.

Holding a Torah is a big deal!

Chapter Thirty-Five

Travel Tales

Why I Travel

From childhood, I knew I wanted to see the world. North, Central, and South America; Africa; Europe; the Middle East — it's an embarrassment of riches, and how blessed I've been to have seen as much as I have.

While sightseeing has been awesome, it's the interaction with people that's memorable, that's fun. Also important are your travel partners.

Without a doubt, Bobby Bostick is a wonderful travel partner. We claim to have more fun on less money than most know how to do. Bobby has the radar to find the Huey's of Memphis, the "in bar," everywhere we go. Since he taught me how to play music, taking our banjos has been a friend magnet. It got us free hotel accommodations once.

Don't get me wrong; we don't rough it, although we have had to share a bathroom with others, and once the water closet was down the hall. I am still enough of a J.A.P. that my potty must be en suite.

Happily for me, I love the company of intelligent, considerate, fun-loving women. A lot of my travel has been either with all women, as in women's weekends or sailing trips, or with roommates.

There's a lesson I've learned in an inconvenient way. If it is possible when you travel abroad, try to travel backward in time. I didn't. Egypt is more climactic than Greece. If Greece gave me goose bumps, Egypt gave my goose bumps goose bumps! Then I went to Israel, so exciting because of its historical import to me as a Jew, but archeologically, it is anticlimactic. Then, the Mayan ruins were amazing, but I'd seen Ephesus and Luxor!

Conjuring up the following tales has been a delight to relive.

Money on a Train, May 1984

My generous baby brother is the greatest! At Christmas 1983 he told me there was a smidgen of a chance he could give Bobby and me a trip to Europe. Every few days he called to say the odds had risen a little bit. By Valentine's Day, it was up to 50 percent, and we had better get our passports in order.

I said, "I know you're having a ball toying with me, but give me twenty-four hours' notice and I'm in."

Ray, a Wendy's franchise owner, was given a free trip for two from a potato chip supplier to Venice and Switzerland. He and Barbie were expecting their first child in May, hence the offer to Bobby and me.

Venice was a treat; we stayed at the Danieli and ate squid in its own ink at La Madonna. Bobby, always the humorist, grabbed the bars in the Bridge of Sighs window in the wall that separated the to-and-fro corridors and pleaded, "It wasn't my dope!"

The art, the "another important palazzo," and the museums were tourist fodder for me. We brought our banjos with us, and Bobby took his aboard the canal ride to entertain the gondolier.

We boarded the train for Lucerne and were treated to lunch aboard the Orient Express dining car. Our hotel in Switzerland was up a funicular train ride to the mountaintop town of Burgenstock. We slept to the gentle sounds of cowbells. We received a telegram announcing the arrival of my nephew Charlie. I had to buy infant-sized suede and leather lederhosen.

This was my second trip to Europe and, not knowing how many trips there would be in our future, we added on a week. Florence, Rome, then home. We decided to wing it for Florence like the cool people do. Bad idea! At the train station in Florence, we discovered there was a huge, competitive run, the European equivalent to the

Boston Marathon. The hotel the travel service booked us in was a fleabag hotel. Maybe literally since the mattresses were horsehair and nasty.

My inner J.A.P. arose, and I told Bobby, "I can't do this." I went out on the streets and found a fairly decent place, but for one day shy of our planned itinerary. I grabbed it. My inner Scarlett O'Hara kicked in, and I would worry about it tomorrow. When Bobby and I departed with our bags to the new hotel, I accidentally took the first hotel key. Somehow we were found in order for the prior hotel's staff to retrieve it from us. Spooky!.

It was on the train ride from Lucerne to Florence that we had our adventure. We were warned not to nap at the same time, lest robbers on the train would steal your purse or carry-on bag. Thieves dressed as priests and nuns victimized passengers, especially those of us in first-class seating compartments. I went to the bathroom with my purse clutched in my hand. Sitting on the commode, I noticed a wad of money behind my right heel. I picked it up and, on the way back, I stopped by each compartment and asked if any woman had lost anything in the women's bathroom. I knew better than to give the money to the railcar porter. I motioned for Bobby to come out into the hall. What we thought was a wad of lira and not very valuable turned out to be the covering for a lot of German marks. A lot of Deutsche marks, as in highly valuable.

"Let's pray it belonged to a drug dealer who ditched the evidence and jumped off the train," said Bobby.

A little bit later, I went up and down the train inquiring again whether a woman had lost anything in the bathroom. No response.

About a half hour later, a frantic-looking older woman knocked on our compartment door, almost begging: "Are you the American who found something in the bathroom?"

Bobby and I stepped out into the hall and said we were and asked her, "What did you lose?"

"Money," she said, now almost praying.

"What kind?"

"Lira and marks."

I reached into my purse and handed her the wad of currency.

Pure relief on her part. She offered us a reward, which we refused.

Then she started her tale: "As a favor to a friend," she said in perfect English, "I took some coins to Germany to sell. I'm German. This is over $5,000 in American dollars. I am so grateful to you for finding it and returning it. Thieves are riding the trains, and I hid the money in my underpants. I forgot when I went to the water closet. Thank God, it was you who found it. Please accept a reward."

Again, I refused, and then she asked where we were going. I told her we were going to Florence but did not have a hotel reservation. She gave me a card and insisted we call her when we knew where we were staying. She wanted to take us to lunch. We accepted that offer.

From the new hotel that we had to vacate a day earlier than we wanted, I called her and asked if she had any connections to get us accommodations for Saturday night.

"It would be like camping, but I would be delighted for you to come to Montevarchi Saturday night. It is about an hour south of Florence and on the way to Rome," she said.

We accepted that offer as well.

Florence was even more of a tourist's delight. While Impressionist and modern art is my passion, I love all kinds. Bobby was getting "Madonna and Bambino"-ed out. We saved Michelangelo's *David* for last, and we may be the only two people ever to go to Florence and not see it. Because of the race, *David* was roped off. We were not allowed across the street to see it. The Pushkin Museum in Moscow has an exact replica, so later I saw *David* in full glory.

Waiting to board the train for Montevarchi, Bobby suggested this might not be so wise. The lady on the train who lost the money knew a lot about us. She knew we were honest people who would not take a reward for the found money. We were substantial enough to be European travelers. What did we know about her? She was a ditzy woman who forgot she was carrying $5,000 in her underwear and lost it. Oh well, we were on our way.

The woman, her grandchild, her son, and her chilly, Connecticut-born daughter-in-law met us at the station. They treated us to dinner in a café and brought us to their ancient Etruscan farmhouse, beautifully appointed. Some walls were six feet in depth. The farm grew Chianti grapes and olives. Our new friend had married an Italian and lived there in her deceased husband's family home. The sole heir artist son and family came home from Paris each summer. The daughter-in-law was working on her PhD in medieval thought of women. She chilled down when she learned I was a lawyer, and we entertained them with our banjos. The sleeping accommodations were two rollaway beds in the library.

I remember this story so well because I believe my dear friends Benton and Betty Fisher loved this story. They held dinner parties for me in DC when I was in town just so I could tell about this adventure.

We arrived Sunday afternoon in Rome in time for its celebration of the big game, the European soccer championship between Rome and Liverpool. You would have thought it was like an SEC football title game. The town was buggy. Cars waved banners in impromptu parades, the buildings were decorated in team colors, and sound trucks blared, "We're number one." We were staying at the Hotel d'Inghilterra at the base of the Spanish Steps. The famous water fountain near the front door spewed water the color of the Roman team. If people were this excited, then we needed to order up a TV to watch this event.

After unpacking, we took our banjos to the Spanish Steps. It is amazing how much people like the banjo, and we have enjoyed sharing our music. We never keep the case open to busk for money. But the police ordered us to stop playing and leave the area. I know a country never guarantees me the same due process laws I have in the United States, so I obey their police!

We walked around this exquisite city full of statuary, churches, and parks. You know you are in a Catholic country.

I don't think I could be a practicing Catholic, as I could not be a practicing Orthodox Jew. Too many rules and regulations I could not abide. But I have always adored Catholic clergy, from Sister Cecile Marie, who served on our Panel of American Women, to the wonderful clergy I met in the civil rights movement.

And I love Pope Francis! He teaches the Christianity I learned at

Southwestern and have seldom seen in practice. I disagree with the Catholic position on not allowing women to have control of their own bodies, nor allowing gays to marry, but I am reconciled that Catholicism and I agree to disagree — not that anyone I know who is Catholic gives a damn.

I have unabashedly flirted with Catholic clergymen. They, so far, have loved it and deserve it. Well, maybe it was more like nonsexual teasing. Experience tells me clergy desperately want to be treated normally in social settings, like men, not just men of the cloth.

It's like my rabbi girlfriend who, when I dropped the "F" bomb, said, "Jocelyn, I feel we really are friends since you can say 'f*#k' in front of me. Most people won't."

Father Paul Clunan was once late to a meeting, claiming the game went into overtime.

"So how much did you have riding on the game?" I asked.

"Oh, how did you know I had a wee wager?" he said.

"I never met a priest yet that didn't make wee wagers," I said.

It was on this trip to Rome that I did my most famous Catholic clergy flirting.

The night before the game, we ate at the restaurant Sabbatini's — with two "Bs," as opposed to the restaurant Sabatini's in Florence spelled with one "B," which led Bobby to say, "Two Bs or not two Bs, that is the question."

At the next table were six clergy-collared men speaking English, so naturally Bobby and I struck up a conversation. I pulled my Catholic clergy routine on them.

"All right, guys, how much money y'all got riding on this game?" And I got the usual answer, "Well, maybe a little bit." The conversation kept up a good pace until it was time for them to leave. They left, but one of the men came back to the table and said, "We want to thank you for showing Aurillous such a good time. He had so much fun talking with you."

"Who is he?" I asked.

"The bishop of Liverpool."

Well, the next day we stayed in to watch the game. Rome lost. When we arrived at our restaurant, the maitre d' met us at the door with apologies. "We can only serve you cold dishes. The kitchen staff was so disappointed with the loss, they went home. Actually, if we had won, they would have done the same thing."

Rome redeemed itself the next day when we saw the repaired *Pieta* and the pope. Not this wonderful man Francis, but a pope, nonetheless. A little background:

I was driving home with the kids one Sunday morning when NPR announced that some nut job had gone into Saint Peter's Basilica in Rome and had done a hatchet job on Michelangelo's *Pieta*. Literally, he took a hatchet and hacked the sculpture.

I barely got into the garage before I welled up in tears. I unbuckled the kids and ran into the house crying, too choked up to answer Richard's "What's the matter?" He followed me into the bedroom and asked again, "What is the matter?" just as I was dramatically flinging myself onto the bed.

"Someone has just gone into the Vatican and destroyed the *Pieta*! Mankind is f*#king up the world, and I haven't seen it yet!"

"Oh," he said. "Is that all?" Not the thing to say to me at that particular time!

Years later, on a plane from DC to Memphis, I sat next to a physician who was Italian. And as sometimes people talk to a stranger about things they might not share with someone they know, I told the doctor my *Pieta* story and that I never got to see it.

"Ah-h-h-h," he said, "Perhaps you didn't know, but the sculpture has been completely restored, and when you see it, you will not know it had been damaged.

"In fact, something very interesting was discovered about Michelangelo in the restoration process. It was learned that Michelangelo was in 1499 a student of palmistry! The lines in Mary's palm said she would have a son and he would be famous; and the lines in the palm of Jesus denoted that he would be important, but would not live a long life.

"So the art and palmistry worlds examined the palms of *Moses* and *David*, and the lines revealed traits commensurate with palmists' predictions. The art world was amazed."

Our Vatican tour was scheduled the next morning. I did see,

along with gobs of people, the *Pieta* — intact, but now behind glass. But having been pushed along with the group, I decided to go back alone later in the day to be able to walk leisurely around Saint Peter's Basilica. I got to stand and admire the *Pieta* as long as I wanted. The experience was too good for Bobby to miss, so the next afternoon we went back together. Regardless of religion, or the lack thereof, it was an amazing place to meditate.

On exiting Saint Peter's, we noticed barricades set up at the outer edge of the famous plaza (country, actually), which had an opening to the street of about only one car width. When we started to exit, a nice guard said in halting English that we might like to stay a few minutes. We walked back to the center of the plaza where two strips of barricades were being set up. Barely thirty or forty people total were divided on either side of these barricades. Within a few minutes, a caravan of vehicles drove into the plaza between the strips. Pope John Paul II was coming home from a historic visit; we later learned from the hotel concierge, with whom we shared our adventure, the pope had visited a head of state of Italy for the first time in centuries!

The pope was standing in his Plexiglas convertible, the "Popemobile." We were less than fifteen feet away, could see his smile, and returned his wave!

I have friends who drove to St. Louis, Missouri, just to be in the same city when a previous pope visited. When I share that Bobby and I stood about fifteen feet from the pope, I feel guilty that the experience was granted to a Jew and a lapsed Methodist.

Nicaragua

In 1984, I received an invitation to travel to Nicaragua to explore the Reagan administration's claims that the Sandinista government was systemically anti-Semitic — against all five Jews who still lived there.

Before the Frente Sandinista de Liberacion Nacional (FSLN) — the Sandinistas — prevailed over the US-supported dictator Somoza in 1979, about 250 Jews lived in Nicaragua. A huge earthquake in the 1970s induced many to leave. These Jews worshiped in a little synagogue that doubled as a Jewish community center. Jews from all over Central America would congregate in centrally located Managua, Nicaragua, for holiday celebrations and so their children could meet other Jewish kids. The little synagogue was the center of Jewish social life for the area.

Abraham Gorn, a wealthy Nicaraguan Jew and close friend of Somoza, was the synagogue's chief benefactor. He was accused of being the liaison for arms deals between Israel and the Contras. The charge of anti-Semitism arose from the Sandinista resentment of Israeli support of the Contras and the Sandinistas' admiration of the Palestine Liberation Organization (PLO). Gorn escaped and joined most of his family, who had fled when Somoza did. Gorn's brother still lived in Nicaragua and ran an electronics store, and he was on the list of folks we sought to interview. He was difficult to reach.

While Congress did not support the counterrevolutionary group called the Contras, President Reagan, the CIA, Admiral John Poindexter, and the likes of Oliver North did. The Iran-Contra scandal emerged when administration officials secretly funded the Contras over the wishes of Congress, a scenario similar to the movie *Seven Days in May*.

To get congressional support for a $100 million aid package for the Contras, the Jewish Anti-Defamation League (ADL) of B'nai B'rith sought Jewish support for the Contras with a claim of Sandinista anti-Semitism, a claim for which the US ambassador to Nicaragua, Anthony Quainton, could find no evidence. The ADL based its claim on testimony from Abraham Gorn and one of his sons in exile.

Enter the New Jewish Agenda, a liberal Jewish organization founded in 1980 that took brave social justice positions before their times — rights for lesbian and gay Jews, Palestinian rights as a path for peace, and sanctuary for Central American refugees. The New Jewish Agenda invited me to visit Nicaragua to try to ascertain the truth. US military action was being weighed.

Why me? I think Dr. and Mrs. Serotta, co-members of the CSA, recommended me to their son, Rabbi Gerry Serotta, the trip leader. Also, since I was a Republican at the time, I guess they were acting affirmatively to include a southern, Republican woman. I often found myself filling a bunch of categories. The trip sounded like an adventure with just a bare hint of danger.

The group met in Miami for pre-departure briefings. Rabbi Marshall T. Meyer, a noted Conservative rabbi who spent twenty-five years in Argentina, introduced himself by saying that his life had been threatened for agreeing to take this trip. While he intended to go, the rest of us might want to reconsider our participation, lest we get hit in the crossfire. That bare hint of danger suddenly loomed larger.

"Just let me know where you're gonna sit, so I can sit on the other side of the room. Okay?" I said.

Several participants were Reconstructionist Jews, a sect of Judaism with which I was not familiar, probably left of Reform Jews, all of whom I found likable and committed.

David Cohen — a leader in all things liberal such as Common Cause, Council for a Livable World, and the Center for Arms Control and Non-Proliferation — was on the trip. So was journalist Hector Timerman, son of the famous newspaper editor Jacobo Timerman, who was incarcerated and tortured by Argentinians opposed to his publications. Hector later became ambassador to the United States from Argentina.

Also on the trip was James M. Statman, who admired a small banjo I brought. When Bobby had begun to teach me to play a banjo, he talked about Andy Statman, a famous bluegrass mandolin player, who was James's brother. It's funny how just a little bit of information can create a nexus with someone — especially when it is so unexpected.

We left Miami on Nicaraguan Air in an old, dilapidated Russian aircraft. We stayed in Managua at the Intercontinental Hotel. Both were adequate and just a bit short of comfortable.

Our days were filled with meetings and day trips. Nicaragua, with a population of about six million people in 1984, is a country with nice beaches and a topography that leaves the shores and rises to volcanic mountains. Being tropical, there were rainbows everywhere. The people were approachable, and I felt safe in the market with others from the trip.

One of our meetings was with a Jewish woman named Michele Najlis, the minister of culture in the Sandinista Cabinet. We learned two Jews were in the Cabinet, hardly supportive evidence of systemic anti-Semitism; we learned that many practicing Catholics claimed to be Jewish. There was a lot of interreligious marriage in Latin America, and the claim of being Jewish meant that you were European and not Indio, denoting a "higher class." But you don't brag about being Jewish in an anti-Semitic state.

Ms. Najlis, a noted poet, gave a presentation on the cultural arts in Nicaragua. Afterward, I was speaking with her and complimented a piece of jewelry she wore. Strung on a string of leather was a tiny painting on a piece of coconut shell. The shell was about three-eighths of an inch by less than an inch, and on the painting was written, "This shall not pass" in Spanish, obviously a revolutionary slogan. She lifted it over her head and placed it around my neck. I was so flattered, and I hope I was sufficiently gracious.

I especially liked one of the women on the trip; Rachael comforted me when I experienced a minor meltdown. We had visited a fascinating woman who lived rather primitively in a barrio outside of Managua. A Maryknoll Catholic order from St. Louis sponsored her and her physician husband. They lived with the people he treated in a Third World environment, and he delivered their own child in the barrio. They had the only generator in the town, and it ran the only refrigerator, which was needed for perishable drugs.

She shared her life with us: the Contra threats, living and rearing their children in such poverty without US amenities, and their commitment to God. It was so impressive and, frankly, emotionally draining. I felt ashamed of my luxurious, selfish lifestyle. She ended the conversation when she needed to get the dinner beans in water to put on the fire.

While driving back to our hotel, I worked myself over pretty well emotionally and barely made it to the lobby bathroom before I cried. Rachael followed me. I was cursing at my image in the mirror.

Selfish bitch! I thought I was doing good things, but I had just seen real goodness in action. Rachael consoled me as best she could.

"Jocelyn, she could no more go to Washington and lobby Congress like you do. Good works is doing what we know how to do best with what we have," she said.

Around her neck Rachael wore a Magen David, the six-pointed star referred to as the Jewish star. Walking out of the bathroom and heading for the gang at the bar, I heard "shalom."

I almost did a comedic double take. I realized the speaker was a large man sitting in the bar. "Were you speaking to me?"

"I was to the woman with the star. Are you Jews?"

"Yes," I said, introducing myself. He introduced himself as Mr. Gorn; he was the brother for whom we were looking, and I induced him to come join our table.

One account of how anti-Semitic the Sandinistas were said that they bombed the synagogue in 1979. The synagogue we saw was in disrepair but still standing. I doubt there were two. There were indentations of Jewish stars on the front doors, indicating the stars had been removed. The ark and the everlasting light were intact, but the Torahs were gone. Mr. Gorn explained that his brother took the Torahs and left the building in the care of his servants. When things were getting bad, they had stripped the building of the copper stars and anything else of value. Fifteen or so people had been living there. The Sandinistas returned the building to the Jewish community, but it remained vacant and in need of rehabbing.

A funny thing occurred when we visited the Jewish section of a cemetery. Rabbi Serotta called us over to view two graves. In Spanish were the names of the deceased and their birth and death dates. Then under the Spanish was Hebrew. Rabbi called over the caretaker, who was so enthusiastic about their stonemason. He had studied in Italy and was so proud he was able to duplicate the Hebrew prayer from one gravestone to the other. Only he duplicated the name and birth and death dates of the deceased written in Hebrew on one grave to the other.

The trip was informative. Our report was met with controversy, but at least it presented a different view from that of the administration and gave some Jewish congressmen and policymakers pause to accept Reagan's position hook, line, and sinker. We Jews don't appreciate the politicization of something we consider as serious as anti-Semitism.

Fast-forward eighteen months. I had a burglary. My good jewelry was in a lockbox at the bank. But the bastards stole my less valuable items: costume jewelry, my mother's Timex watch, and my little piece of painted coconut shell given to me in Nicaragua.

Shortly afterward, I accepted an invitation to serve on a panel at UCLA and discuss my venture to Nicaragua. The panel convened likeminded persons with concerns about Central America. My participation was received well: "Maybe not every country is ready for American-style democracy and capitalism. Perhaps it has to evolve. Doesn't it need to be a self-determination thing?" They had not heard a Republican speak as I did.

I arrived late to the cafeteria afterward and found a seat at a vacant table. I was deep in thought, recapping my participation. My mind wandered to the burglar. Son of a bitch, he stole my coconut necklace, and this would have been a perfect place to wear and explain it.

I was tapped on the shoulder. "We have a guest speaker from Nicaragua who would like to smoke. Do you care if someone smokes at this table?"

I turned around, and Michele Najlis was sitting there.

Cuba

Hooray for President Obama! He did it! He loosened the noose. What a bully the United States had been to Cuba. We trade with China and Russia but refused to trade with communist Cuba? In 2018 President Donald Trump sought to reinstate this embargo. I bet if we keep this embargo up another fifty years, we will bring the Castro regime to its knees.

I visited Cuba in 1995. I went on a religious mission to take Passover to the 1,500 Jews who still lived there. At one time 15,000 Jews lived there, and four synagogues served them.

Bobby said, "I can't believe that you are going to an island surrounded by sea critters delicious to eat, and you are taking them that nasty fish in a jar." Gefilte fish is an acquired taste.

Mexico had supplied the Jewish Cubans with plenty of matzo, horseradish roots, gefilte fish, and haroset. Our Seder was marvelous, if not lengthy, with everything being said in Hebrew, Spanish, and English. It was held in a synagogue, probably Conservative. Earlier that day, we toured a huge Reform Jewish Temple; the shelves held Sunday school books from my Temple youth.

The synagogue had a "medicine cabinet," and we had been asked to bring prescription drugs to donate. They should have asked us to bring spark plugs for the 1950s cars.

Anything inexpensive to us is a luxury to the Cubans. With little profit, shipping cheap items to Cuba is prohibitive. I was struck that the children begged for pens and pencils. Toilet paper and Kleenex were a luxury. I snuck a roll of toilet paper from the hotel in my bag when I went out and gave it along with a tip.

We stayed at the Hotel Nacionale de Cuba, an elegant old place. Portions had been rehabbed beautifully; other parts looked a bit tired. But it was still a resort with sufficient bellmen and doormen. I later learned the doormen doubled as guards and surveillance.

On the breakfast table was butter from France and jelly from Japan. Ninety miles away and our farmers are not allowed to sell them butter and jelly!

My first room had a commode with problems, so I was moved to a luxurious corner room. The maid came in, and when I spoke to her in English, she asked, "Canadian?" When I said, "No, United States," she threw her arms around me. "Americans, Americans! Gracias, gracias!" She ran out into the hall to whisper to the other maids. My presence must have represented some hope.

My friend Joyce Lazarov was my traveling companion and former neighbor. Joyce is a stunning woman, tall, slender, with a natural shock of white hair, an inch and a half wide, from her forehead over the top and back down her dark hair. Her mother was a friend of my parents. Daddy adored her. She was an elegant-looking woman who smoked with a Hollywood long cigarette holder. When Daddy saw her, he would say, "Is that Hortense? You look pretty calm to me." She loved it, but everybody loved Daddy.

Previously a travel agent, Joyce is a seasoned traveler. So clever, she brought an instant Kodak to take pictures of the children as gifts. She also arranged a day outing for us to Varadero Beach, an exquisite beach lined with hotels, each built by a different country as a statement of support for Cuba. The beach was sparsely populated. We almost had it to ourselves.

At the Seder dinner, Joyce and I sat with a young couple, he a physician, and they were leaving to make Aliyah in Israel in the next few days. I don't know how they got permission to leave Cuba. I saw Joyce slip him a few hundred dollars.

One of our Jewish Cuban hosts was Arturo Levy, nephew of Delvis Levy, a Cuban American, who headed a Cuban-American cooperation group that worked to ease tensions between our countries and who helped arrange the trip. Joyce and I got Arturo to take us to the still-performing *Tropicana* in a huge 900-seat outdoor theater. Now that it is government-owned, the dancers are no longer seminude, but it is an entertaining variety show. The last we heard, Arturo got permission to come to the United States to study for the rabbinate.

Joyce and I felt comfortable out wandering the streets alone. We had an adventure when some men hailed us from a balcony of an authentic colonial building. Beautiful architecture, but like most of Cuba, it desperately needed a scraping of peeling paint and a fresh coat.

Lord knows why we accepted their invitation, but we went inside to what looked like an upscale antique store. There were magnificent pieces and extraordinary chandeliers, one of Murano fruit-shaped glass. We were champing at the bit to buy stuff but feared shipping and customs issues. We exchanged cards and contact information; they called me, but we didn't follow up.

Joyce and I went to lunch atop a building in a hesitating elevator. A guitarist playing during lunch was quite good. We invited him to come to the Nacionale later that night to play for our departing party on the rooftop. The hotel trio of musicians came up and created a memorable evening.

Our hired guitarist arrived at the hotel and was denied entrance. The Hotel Nacionale didn't allow Cuban nationals to come into the hotel without a "sponsor." We had met with members of the Jewish community to discuss the political situation of Cuba opposed to by the United States, and getting the meeting held at the hotel took a bit of diplomacy.

The hotel kept tabs on us; our invited musician convinced the doorman or guard to summon me. Somehow they knew we were on the rooftop. I had to go down to vouch for him. The hotel trio loosened up a bit, and we had a great jam session with me playing a tune or two.

Good music is everywhere in Cuba. Melissa Daar, a woman in her late twenties from San Francisco, was our group guide. Most of her trips to Cuba were labeled cultural exchanges; her not-for-profit group was called the Caribbean Music and Dance Association, or something similar. Ours was a cultural and religious exchange.

One night the group went to another hotel for a night of salsa instruction and dancing. Great band! On the way back from the "banjo," I peeked into the bar and heard jazz being played. Not the Buena Vista Social Club or Ruben Gonzales jazz, which is wonderful, but straight-ahead American jazz. As the Jazz Society of Memphis founder, I found my niche and told Melissa I was going to hang in the bar.

We were in Cuba at an auspicious time. Fidel Castro had just allowed craft fairs with private individuals selling their wares. If you owned a card table and an umbrella, you could go into business. And there were nice crafts. Our group helped the Cuban economy. American dollars are valuable and are at a premium to the average Cuban.

Upon my return from a day out shopping, Melissa called me to her room. "We have a problem. The Treasury Department (of the United States) has denied permission for this trip. I just got the fax." I must have blanched or turned purple because she asked if I was all right.

"No. I'm not all right! Damn it to hell, I'm an officer of the court! I'm on an illegal trip to Cuba! Damn, woman, how could you do this?"

Melissa explained she had come often and never had been denied before. It was pretty pro forma. She just thought they were late in getting back to her.

I asked, "What does this mean?" She said they might abscond with our purchases. I told her she had better convene the group; that was our souvenir-shopping day. I was so furious with that girl!

Melissa got the group together. Her advice was, "When you go through customs in Nassau, try to get to the Black guy, and if he asks about this trip, tell him I will come down and explain everything as soon as I can."

Well, I made sure I was the first in line, and I went directly to the Black officer. He asked if we had gone anywhere other than Nassau.

"Yes, sir, we went on a religious mission to Cuba," I said.

"Let me see your letter," he said.

"Well, that's a bit of bother. Melissa Daar said to tell you that she would be down in a minute to explain everything. We just got notice our trip was not sanctioned."

"I don't have time to wait on Melissa. Do you have any cigars or rum?"

"No, sir, I do not."

"Well, next time don't go anywhere your country says you can't go to."

"Yes, sir, I promise."

Joyce was behind me. He broke her cigars in half, took her rum, and sent us on.

But it was quickly ascertained up and down the customs lines that our group was an illegal trip. Others had all their purchases taken. But that wasn't the half of it.

On our trip was a fascinating older couple from San Francisco. Both were Holocaust survivors, the husband of the "forced march," the wife of the ship *St. Louis*. The woman had come on the trip so she could visit her father's grave in Cuba.

It seemed her father had escaped to Cuba in 1938 and

awaited his wife and daughter's arrival. According to the Holocaust Museum in DC, the *St. Louis* departed Hamburg, Germany, on May 13, 1939, for Havana with 937 passengers, practically all Jewish. Cuba said the passengers' papers were not in order and wouldn't let them debark. Our new friend shared that for weeks she and her mother stood at the bow of the boat and, with sign language and blown kisses, tried to communicate with her father.

After Cuba and then the United States denied these refugees entry, the *St. Louis* was forced to return to Europe on June 6, 1939. Following difficult negotiations initiated by the American Jewish Joint Distribution Committee, the ship was able to dock in Antwerp, Belgium, and the governments of Belgium, the Netherlands, France, and the United Kingdom agreed to accept the refugees. By 1940, all of the passengers, except those who escaped to England, found themselves once again under Nazi rule.

The customs officer heard our friend and her husband's accent, and for some reason theirs were the only passports picked up and taken elsewhere for ascertaining validity and copying. According to the others in her line, she went into a psychotic state, screaming about "the selection," and collapsed. When we gathered outside the customs area to give our hugs and kisses goodbye and to head for our forwarding gates, we all tried to console our friend. She was inconsolable.

I don't think Fidel Castro is one of the good guys. He betrayed a lot of American supporters in his quest to oust the dictator Fulgencio Batista Zaldívar. Batista was the elected president of Cuba from 1940 to 1944 and a US-backed dictator from 1952 to 1959 before being overthrown during the Cuban Revolution. Castro claimed he would set up a democracy. In 1995, he was claiming 100 percent literacy and 100 percent medical coverage under his Communist regime.

I am just saying that the embargo seems counterproductive and hypocritical since we trade with Russia. And it is hurting the people of Cuba, not ousting Castro. Both political parties have bowed to the hardcore émigrés in Miami for political gain. I found the people of Cuba to be a proud people. They just don't want to say "uncle" to someone who they feel is a bully.

When we arrived back in the United States late in the afternoon of April 19, the Atlanta airport was abuzz. TVs showed the remains of the Murrah Building in Oklahoma City — the dastardly work of anti-government terrorist Timothy McVeigh. I had not heard a word about it while traveling.

Castro? McVeigh? I came home a helluva lot more pissed at McVeigh.

Chapter Thirty-Six

Music Tales

Ted Lewis

NPR asked its listening audience to submit the music we heard on our family's record player while we were growing up. As mentioned earlier, my first musical memories are of my father and me performing skits for the family. Remember, this was pre-TV. I was probably five or six.

One skit was his soft-shoe dancing to Ted Lewis's song, "Me and My Shadow." Daddy would dress me all in black and then blacken my face and hands with charcoal. Then I would become Eddie Jackson, Ted's "Shadow," and we would perform a dance routine while lip-syncing the song.

Telling this story to Dr. Vasco Smith to share my early jazz bona fides, I learned more about Ted Lewis from him. "On one occasion, while engaged to perform at a southern segregated hotel, Ted Lewis refused to do the gig unless his 'Shadow' could stay at the same hotel. He stood his ground, and he won."

Thinking about sending this story to NPR, I Googled Ted Lewis and found his daughter Dawn. I wrote to her to verify the story and the "Shadow's" name, Eddie Jackson. She was delighted with my email, confirming the courageous story. She said that her father had several "Shadows," but she specifically remembered Mr. Jackson.

I wrote all this to NPR. They wrote back that they would call me, but I never heard from them.

Give My Regards to Broadway

My brother, Ray, did the coolest thing for me. He gave me the CD of *Hamilton: An American Musical*, by Lin-Manuel Miranda, with words to read along. This Broadway play won a Pulitzer and eleven 2016 Tony Awards, including for best musical. Its fan base has become a cult!

Ray's gift has brought back marvelous memories of my Broadway play experiences. When Daddy was in the advertising business as a newspaper representative, he would go to New York often. He loved Broadway theater. Daddy would bring me home the playbill from the show he saw and the record album, originally in 78s and then later in 33⅓ records. I would go to the library and check out the book form of the play. I would read the book for a bit and then play the song on the record. Then I would raise the needle off the record and read some more. Listen and read, listen and read. So when the road show came to Memphis, I knew all the songs by heart.

The first album I recall was a play about World War II. Irving Berlin's *This Is the Army, Mr. Jones*. "You gotta get up, you gotta get up, you gotta get up this morning! Someday I'm going to murder the bugler; someday they're going to find him dead. And then I'll get that other pup, the guy who wakes the bugler up, and spend the rest of my life in bed."

Daddy really gave me a love of Broadway, and when I married Richard I was lucky to learn that his mother loved Broadway, too. She was delighted to take me to New York. We would go to the theater nonstop. One night we had difficulty getting a taxi after the play ended, so when Mom got older, she hired a driver to take us to dinner, then to the play, and then back to our hotel.

Mom was a good sport; we even went to see *Oh! Calcutta!* Outrageous! For a Saturday matinee, we went to see *A Funny Thing Happened on the Way to the Forum*. I later saw Zero Mostel do the role he created at the Arena Stage in DC, but that afternoon on Broadway, Dick Shawn played the role of Pseudolus. There was a marvelously funny line in the play when a eunuch displays anger, and the response was, "Don't you lower your voice to me!"

Mom and I were sitting on the front row and, as bizarre as it sounds, no one in the entire theater laughed. Not a soul, except me. Dick Shawn literally walked over in front of where I was sitting and bowed!

When I got the appointment to serve on the CSA, I went to New York and Washington a lot and went to the theater by myself. Some plays were not very good; disappointed, I walked out of a play with Sigourney Weaver, who I think is a terrific actress, and my assessment was proven correct when the play closed shortly afterward. The same thing happened of a little-known Tennessee Williams play performed in Washington. The setting was Memphis, and it was awful.

Obviously I was wrong about *Sweeney Todd*. I walked out — even on Angela Lansbury — and it became a major hit. Lansbury won her fourth Tony Award in her role as Mrs. Lovett.

I couldn't imagine why theater wasn't as good as what I was used to. Then it occurred to me that only the really great plays went on the road. These road companies that would go across the country were only the tried and tested successes. So until I got older, that was my theater experience: Rodgers and Hammerstein, Alfred Drake, John Raitt, and even Mary Martin washing her hair on stage — on the road.

Oscar Hammerstein may have helped program me for civil rights. He considered himself a social activist, and I grew up listening to his and Richard Rodgers's moralistic music. "When you walk through a storm, hold your head up high and don't be afraid of the dark"; "We kiss in the shadow ... afraid to be heard"; and *South Pacific*. Its music includes a song on racial prejudice: "You've got to be taught to be afraid of people whose eyes are oddly made and people whose skin is a different shade, you've got to be carefully taught ... to hate all the people your relatives hate, you've got to be carefully taught."

I took the kids with me to local theater. It took, but symphony didn't. I fear I did it too early, and it bored them. When I took Cheryl to *Porgy and Bess* when she was eight, I explained some folks considered it a Broadway musical and some called it grand opera. I had already taken her to both. When we left, I asked what she considered it to be. "Oh, Mama, it's grand Broadway."

Ray and Barbie and I found ourselves in New York at the same time, so they invited me to the theater, *La Cage Aux Folles*. We were standing in line to enter the theater and realized we were in front of Carl Reiner. Our father described him to us as clever, sophisticated, and an icon of comedy. He is also the father of one of my civil rights heroes: Rob Reiner, a famous writer and comic actor himself, helped fund the lawsuit tried by David Boies and Ted Olsen (an odd couple for justice) in support of gay rights. Carl Reiner was sociable; we chatted, and he was interested when we told him that the play's star, George Hearn in the role of Albin, sang in our Temple choir with Dixie Carter. Dixie, who went to Southwestern College while I was there and went on to be a TV star, and George were in repertory theater in Memphis and were paid members of our choir. Mr. Reiner was tickled when I told him George Hearn sang a mean Kol Nidre.

Once Bobby and I were at the play *Reminiscences of My Father*, which starred Gabe Kaplan. Heavily Jewish-themed and laden with Yiddish words, the play was about a dark father-son relationship. Bobby sat on my left next to a woman who kept whispering translations to him. I was sitting next to a man, and we spoke a bit at intermission. After the play, the wife of the man to my right leaned over to me and asked, "Not being Jewish, could you enjoy this play?"

"Well, I am, but Bobby's not. Let's ask him."

After each of my children graduated from high school, I treated them to New York. My New York boogie was to take them to Windows on the World for lunch, sunset on the sculpture rooftop garden of the Metropolitan Museum of Art, Le Perigord for elegant dining, and theater. We stayed in a bed and breakfast on the upper West Side on 80th between Amsterdam and Columbus. We did Zabar's, the New York grocery store on steroids, and the entire bit. It felt like being a New Yorker for a few days. Well, I'm here to tell you, for all three of my kids, New York took!

Elvis Tales

Southern girls were actually taught how to be a good date. That's what northern boys told me frustrated them. "She seemed to have such a good time with me. I never thought for a moment she wasn't having as much fun as I was having."

Some instruction included:

1. Don't order a sliced chicken sandwich. We're talking 1950s, and that cost a whole lot more than a hamburger at the Pig and Whistle.

2. Don't kiss on the first date, but act as if you really wanted to, and would, but for your moral code's prohibition on first-date kissing.

3. Talk about him. Dummy, you never ask a question that can be answered "yes" or "no." Hell, mediation training demonstrating the benefits of "open-ended questions" didn't compare to your mother's lectures.

4. Show him a good time! Whatever you do, show him a good time. And even if he's a nerd, you'll run into someone you really like.

What one gleaned from all that was that a date (the event, not the person) was like a contract. He was going to take you out, spend his allowance or earnings, make arrangements, and try to impress you. The least you could do is be pleasant, funny if that's natural; show some intelligence, but not so much as to use it as a putdown. Sarcasm was the order of the day, but not hurtfully so. Be appreciative of his largesse. However, his spending never obligated you to anything. Hence the first-date kiss prohibition was actually making a stand, even in light of an expensive evening. In other words, the two of you equally entered into a contract for a successful evening with equal rights and consideration.

The best "open-ended question" on a new date was "Okay, tell me your Elvis story." I had a bunch. I sat behind Natalie Wood when she had a date with Elvis in the movie *From the Terrace* with Paul Newman and Joanne Woodward at the Loew's State. My dentist was Elvis's dentist, and he gave my dentist a Cadillac!

Leaving the movie late one night at the Memphian Theater, my date and I found ourselves the last folks in the parking lot. Suddenly there was this roar. A bunch of motorcycles appeared. Elvis pulled in first. And then cars pulled up and men, women, and children of all ages hopped off the cycles and out of the cars. Elvis pranced. You could tell that he just knew he was hot stuff!

I was not immediately an Elvis fan. After all, he went to Humes High, and I went to Central. Humes guys didn't wear khaki pants with little useless buckles in the back, nor button-down collars. They wore T-shirts with a package of cigarettes rolled up in the short sleeve. They wore the back of their hair in ducktails. We called them "rogues." Elvis looked like a rogue.

I bought his first record by accident. No one told me I couldn't go down to Beale Street. Beale Street catered to Black customers and was still lined with pawn shops attracting less than the elite, not exactly a place for young girls to go. Surely if I had asked my parents if I could go down there, they would have said no, so I just didn't ask them. I guess it never occurred to them that I would until one evening they heard strange music emanating from my bedroom. We white kids loved the rhythm and blues music that Black radio played. And Dewey Phillips was promoting this new rock and roll.

I went down to Beale Street to the Home of the Blues record store to get "Lovey Dovey." Larry Shainberg, an older boy — he was in high school and I was still at Snowden Junior High — was at the counter. He later authored the novel *One on One*. "Jocelyn, you got to buy this new record! It's by a guy here in Memphis named Elvis and Dewey's playing it." Trying to be "hip" in front of Larry, I bought Elvis's first Sun Studio record.

On the first date with my husband-to-be, when I asked him for his Elvis story, he said he sat behind Elvis Presley when he had a date with Natalie Wood in the movie *From the Terrace* with Paul Newman and Joanne Woodward at the Loew's State. We learned we had sat beside each other five years before we met.

Elvis used to drive a truck for MARL Metal, a dinette manufacturing company, and frequented Wurzburg Brothers' loading dock to pick up a product called Tuflex, a chair stuffing. My husband started off working on the dock before his meteoric rise to president of his family's business. Elvis kept Richard apprised of his performance schedule and career advances.

In 1982, newly divorced, I remet and started dating Bobby. When re-entering the dating scene, most newly divorced confess to listening to those old teen-dating-behavior tapes resurrected and now playing in their heads. Since we used to bop at the rainy-day sock hops in the Central gym, I reverted to the 1950s. "What's your Elvis story?"

His Elvis stories were much better than mine. His favorite was this: Someone had asked him to return a book to Alan Fortas's father, who lived close by. Alan was a bodyguard and companion to Elvis. Mr. Fortas asked Bobby if he knew Alan. He did. "Do you know this singgg-ger he's running around with?" in an old country accent tinged with snobbery. "I can afford to send him to any school he wants to go to, send him to law school, but he runs around with this singgg-ger."

"Well, if it's any consolation to you, Mr. Fortas, this singer is really big!"

"Bigger than Sinatra?" he challenged.

"Well, yes, sir. You may not believe this, but right now he's bigger than Sinatra."

Bobby says Mr. Fortas told him to leave the book and flipped his wrist at him as if to say, "This kid is as crazy as my son Alan."

Actually, Bobby had the ultimate Elvis story. At age sixteen, he got invited to Elvis's house off Park Avenue. Scotty Moore was late and Elvis, who was trying to impress girls, was anxious to get the playing out of the way. It was suggested that Bobby knew Scotty's licks, and he could sit in. He did. For two whole songs and then Scotty arrived. Bobby said that was good for getting girls' attention for six months.

It was good for getting my attention. I kissed him on that first date. I was freshly divorced and wasn't sure what the new code was, so he left with just that kiss.

When you walk into my house, on the right you will see a Robert Dye photo of Elvis at the 1956 Variety Club fundraiser concert held at Russwood Park. He's photographed surrounded by teenage women in dresses and some with white gloves. Elvis was explosive, at the beginning of his huge career!

If I tell you to look up to the ceiling, you see what looks like — and is — one acoustic ceiling tile framed and mounted. It is the source of Bobby's and my continuing Elvis story.

In 1977, Bobby had the leasehold on 706 Union Avenue. While he worked for his father at Bostick Enterprises, he sold used sports cars on the side. They were stored in what was Sun Studio. He and fellow musicians used to jam there, feeling the place was magical. A few acoustic tiles had fallen off the ceiling, and Bobby kept them. When Elvis died, Bobby pleaded with his father to buy the property. Really fearing his son would devote even more time to music than his business, Mr. B dismissed the idea. "No one will remember this Presley person in six months," he said.

When people come to our house and inquire about what that thing is on our ceiling, we tell them it is an old acoustic tile from Sun Studio. And on a full moon, if you're real quiet, you can hear "Blue Moon of Kentucky" — "keep on shining." And if you turn it over, you can hear "That's All Right, Mama."

And All That Jazz

Jazz is my favorite music. I love all music genres, but jazz is the ultimate expression. It requires the facility of a classical player, but with the added ability to improvise while playing. How jazz musicians can think of how they want to play the next few phrases while playing the current one is beyond me.

While my father introduced me to jazz, it was the Jazz Society of Memphis that gave me the greater appreciation of this art form. A favorite jazz exercise for me is to know the song, mostly the old jazz standards, and hear what the musician is doing with it. It was said that Cole Porter was ecstatic going up to Harlem and hearing what the jazz greats were doing with his Broadway compositions.

In 1982, we Jazz Society of Memphis members would go hear Jamieson Brant jam at the Belmont Bar and then come back to my condo to discuss how we could promote more jazz in Memphis. One loyal member created a jazz hotline listing where jazz was playing that night.

To raise funds, JSOM held a tribute at the Peabody Skyway to Benny Goodman. The locale was appropriate since radio broadcasted jazz bands, including Goodman, from the Skyway back in the 1930s and '40s. "High atop the Hotel Peabody in beautiful downtown Memphis, Tennessee, the Skyway presents —." The professors recruited clarinet players to play tunes from different periods of the Goodman era. We pulled off a coup. Our new maestro of the Memphis Symphony was a clarinet player. He agreed to play the young Benny Goodman. Maestro Balter didn't improvise, so a member, Allen Rippe, transcribed a recorded song so Mr. Balter could play it. The master musician he was, you couldn't tell he was reading music.

Tickets were almost sold out the day of the tribute when the morning paper had a front-page picture on the entertainment section of the new maestro playing a clarinet and touting the event. My phone rang off the hook with folks seeking seats. I had been working well with the catering director of the hotel, who will remain nameless since I thought I would kill him that morning. I called to give him our final number and beg for an additional thirty seats.

"Hi, dear. We have a sellout for tonight, and is there any chance of squeezing any more folks in?"

"Tonight?"

"Yeah, for the Jazz Society event in the Skyway tonight."

"In the Skyway? Tonight?"

"John, the Jazz Society tribute to Benny Goodman. Tonight! We have hundreds coming!"

"Tonight? Jocelyn, I'm putting you on."

John's left leg was in a cast for months. "John, when I see you tonight, I'm going to break your other leg! Not funny!"

I milked the presidency of the Jazz Society. When I dropped that to the maitre d' of the Blue Note in New York, I got front-row seats and was allowed to purchase the second set. When I saw Stephane Grappelli there, he kissed me instead of giving me an autograph.

I sat in the front row for two sets of Oscar Peterson when he played and recorded live a four-CD album, *The Legendary Oscar Peterson Trio Live at the Blue Note.* He played with Ray Brown, Herb Ellis, and Bobby Durham.

Getting to New York once or twice a year, I became a Blue Note regular. New York was jazz mecca. The JSOM counted thirty Memphians playing jazz there since they couldn't make a living as a jazz artist in Memphis. Our Memphis greats — James Williams, Mulgrew Miller, Donald Brown, Harold Mabern, Bill Easley, and Bill Mobley — held court at Bradley's in Greenwich Village. It was a thrill to see Les Paul at Fat Tuesday's, and I talked myself into a sold-out performance at the Waldorf Astoria to see the fabulous Ella Fitzgerald. It was such a sophisticated feeling seeing Bobby Short and the Modern Jazz Quartet at the Carlyle. I even saw Hazel Scott perform live at a Holiday Inn. Having been taught jazz appreciation was an extraordinary gift for which I am still grateful.

The Jazz Society pulled off another terrific coup. The famous Mitchell-Ruff duo was still playing and was reputed to be the longest-existing duo playing in America. Dwike Mitchell played beautiful jazz piano. Willie Ruff was a phenomenal personality. He played bass and jazz French horn. The duo started in the armed services in 1947.

Willie Ruff, a professor of jazz and Black history at Yale, learned the language of every country he visited well enough to lecture in it, including Chinese and Russian. The duo's performance in Shanghai was claimed to be the first jazz brought to China. I own a pirated copy of a tape of him playing Gregorian chants solo on his French horn in Saint Mark's Basilica in Venice. He told me he pulled the Black card to get to do this. Fearing embarrassment, the Italians didn't want to refuse this Black American's request. He has a terrific public persona, engaging and witty. He agreed for the duo to perform for the Memphis Jazz Society. We joined with the Yale Club of Memphis and held a true musical happening.

Another wonderful jazzman was Dr. W.O. Smith of Nashville. Dr. Smith was the husband of Kitty Smith, a known civil rights activist and political operative. I thought her the Maxine of Nashville. He was the first African American member of the Nashville Symphony. Kitty bunked me at her house one night when I was coming to Nashville weekly to sell my legislation. Dr. Smith offered to take me to the airport the next morning and shared the most delightful story with me. Pre-Kitty, he lived in New York and stayed in the home of Duke Ellington. He had a job and went to school, but in lieu of rent, he was to tutor Mercer, Duke's son. Billy Strayhorn lived in the house as well.

"I stayed in a little room off the living room where the piano was. Billy Strayhorn's habit was to compose pieces on the piano in the wee hours of the morning. I loved it, but I had to move out. How could I sleep when such genius was going on in the next room?"

A teacher of music at Tennessee State University and Vanderbilt, Oscar Smith wrote *Sideman*, his book that is like an anthology of jazz. His most wonderful contribution to music may have been his W.O. Smith Music School for poor kids in the community. He had Nashville musicians volunteering their talent to teach children for fifty cents a lesson.

Jazz is universal, and the discovery of a fellow lover of it makes for enhanced friendships. A great gift I often give people is the link to our University of Memphis jazz station, WUMR. I sit on its advisory board.

On one European trip, I met up with my sister, Libby Lavine, in Barcelona. Libby had arranged for us to have brunch at her exchange student's home. The parents were cordial, cutting their vacation a day short to have us over. All the family members came in from around Spain to see Libby.

I noticed an opened room with large photos of famous jazz musicians. When I mentioned, "I see you have Miles, Dizzy, and the Bird on your wall," a gift of gold couldn't have made the father light up any brighter. He had given us a brief tour of the city. All the while he was a gracious host. But when I knew his jazz heroes by name, he became animated.

"You must come see my jazz collection." He had a large man cave another flight up. The walls were lined with records, tapes, and CDs. His speakers were superb. He was in seventh heaven showing me all this. Jazz is a universal language.

Jazz lovers are concerned for the continued existence of this American-created art form. The Memphis Jazz Workshop has an idea we hope to implement: a jazz concert for children, similar to those classical concerts for kids in major cities. Won't it be fun to teach an audience of children what jazz musicians, playing various instruments, can do with "Three Blind Mice"?

'300 Feet of Fun'

When I sought rental space in downtown Memphis for my new law and mediation practice, I was immediately smitten with the Lincoln American Tower, which was a replica of the Woolworth Building and was Memphis's first skyscraper of twenty-two floors. Don Lovelace, the office manager, showed me the north half of the nineteenth floor, a space twelve by twenty feet. Framed perfectly by the northwest window was the Martin Luther King memorial sculpture by the renowned artist Richard Hunt. The late Lucius Burch, the late Rev. D.E. Herring, and I chaired the drive to erect a memorial to Dr. King, and there it was right down the mall in front of Ellis Auditorium in the civic center. I rented the space on the spot. This was 1984, and I paid ninety-eight dollars per month.

The space was the northwest corner office, giving me an unobstructed river view; Hotel King Cotton had been demolished, and the Morgan Keegan building, not completed until 1985, wasn't up yet. There was a great view of North Memphis and the Hernando de Soto Bridge. The women's bathroom, the room just east of mine, had a fabulous view to the north and of Memphis east of downtown. It was a treat to go to the john!

We combed the basement and found the original light fixtures. I was only the second tenant in that particular space since the building opened in 1924. The previous tenant was a draftsman and had the originals replaced with fluorescent lighting when it was developed. Gold foil lettering denoting my name and profession on the translucent glass door helped maintain the feel of the 1920s. The elevator opened into a not-so-spiffy hallway; the first view was a folded fire hose on the wall, raising doubts about whom the visitor was going to meet. Entering my office was an artistic surprise.

The management raised half of the space nine inches so I could have my clients seated in a "living room setting" conducive to amicable problem-solving and allowing them to look out the windows, which could be opened for fresh air. For the furious, aggrieved divorce client wanting her day in court just so the judge would hear what a stinker her spouse was, I would raise a window and tell her to stick her head out the window and yell to everyone down on the mall what a M...F..., son of a b... he was. And if I could get her to do it, I would then tell her, "Now that all of downtown Memphis knows, you don't need to spend $50,000 to tell some judge who doesn't want to hear it."

The night I moved in, Bobby and I opened a bottle of champagne and sat with the windows open, enjoying the view. Suddenly, fireworks erupted from Mud Island. FedEx had some affair going with fireworks. Lord, I loved this office.

And I loved the building. The management allowed tenants to use the top penthouse for special occasions. This was the same space where Memphis's infamous Censor Board chair, Lloyd T. Binford, would show his friends the dirty movies he censored for the Memphis public. He censored all Ingrid Bergman movies because she had a child out of wedlock and all movies about Jesse James (unless portrayed as a dirty rotten scoundrel) because he was in a train robbery in Mississippi when James was rumored to be in the state. Binford banned *The Wild One* with Marlon Brando because it flaunted social disorder. But most of all, he banned any movie showing Blacks and whites in any situation other than Blacks subservient to whites.

The penthouse was decorated in traditional style with draperies and occasional tables and chairs, suitable for me to host bridge parties, to the delight of my friends.

One day I went to Mr. Lovelace with an idea. I wanted to throw a party with bluegrass music in the Yellow Rose Cafe on the ground floor, zydeco and blues music on the second floor, jazz on the empty tenth floor, and in the penthouse would be a Kansas City jazz banjo and guitar duo alternating with a flamenco guitarist. We would distribute only forty tickets per set in the penthouse. The cash bars would benefit the American Civil Liberties Union. Would he ask the leasing company if I could do this?

He came back to me and said the building had just changed its management company and they would like to give the party if I would put it on. They would give me $10,000 toward it, but there was one hitch. "Would you be willing to change the charity?"

I am ashamed to say how easy I was! I asked, "How 'bout the Jazz Society?"

We held the party on September 9, 1989. Our invitations invited people to "300 Feet of Fun." Okay, we fudged since the building was 290 feet tall. Kathy Chiavola brought her bluegrass band from Nashville; The Blue Runners came from Lafayette, Louisiana; Memphis Bob and the Jug Busters featured my Bobby and Lee Baker playing blues; in the penthouse, John Blackburn, a noted flamenco guitarist from Amarillo, Texas, alternated sets with a master tenor banjo player, Epp Roller from Mountain View, Arkansas. But the tenth floor was the happening! It was a jazz jam with Gene Rush, Alfred Rudd, Charlton Johnson, Joyce Cobb, Jamieson Brant, Floyd Newsom, and anyone else who wanted to come sit in. It was an extraordinary musical treat. And in the Yellow Rose, the Cluster Pluckers crashed the party to jam bluegrass.

We limited the party to the first five hundred responders. People called to volunteer as bartenders just to get to come. Cecilia Chilton donated lighting, and Ham Smythe donated a taxi ride home if anyone imbibed too much. The building looked great, and for many party guests it was their first time inside to see the marble entry and brass appointments. What a great night!

One day I walked into the building, and there was a sign on the elevator: "The utilities will be cut off in ten days. Sorry for any inconvenience this may cause." The tenants were flabbergasted. Mr. Lovelace said the new management company was "deserting" the building and had not paid the utility bill in months. I immediately called Joyce Blackmon, vice president of MLGW, and asked for a stay on this order. She invited me to come to the board meeting to be held that afternoon and plead my case.

We were given a few more weeks, but I, like others, realized that if the utilities hadn't been paid, surely the elevators had not been maintained. Only the center elevator rose from the thirteenth floor to the top. The staircase was a problem. Like most of the building, it was not up to code. The stairs were an open winding staircase, which would work like a flue in case of fire and would make it impossible to manipulate the removal of office furniture. We all agreed it was time to vacate. But before I left, Mr. Lovelace took me up to the glass cupola atop the building to see a spectacular, 360-degree view of Memphis. Please, don't let this building be torn down.

Pete Seeger

On January 27, 2014, Pete Seeger died. America's most famous folk singer, he was an icon, from his Woody Guthrie days to his time as a Weaver. He's inspired us with "Where Have All the Flowers Gone?" and "If I Had a Hammer."

The first time I met him, I took Bobby's red Pete Seeger banjo instruction book to the Orpheum, hoping to get him to autograph it. I was lucky. I handed it to him at the stage door. He held it high and said, "Ah-h-h, this may not be the best book ever written on how to play a banjo, but it is the cheapest." He popularized tablature as a string instrument learning tool.

The next time I met him, we were attending the third Tennessee Banjo Institute in 1992, a phenomenal music project funded by the National Endowment for the Arts. It was a convocation of banjo players of all varieties of music played with a five-string banjo — nineteenth century classic, mountain frailin', clawhammer, bluegrass, three-finger picking, and jazz. Everyone was there! Bela Fleck, Doug Dillard, Tony Trischka, Pat Cloud, John Hartford, Grandpa Jones, Taj Mahal, a Grio from Africa, the Thompson Brothers, Eddie Adcock, and Danny Barker. It was a banjo picker's paradise: concerts, instruction, and workshops ending with a show open to the public at Middle Tennessee State University. They call it a "Banjo Meltdown."

Being really late-night people — Bobby is nocturnal, and I don't do mornings — we found the late night hardcore. Doug Dillard, Bobby, and John Hartford picked to three or four in the morning. None were strangers to a bit of marijuana. Hartford had a strange way of looking at you, almost in a trance. Not intimidating, but piercing. And then he would give you an approving nod at a break you just played. He shared stories of being a riverboat captain on the Cumberland River. He was a genuinely gentle soul — and a skilled flirt. In front of all, he wanted to hold hands. It was more like caressing than handholding. It felt adulterous. When it morphed into discomfort, I laughed and turned to him and said, "John, you give great hand!" John died much too young.

I hate to say this, because Daddy always said, "Don't speak ill of the dead," but Pete Seeger was not a very nice man. When your heroes aren't pleasant, it is a disappointment. We probably expect too much from our celebrities, but they asked for the adoration, and the least they can do is be nice to fans. He was dismissive, and no one was being a pest.

But I'm being small-minded: Pete Seeger genuinely cared about the working man, minority persecution, the environment — and his long-necked banjo and music were his tools to construct a better platform on which to stand and speak out.

We convened at Tennessee's Cedars of Lebanon State Park. Too much a J.A.P., I wanted to stay with Bobby in a nearby motel instead of separating into single-sex group sleeping quarters. I left the hotel room, and coming out next door was a man with a banjo.

"Oh, I hope I didn't disturb you with my playing," he said, just before Bobby walked out the door with our two banjos. "Oh, never mind," he laughed.

Bobby recognized him, Mike Seeger, Pete's half-brother.

Pete did have a sense of humor. All 180 some-odd players met for a group photo. The photographer had an antique camera that swiveled almost 180 degrees from one end of the group to the other that was stretched out about twenty-five yards long and six rows in depth. The result was a 46" x 8" photograph. We were instructed to remain as still as we could, and it took a few minutes for the camera to swivel its base to capture the people. That was enough time for Pete Seeger and Bela Fleck to sneak behind the group after being photographed on one end and run to the other end, thus being able to bookend the entire conference participants in the picture.

Pete Seeger was honored at the National Civil Rights Museum award banquet in Memphis. At the pre-reception, I had another chance to meet him and correct my impression, but I couldn't. He snubbed everyone, it seems. Oh, well, born and reared in Manhattan, he just didn't come naturally to any southern charm.

Tchaikovsky

I am a certified fag hag. I'm promised it's a term of endearment.

Service on the CSA gave me the opportunity to make so many wonderful friends. Jewish and liberal. I had not known too many Jewish liberal men down here in Memphis. A horrible metaphor for Jewish civil service, but I was in hog heaven. I loved the fabulous women I got to know on the commission, but liberal Jewish businessmen? Who knew they existed? I certainly didn't. My new world into which I had stepped didn't have too many Temple members. I was always walking on eggs around the Jewish businessman I married.

The commission had a number of homosexuals as members, and they allowed me to hang with them, especially John and Herb. Their rabbi drove them up to Vermont to allow their thirty-five-year relationship to become a marriage. John was a theater scene creator; Herb was an attorney. Herb's pleasant demeanor and countenance belie his strong lawyer accomplishments.

One subcommittee of the SAC was on youth suicide and drug abuse. A father grieved by his son's suicide funded a seminar on those subjects, and he was convinced the topics were related in that instance. The seminar was held at his beautiful estate in Greenwich, Connecticut. Michael and Kitty Dukakis were there, sharing their experience with alcohol abuse. Kitty said she would go across Boston to a Baptist church for AA meetings only to find a bunch of Temple members there.

John and Herb's best contribution to the work of the committee was to inform us that youth suicide probably had less to do with drug and alcohol abuse than with sexuality. These two guys opened my eyes to a different mindset and gave me a remarkable treat: The men invited me to the finale performance of Tchaikovsky's *Swan Lake*, performed with male swans. We had front-row center seats. They explained this rendition was autobiographical of Tchaikovsky's life, being forced to live straight when he was a closeted homosexual. He was forced into a marriage attended with all the frustrations of living a lie. This version has been shown on PBS and is probably available.

The ballet had the same theme. The audience was mostly male and gay. The dance was potent, and the response electric. Never had I experienced such a oneness of art and an audience. And I was thrilled to share it with friends I really adored. I felt so accepted that they would share the evening with me.

On my bucket list is including LBGT rights as a protected class under the legislation I wrote, the Tennessee Human Rights Act. In Tennessee, an "at will" termination state, an employer can fire someone just because they're lesbian, bisexual, gay, or transgender.

When I was a newlywed and required to pick my charity of choice, as young Jewish marrieds were expected to do, I volunteered at the Variety Club Metabolic Endocrine Clinic. My job was to transcribe doctor's notes into a file. Scary because no one seemed to care when I couldn't read some handwriting. "Just do the best you can," they said.

I came across something called adrenogenital syndrome. I learned that a lot of babies are born with two sets of genitalia, and the attending physician would guess what the baby looked more like, a boy or a girl. They would pick and either snip off a penis or sew up a cervix. I am sure it was not that simple, but I am talking 1961, and this was a charity hospital.

Accomplishing LBGT rights in Tennessee would honor my friends and the memory of Tchaikovsky, who took his life to escape the shame his society imposed on him for being gay.

An Evening of Soul

I tried to start a project back in 1972 that failed miserably. And it was so worthy! Erma Clanton, a professor at Memphis State University, now the University of Memphis, created and produced a play called *An Evening of Soul*. It traced Black music from slave chants to gospel, to blues, to soul, to jazz. It was an anthology of music that traced the Black experience from slavery through the civil rights movement and into the world of entertainment.

The talent was terrific. The play was spellbinding, and it was a huge success. Greg Seegers was narrator, and Deborah Manning's singing was inspired. Vasco Smith and I had agreed that the survivor of the first of us to go had to get Deborah Manning to come sing at the funeral. She did a beautiful job.

My crazy idea was to get the play on Broadway; it was as good as anything I had seen on Broadway in a long time. I just knew it was of that quality. My alternative idea was that it should be on Beale Street playing every Wednesday through Saturday night with a Sunday matinee. Students of theater would get college credit, experience, and a stipend. It would give the university visibility downtown. Thirty-five years later, the law school filled that role.

I failed on several fronts. First, I knew nothing about how to go about selling a play to Broadway. Second, I am a lousy fundraiser, and I could only raise $1,000, hardly enough to hire a pro who knew how. I was in no position to stake this idea financially. I was cocky even to think I could pull this off.

In December 2016, Ms. Clanton won a Black Heritage award for her production of *An Evening of Soul* forty-five years earlier. Hurrah! I wasn't the only one who recognized how special it was.

Country Music

Country music radio stations are not in my car's push-button selected stations. It's not that I don't like it; it's just not the music I usually listen to. Mostly I listen to classical in the morning and jazz at night. Jazz instrumentals are my dinner-party music.

In the early days of radio, WSM, which carried the Grand Ole Opry, didn't reach Memphis. On clear nights you could get the country music station WLAC from Nashville. Nashville has made the Opry world-famous. The Ryman Auditorium, from which the Opry was broadcast, has been rehabbed and is worth the visit. Nashville has three music meccas: the Station Inn for bluegrass and the Bluebird Café and Ryman Auditorium for country.

Since the Opry was mostly broadcast over radio, pre-TV, I was fascinated that the biggies were not necessarily attractive-looking people. It was the voice that counted. Now the stars have to be pretty, talented, and photogenic.

Marty Stuart, a country music star, is the total package. He's a great singer, a terrific showman, an accomplished mandolin player, handsome, and mature beyond his years.

Bobby and I met Marty Stuart at Bobby's old movie theater in Millington, a small town north of Memphis about twenty-five minutes up the road. The movie house used to cater to the sailors at the naval base in Millington decades ago, but for the last thirty-seven years, it housed a gospel music show on Friday nights and a country music show on Saturday nights. When I remet Bobby, he played banjo there every Saturday when banjos played a more prominent role in country music.

We went up one Friday night to hear the Sullivan Family, with whom Marty started playing as a child prodigy. It was rumored he might be there that night, so we went in hopes of hearing him play. He had a reputation as a terrific musician, a young prodigy, but he had not yet made it big.

Marty was a delight. We invited him for a late dinner, but he said he was leaving for Mississippi right after the show. But he would be back in town Sunday and would love to be with us. We agreed to bunk him and gave him directions to a friend's Super Bowl party that Sunday evening.

Only Bus, our hostess's brother, and also a mandolin player in Bobby's Jug Band, recognized who Marty was. Marty, for all his experience, was still considered a young up-and-comer. Bus was thrilled, and we asked him to join us for dinner and jamming later.

That's when Marty let me play his extremely valuable pre-war D-45 Martin guitar.

Marty was interesting, and I commented on how well-read he was. "I started on the road playing mandolin with Lester Flatt when I was only thirteen. I got to read; I was too young to drive the bus," he said.

Marty is not only a gifted musician, but he has showman qualities on stage. He tells a cute story: "When I was ten years old, I saw Connie Smith on a stage in Philadelphia, Mississippi. I told my mother, 'I'm going to marry her when I grow up.'"

And sure enough, he did. A cute shtick Marty shares at performances was how fans would greet the bus with, "'Did Connie come with you?' One fan mocked me and asked how it felt being married to a superior performer. I said, 'I don't know. When I get home, I'll be sure to ask her.'" Connie had just been inducted into the Country Music Hall of Fame.

Marty is also a fine photographer and gifted writer. He has produced two beautiful coffee-table photo books of country music stars and historical events. He also has a rare and copious collection of country music memorabilia. We donated one of Bobby's Sun music acoustic tiles to him.

Another country musician friend was the late Paul Craft. He was from Memphis originally and was a friend of Bobby's and his wife. His most famous songs were "Dropkick Me, Jesus (Through the Goalposts of Life)" and the exquisite "Keep Me From Blowing Away." Linda Ronstadt has a beautiful version of that; they dated a bit.

Paul never accepted me out of loyalty to Joella, but he flattered me by asking me to mediate his and his second wife's divorce. Paul would include Bobby and me in his jam sessions or take us bar-hopping when we were in Nashville.

He introduced us to a marvelous singer, Kathy Chiavola, who befriended us. Operatically trained, she is a well-respected Nashville country singer and brought her group to the "300 Feet of Fun" party.

Paul was an anomaly. A sensitive man he was not, yet he could write the most beautifully sensitive songs. When we teased him about it, he would say, "I'm an English major graduate of UVA, damn it. I know how to write sensitive music. That's my job. I don't have to be sensitive."

It was disconcerting for Paul that he never got inducted into the Country Music Hall of Fame; he was nominated often but not selected until 2014. He participated in the pre-ceremony activities. While speaking on a panel program just prior to the induction, Paul had a massive stroke and died before he received his award.

Bobby played country music at the Saturday night show in his Millington theater for years. Banjo fell out of favor in country music, so he quit. His favored music on the banjo is blues and rock, with bluegrass a distant third. That's so Memphis of him!

The Banjo and Me

The banjo is a marvelous instrument! It's a happy sound, and I have been fascinated by how children are attracted to it. I've not played in public often, but when I have, little ones run up and ask to strum it. It's fun to let them sit in my lap and strum while I fret it.

It's really a drum with strings. Originating in Africa as gourds with attached necks and strings, American banjos have been studied as an interesting engineering design. The Massachusetts Institute of Technology once held an exhibit on the development of the banjo, *Ring the Banjar*, an early name of the instrument. The banjo consists of a pot, a wooden rim covered with skin or plastic with a metal tone ring and hooks to adjust the tension; a neck along which to fret strings to raise or lower the sound; and a peg head that holds the pegs around which the strings are wound. The strings run from the peg head to a tailpiece at the bottom of the head of the pot.

The banjo comes in four-string tenor or longer-necked plectrum sizes. It went from a strumming instrument to Earl Scruggs's three-finger picking a five-string banjo. There are six-string guitar banjos, eight-string mandolin banjos, and other configurations.

Too often, the banjo is associated with early minstrel music. Despite its African origin, most Black folk find the instrument to be off-putting, associating it with slave days.

By the time I was introduced to the banjo, musicians such as Bela Fleck, Alison Brown, Tony Trischka, Eddie Adcock, and Pat Cloud were taking it far beyond folk, bluegrass, and Dixieland jazz music. The New Grass Revival played rock banjo, and my Bobby is a blues banjo player. Jazz on tenor banjo has been around since jazz was created, but listening to the melding of jazz and a five-string banjo is pure delight.

Bobby claims I picked it up remarkably fast, especially since I had never played music before. But like everything, one needs discipline to practice to make good progress.

"Joselynda, you would get much better if you would practice more than fifteen minutes a month," Bobby said.

After thirty-five years, I'm still a beginner. And I can't read music, which is crazy since I was a math major in high school. All I do is play just enough rhythm so Bobby can play lead or harmonica. Thank God, I can keep a good rhythm.

The best part about learning to play music is learning to listen to music better. While I always played a competent stereo, listening to music is so enhanced by knowing how music is made.

Traveling with banjos has been rewarding. Though not busking, we make friends by giving away the music. When I attended school, we had music appreciation, listening sessions with instructions on what to listen for. You could learn to play if you joined the band.

So many of our public schools have dropped art and music programs. Recently, I have been visiting an "Alt" school to meet with kids who have been incarcerated for crimes. They don't have art and music; they have no sports at these schools. I asked if the students thought things might have turned out differently if they had learned how to play music. They all said "yes." Music takes cooperation to play together.

The first song I picked up was "Will the Circle Be Unbroken?" While I was playing with Bobby one afternoon at a nursing home, a woman came up to tell me she just knew what a good Christian I was by the way I played banjo.

Chapter Thirty-Seven

Art to Love and Collect

What can I say? I love art, and I collect it. My collection is not all that valuable, but each piece has a story and speaks to me. I've overdone it; my husband once said, looking into the bathroom, "Jocelyn, you've missed a wall!" I've fixed that.

My taste begins with Impressionism, when art didn't have to look like a photograph. When traveling, I seek out the locale's Impressionist collection. Europeans were particularly sharp to collect the art coming out of France during that period, and the artists were prolific in output. When I walk into a city's Impressionist salon, my first impression is: "The gang's all here." Monet, Manet, Renoir, Degas, Pissarro.

My taste includes non-representational art. Helping the Mallory Knights with a Martin Luther King memorial was a kick. Richard Hunt, the renowned, commissioned sculptor, sat with the men to explain that what he would create would speak to the soul, not necessarily just the eye.

I started a collection of gallery and exhibition books with the intention of reliving the experience in my older years; it's become a compulsion. I have been in major art museums around the world — the Hermitage, the D'Orsay, the British Museum, the Prado, the Egyptian Museum in Cairo, the Metropolitan Museum of Art in New York, and the Detroit Institute of Arts. The collection of books is now large, and the number of my remaining years to reread them isn't.

A new experience to talk about is Crystal Bridges. It is a gift to mankind from Alice Walton, as in Walmart's Walton. What a gift it is! Designed by the Israeli architect Moshe Safdie, five buildings, mostly glass, straddle a body of water in a beautiful wooded setting. It is located in Bentonville, in the northwest corner of Arkansas, where Walmart is located. Crystal Bridges houses Ms. Walton's collection of American art. Detractors call her a "culture vulture" since she can outbid everyone when a treasure comes up for auction.

When I walked in, volunteers welcomed me to Crystal Bridges. When I asked where you paid to enter, they responded, "It's free. It's compliments of Walmart."

"Sure," I said to myself. "Compliments of all those low-wage employees." But I went in anyway.

The collection is fully comprehensive, pre-Revolutionary War to Andy Warhol, Rothko, Calder, Pollock, Hopper, and O'Keeffe. It is truly a treat for any lover of art.

On my last visit there, I took a tour of the Frank Lloyd Wright house, moved from New Jersey piece by piece, compliments of the J.B. Hunt trucking line. Duh! Seventeen hundred square feet of pure, clean art. Costing $30,000 in the 1950s, it was one of Mr. Wright's series of Usonian houses, his attempt to bring good architecture to the middle class. He also created all the furniture in the house; they were mostly built-ins. The guide said she doubted he selected the sofa pillows displayed, since he didn't like pillows. The house owners probably put the pillows there. I thought of my friend Joseph and shared the story of Mr. Wright's sister, Maginel.

Crystal Bridges has a Milton Avery painting. Seeing it reminded me that Bobby and I struck up a conversation with his widow, Sally Michel Avery, also an artist, when we visited the Guggenheim in New York. She gave us a card and insisted we come to her studio on our next trip, so we did. Her studio was in an old office building in Union Square that had been converted mostly to art studios. When we walked in the door, the smell of paint assaulted us. Still working, Ms. Michel must have been in her eighties. We invited her to go out for a drink. She did. And did, and did. She regaled us with art and New York stories. She died in 2003 at age one hundred.

Also, Ms. Walton, you are my new feminist "shero." The museum now includes historic timelines painted on the walls contemporary with the art in that particular gallery. Most historic timelines reflect wars. Jackie Kennedy insisted the timeline in the Kennedy Library in Boston Harbor note historic art accomplishments. For example, hers notes the creation of the Dance Theatre of Harlem. In the Crystal Bridges gallery featuring women artists was a notation of the IWY National Women's Conference 1977. Good for you, Alice!

In the last few years, I've taken art lessons from some of our local biggies, Jeannine Paul and Nancy Cheairs. Unfortunately, I've been as successful at that as I have been with my music lessons, which is nothing to brag about. I think of good art and music, but I can't execute it. Only one piece has been worthy of the living room. The rest are in my bathroom — thank you very much, Richard, for that idea.

What art and music lessons have done for me is to teach me how to look and listen better. I can appreciate even more what real talent is.

Chapter Thirty-Eight

I Miss Sports

Oh, I miss sports — playing them, since I watch them a lot. I never was any good, but I did enjoy the action and the competition. Golf was frustrating, but not enough to make me practice at it. I had the highest handicap at the club, which meant that I got to play with the best players when we had "scrambles." A scramble is a tournament whereby the worst player is paired with the best and then two mediocre players are included in a team of four. Each takes a shot from wherever the lie is, and we use the best one. Hell, even I could have a lucky shot sometimes.

Our golf pro was Buddy McEwen, who, I later learned, was also a terrific bass player with Memphis's iconic bluegrass band, The Settlers, and a friend of Bobby's. Buddy said, "Jocelyn, you have a good swing. All I want you to do is swing the club one minute a day."

Since I couldn't handle that, I would hit every sand trap and water hazard. Cussing at myself coming out of a creek, I didn't notice this man. In a South African accent, Gary Player entreated me not to be so hard on myself.

Tennis, on the other hand, is a sport you can get better at with time. One of our panelists, Bernice Cooper, had a tennis court in her backyard, and we played a lot until I went to law school. Later, I got too heavy to play with agility.

Baseball just got too slow. Daddy had a great idea for the sport. He thought innings should be timed, even leaving men on base if time ran out. All saved minutes — three up, three down — could be used for the ninth inning. Basketball's my sport of choice. I played it as a kid and love the ballet of it. I think the shot clock in college basketball is way too long. The shorter time for the pros makes the game move so much faster.

The Memphis Grizzlies games are a hoot. There is even entertainment during timeouts and halftime. I had a Grizzlies T-shirt attached to a parachute fall from the ceiling right into my lap. It was on Dr. Martin Luther King's birthday, I had been to Mason Temple that morning, and I was sure I was the intended target for the gift from heaven — or from the ceiling. Any city that wants to integrate its population should bring in a professional basketball team!

There was a time in my life that I got into hunting, fishing, and sport shooting. I went fly fishing once but only caught a tree branch. I never caught a bass topwater, but I did catch some underwater with a purple worm. Somehow I didn't mind baiting a hook with worms or crickets.

Richard collected guns, and he taught me how to handle one. He owned consecutively numbered Smith and Wesson 357 Magnums. He thought it was cool we had "his and her pistols." I didn't take mine in our divorce.

Eventually, I took up hunting to be with him more. I only hunted quail — once on horseback, which was fun — and doves. I felt dove hunting a bit unfair. Farmers and land-owning hunters would not harvest all their corn crop. They would leave some to attract the birds. It's called baiting the field.

A dove hunt could consist of fifty people or more if the field was large enough. The hunters lined the perimeter of the field, hopefully out of range of buckshot from those across from them. We often cheered a bird that could traverse the field unscathed.

Doves are beautiful birds, a warm tan in color. There is a heart-like quality to their wings when spread. They never glide when they fly, so you can tell a dove from the distance.

When my CSA Yankee buddies learned I was a gun enthusiast, they were amazed. Some of them had never held a gun, much less shot one, and never knew a Jew who hunted. One friend teased, "Jocelyn, you are a Jewish Republican civil rights worker who shoots guns for a hobby?"

I shot a 20-gauge Remington 1100 automatic shotgun and, yes, I belonged to the National Rifle Association — until it got into the anti-abortion business.

At one time, I was a special deputy for the sheriff's department. After qualifying with a handgun, I had a permit to carry. Leaving my downtown office after dark, I felt a bit more secure with my pistol. I had a .22-gauge Beretta. Whether I could point a gun at a person I will never know, thank God, because I was never tested.

After Richard took his life with a handgun, I gave up my permit to carry.

Chapter Thirty-Nine

My Beloved Israel

I do love Israel, but I am conflicted about her policies. In November 2014, my rabbi, Micah Greenstein, held a membership meeting at our Temple to discuss them. It was a brave thing to do, and he asked for questions in advance. I sent one and used the dreaded word "apartheid." At what point does occupation become apartheid?

At the meeting, the rabbi said, "A few of you asked, 'Is Israel practicing apartheid?'" The room erupted into a shitstorm.

That night I wrote him the following letter.

> November 23, 2014
>
> Rabbi Honey,
>
> I am a committed Zionist, a charter member of ARZA. I love Israel and its importance to Judaism. But I also need Israel. It may be the only place in the whole wide world I can count on not to deny me entrance if I need it. So Israel's existence is personal to me.
>
> I was so conflicted tonight. I was chomping at the bit to out myself as one of the three folks to be so concerned about our beloved Israel and its occupation of the West Bank. I feared being drawn and quartered — there was a whole lot of vitriol among our flock — or, more importantly, diverting the conversation into personalities and not the subject.
>
> I was unaware that the word "apartheid" could draw such ire, nor how much concern Israel gave President Carter's book,

Palestine, Peace Not Apartheid. Israel felt it needed a PR campaign to address the book. Every single person who told me of their fury at Carter's book also told me they didn't read it. "I wouldn't read such trash." I wonder if you and I were the only ones in the room who did!

My question wasn't pertaining to the State of Israel proper practicing "apartheid." While there is a lot of prejudice within Israel toward race, ethnic groups, religious groups — hell, I was even spit on and the target of rocks in Mea Shearim — Israel is a young country and still growing into its covenant. I feel we Jews are supposed to know better, but ...

My question and concern is the occupation. We can't annex the territories because if we do, we have to give Palestinians the vote, and we can't do that or a Jewish state could be voted out. We can't take it over and not let the occupants vote because that is apartheid. So what do we do?

I know all the arguments: God gave us the deed, we have won it three times in war, and we are better stewards of the land. But it's not ours. And we are treating the people who ended up there terribly. So, again, what do we do?

Of all the Arabs in the world, the Palestinians could have been our best hope for neighbors. They are secular, educated, business savvy, and culturally sophisticated. A big fear is all that may be changing and quickly.

We have got to secure peace somehow. And we can't let the nut jobs — ours or theirs — veto every peace initiative with a dastardly act.

Micah, two more issues: When I hear, "They hate us more than they love their children," I think of Golda Meir, who not only sent letters to the mothers of our slain in war, she sent letters to the mothers of soldiers we had to kill. As a mother myself, I can promise you there isn't a Gazan Muslim mother who would rather have a dead martyr than a live son. The other sad thing is she has to convince herself she's proud in order to cope with her loss.

And second, showing advertisements in Israeli media

claiming diversity in Israel proves Israel isn't racist would be like my waving a photo of Mayor A C Wharton and proclaiming as evidence, "See, there's no racism in Memphis."

My love, you were courageous to have the session. You are the best thing that has happened to our Temple and our town.

Love, Jocie

The salutation, "Rabbi Honey," requires an explanation. My grandchild Josh was born unable to keep formula down. I held him in my arms at Le Bonheur Children's Hospital's intensive care with an IV port attached to the top of his head. Priests and Protestant ministers were praying for this child. I called Micah when I got home to ask him to pray as well. While not strictly observant as a Jew, I do understand the concept of there being no atheist in a foxhole, and I wanted to pray Jewishly.

Rabbi Micah and I liked each other. We still do. About the first week or so he was here, I called him.

"Rabbi, we haven't met yet, but I have an extra ticket to the Rolling Stones tomorrow night. Would you like to go?"

"YES."

He returned my call regarding my grandchild Josh when Bobby was sitting beside me on the sofa. Bobby heard: "Thank you, honey. Yes, honey. I will, honey. Honey, I really appreciate this."

When we hung up, Bobby said, "Joselynda, you Jews are a strange bunch. Catholics call their spiritual leaders 'father.' We Protestants call ours 'reverend.' But you Jews call your rabbis 'honey.'"

Meanwhile, Josh recovered after two surgeries and lots of interdenominational prayers.

So later I told Micah about Bobby's comment, and we commenced my referring to him as "Rabbi Honey," and he signs off emails likewise.

One time he signed off, "Rabbi Baby."

I wrote him back, livid. "Baby? Baby? Are you two-timing me?"

Despite my criticisms of Israel's policies, which I consider being able to give as a valid member of the family, I love and need Israel. My two trips so far were spiritual to my Jewish psyche.

Chapter Forty

If Maimonides (1135-1204) Lived Today

We know his famous quotes: "Give a man a fish and you feed him for a day; teach a man to fish and you feed him for a lifetime."

"Anticipate charity by preventing poverty."

"No disease that can be treated by diet should be treated with any other means."

This is pretty modern thinking; the organic farming industry would like this.

Maimonides (1135-1204) was born in the exquisite town of Cordoba, Spain, about an hour's beautiful ride from Seville. Cordoba is proud of its native son and demonstrates it in preservation of his synagogue and in statuary. He was a celebrated medieval Jewish thinker, jurist, physician, and philosopher. He is known by other names: Rabbi Moshe ben Maimon and Rambam. In Torah class, we studied his *Thirteen Principles of Jewish Faith*. For example:

"Principle 10. I believe by complete faith that the Creator, blessed be His name, knows every action done by each human being as well as all their thoughts, as it was said, 'It is He that fashions their hearts together and He ponders all their deeds.'

"Principle 11. I believe by complete faith that the Creator, blessed be His name, rewards all who keep His commandments and punishes all those who transgress His commands."

Others are quite brief, so if he lived today, he could communicate well in the Facebook and Twitter world.

As an exercise in chutzpah, I decided to propose some new

principles. My rabbi and class were less than impressed. I love my religion and love being a Jew. So, respectfully, I'm trying again:

JOCIE'S PROPOSED TENETS OF REFORM JUDAISM

• God is. But the concept of God may vary with the individual Jew.

• The individual Jew's relationship to God is personal and may take differing forms — although none superior to the other.

• Our benevolent God revealed to Jews the code of how humankind should coexist with each other; as consideration, we Jews should behave in such a way as to be an example of good coexistence.

• The universe and its nature are worthy of our awe and appreciation.

• Humankind and all living creatures deserve acknowledgment for their role in the universe.

• Where humankind and the universe intersect, humankind must uphold good stewardship of the universe.

• Jews must be charitable and kind toward the less fortunate and seek knowledge from them as a way of showing respect.

• Jews must ensure justice for all.

• Jews need to be aware of our history as a way of ensuring Judaism's continuation.

• Jews should support "kehilla," a community of Jews, as a way of ensuring continuation.

• Jews should support Israel, the birthplace of Judaism, if for no other reason than that there must exist a place that won't deny entrance to a Jew.

• The Torah is a highly inspired, remarkable document that is intended as a helpful guide to practice Judaism.

• As humankind advances toward self-actualization, so does the Torah. It should be reread for applicability as we, and it, grow.

• Jews should treat others as we wish to be treated.

I also have reduced the Ten Commandments down to two:

I. Thou shall not hurt on purpose.

II. Let there be spaces.

P.S. My two grandsons, Joshua David and Noah Aaron (similar to Elvis since Noah was born on his birthday), were in the midst of their parents' miserable divorce and never got to be Bar Mitzvah. I conjured up a plan: In September 2016, I started taking Hebrew. I didn't tell a soul.

In April 2017, I met with the boys and shared my idea. I wanted them to be B'nai Mitzvah with me. We would do it at Temple Adas Israel in Brownsville, Tennessee. Just a family thing. I wanted to keep it a secret until Passover, at which time I would reveal my plan by reading the 4th Question in Hebrew, traditionally asked by a child at the Passover Seder.

Passover is a big deal in our family. It's my favorite Jewish holiday. Sixteen or more are seated at dinner, at which we eat ceremonial foods prior to the meal. Tradition says Jews eat matzo ball soup on Passover; matzo balls, in my family's Reform German Jewish tradition, are made from matzos, not matzo meal, which resembles white cornmeal. Ours are chewy, have a diameter the size of a nickel, and it would be best not to drop one on your toe. First my nephews, Charlie and Barry, and then, after they left for college, my grandsons have always helped me roll hundreds of these balls. As Tevye said, "TRADITION!"

I was so excited. I rehearsed my Hebrew endlessly. I was going to blow my family's socks off. My brother asked my grandchildren to read. My granddaughter Sydney, age seven, read the first. Josh read the second, and Noah was to read the third and fourth. Only I interrupted and said I would like to read the fourth one.

My children and brother's response was totally underwhelming! I was crushed. Thank God for my two sons-in-law. After the pregnant pause, they expressed excitement and approval for me. They complimented my achievement and delighted in saying they would be attending our ceremony.

The B'nai Mitzvah took place January 20, 2018. And I am happy to report our portions, Exodus chapters 10 and 11, tell the story of Passover!

Chapter Forty-One

Racism

Hundredth Anniversary of the Memphis Branch of the NAACP

Nothing was ever said about me receiving an award. I knew I was an honorary co-chair, but neither of the other two knew about us being honored. Happy bought a table, but I didn't include Bobby or the kids. Oh, I wish I did. I channeled my father that day, and I nailed it.

I got the notice they wanted me to speak for two minutes the day before, and I knew immediately what I wanted to say — if I had the nerve. I found the nerve.

"In the 1970s, my mama surprised me: 'Jocelyn, I've signed you up for the Daughters of the Confederacy.'

"'Mama-a-a, why in the world would you think I would like to be in the Daughters of the Confederacy? I'm a Golden Heritage member of the NAACP! I don't wanna be in the Daughters of the Confederacy.' She unsigned me.

"Fast-forward to three weeks ago. I was in New Orleans at the New Orleans Museum of Art. On leaving, I had the staff call a taxi to go back to the Vieux Carre. It was dreary out and sprinkling a bit, so I was under the portico. And there was only one other person standing in front of the museum.

"This woman walked over to me and said, 'Well, they took down our monuments, didn't they?'

"'I'm glad they did,' I told her.

"'You are? Why?' she asked.

"'Because they're hurtful,' I said.

"'They're history! Our Robert E. Lee was a graduate of the military academy and a hero!' she said.

"'And he led a war in order to keep slavery!'

"'That's not what that war was about!' she said.

"I walked over to the woman and I said, 'Lady,' and I lied through my teeth. I said, 'Lady, I'm a Daughter of the Confederacy! And that's exactly what that war was about!'"

I turned away toward my two women friends Deidre Malone, president of the branch, and Gale Jones Carson, who put on the event with Deidre. I didn't realize the audience was standing, laughing, and applauding.

Congressman Steve Cohen and former congressman Harold Ford Jr. came up to hug me and give me an "attagirl."

But the thrill of the afternoon for me was Melissa Harris-Perry, once a Princeton professor, now at Wake Forest, and former MSNBC commentator. And a real "SHERO" of mine! Melissa is brilliant, academic, entertaining, funny, and a natural beauty; she is one of the best speakers and teachers I've ever heard.

And she came up to ME to hug ME! All I could say was, 'I'm being hugged by Melissa Harris-Perry. Yea!'"

Race and Extra Money

Carl Glatt, one of my civil rights gurus, said the best argument for non-discrimination in the workplace is money. If someone has extra money, after food, clothing, and shelter, they may go to the hardware store, buy a can of paint, paint the outside of the house, and make the neighbors happy.

Reading Isabel Wilkerson's *The Warmth of Other Suns*, Michelle Alexander's *The New Jim Crow*, and J.D. Vance's *Hillbilly Elegy*, it's all about money. And if you put together race and money, or the lack thereof, we see how racism works.

When Black folk migrated to the North, they were relegated to the poorest parts of town and paid obscene rent. Yes, they made more money, but it took all their money to pay for food and shelter.

Mass incarceration of people of color is the new Jim Crow. I just learned that when prisoners get out, they owe past rent for the jail cell and must pay to report to their probation officer, and perhaps past child support. Where does a parolee get the job to pay for this? He now has a record and can't get a job. So where does he get the money? Crime!

We've created a permanent underclass. And we all lose! We of white privilege are paying the price for our racism. Sick people running around may infect me with their sickness. Poor people needing money may rob me. Addicted people drive impaired and may run into me. Uneducated people do dumb things. Frustrated people do frustrating things and may frustrate me. Why don't we understand that?

When first learning about civil rights, I learned that when you keep someone in a ditch on purpose, you've got to stand by the damn ditch and keep them there. Who doesn't have to stand by the ditch? Rich people! They pay poor people to have to stand there.

And sadly, when we have elected intelligent Black leadership as mayors, one governor, and even president of our United States, white folk just couldn't stand it. A Black man in the White House! Instead of seeing if Black leadership may have some insight and perhaps some solutions to break the permanent underclass, we white people just couldn't allow success. Enter Mitch McConnell.

And now we have elected Donald Trump president. So now folk don't even have to be subtle with their racism and prejudice.

Black Lives Matter

All lives matter, but if that is your retort to Black Lives Matter, then you don't understand the problem. Nobody ever had to assert that white lives matter. The Black Lives Matter movement arose from police brutality on minorities. The deadly retaliatory attack on Dallas police was then labeled Blue Lives Matter.

I grew up knowing that the policeman was my friend; I could depend upon him to help me when needed. It took Dr. King's assassination and the attending unrest to learn that half my city didn't grow up thinking that. Prejudiced policemen could dick around with Black folk just for the hell of it and with impunity.

Richard was a sheriff's reserve officer. While I wished he had been enamored with a different hobby, I couldn't criticize his choice any more than I would tolerate his berating my interests. I never was anti-police. His father eventually told him he could ride in a squad car or be president of the company, but not both. Richard quit riding and taught marksmanship instead.

For Black folk, police brutality is a reality. Racism and guns, and especially the authority and power to have one, is not a good combination. Policing, in part due to its attending pay, has been known for not drawing from the top socioeconomic ladder. On September 16, 2017, the Bureau of Labor Statistics (BLS) reported that the national average wage for a police officer in the United States was $29.45 per hour, or a salary of $61,270 per year. But even today, the BLS shows that Tennessee ranks tenth in lowest salaries for police officers across the nation. The average pay in our state is $43,090, with Memphis having its highest pay at $47,450. Tennessee also has one of the highest assault rates per capita. In California, with the best pay for officers, the average salary is $93,550, which is related to the cost of living.

But some years ago, with school segregation, Black and white folks of the same rung rarely interacted. So police, who used to be only white men, never knew Black folk; they never ran around with anyone Black or had a Black friendship. They couldn't harass white folk; you might be harassing a cousin of the mayor!

While serving on the State Advisory Committee of the USCCR, we studied and held hearings on police brutality across the state. The Memphis chief of police at the time invited us members to ride with the police. I jumped at the chance, not just because I thought it would be an adventure, but a squad car experience might give me more insight about why Richard found his hobby so fascinating.

To the man, every policeman I rode with expressed the thought: "Nobody likes us but us." They do feel maligned. When I asked about their social lives, some of the men were committed to their church and its activities. Others told me they socialized with other police or firemen. One of our Shelby County General Sessions criminal court judges, designated as the domestic violence judge, shared her anecdotal experience that firemen were disproportionately before her, but the arresting policeman was all too often absent on the court date.

"They don't want to testify against their brethren," she said.

The job can be surprisingly dull most of the time, driving around an assigned district. There is a constant drone of indistinguishable talking on the police radio. My patrolman was attuned to it and could actually hear when the call was meant for him.

When the serious call comes in, there is a palpable rush when the siren comes on and the lights flash. My patrolmen were calm, matter of fact, but I was on the edge of the car seat with excitement. Most said they had never in their career removed the gun from the holster. When I asked if anyone had ever been scared, they said no, but they had been in scary situations.

Of recent influence on my way of thinking is the movie *Crash*. It covers all forms of prejudice and how we overtly or covertly act on it. The portrayal of the Los Angeles police is interesting. No spoiler here, but the relationship between the police and the policed in the movie shows the complexity of the job, trust issues, and human nature. Another influence is Michelle Alexander's *The New Jim Crow*, in which she connects the dots between post-slavery Jim Crow laws, the struggle for civil rights, the political conservative southern strategy, and the war on drugs. The result is disproportionate mass incarceration of Black and brown peoples.

The Black Lives Matter movement raised a potent protest in Memphis. I regret I am too old and gimped up to participate these days. The protest started downtown, but it gravitated to the Hernando de Soto Bridge over the Mississippi River at Memphis. It had the effect of shutting down Interstate 40 for three and a half hours. The protesters allowed one sick child to get through to St. Jude Children's Research Hospital, but back too far in Arkansas, another child's emergency took hours for the police to reach, back up traffic, and get that child to a hospital over another bridge.

The protesters appeared leaderless and mostly young. It got everyone's attention! The chief of police and the mayor invited the protesters in for an open conversation the next day in exchange for getting off the bridge.

Terri Freeman, president of the National Civil Rights Museum, was delighted to see so many young people involved, but she suggested they might want to let some old folk in to perhaps enlighten them on what works and what doesn't. My thoughts were to use Aikido, the process of taking the force of another and turning it around on them. For example, rather than being the one to stop traffic in such a strategic location, stand there en masse with signs, and the traffic will slow down to read the signs and rubberneck to see what's going on. Then the protesters didn't stop the traffic; the drivers did.

While I didn't think obstructing I-40 was cool, I couldn't help but wonder what might have happened in 1936 if Jews had blocked the autobahn and protested, "Hey folk, there's this guy Hitler who says Jewish lives don't matter!"

A few days later, the movement protested in front of Graceland, and it has threatened to spoil Elvis Week, which is held every year around August 16, Elvis's death date. Even some Black Lives Matter supporters have said, "Okay, it's proper to f*#k with the mayor, and even the chief of police. But gang, we don't f*#k with the King."

Racism in the Twenty-first Century

Post-racial my ass! The election of Barack Obama did not put an end to racism. In fact, it unleashed a lot of pent-up racial resentment. It saddened me to learn that in the twenty-first century, some people just couldn't get over the fact that we elected a Black man president of the United States.

Then the campaign and election of President Trump gave permission to the hardcore to express that resentment in the most vile and ugly words and actions. So emboldened, the Klan, neo-Nazis, and other white supremacist groups called for a gathering in Charlottesville, Virginia, of all places — the birthplace of American democracy. They wanted to show force, with guns attached to their bodies, as permitted in Virginia, to protest the removal of a statue of Robert E. Lee. Violence erupted, and a young woman counter-protester was rammed by a car and died of her injuries in an event like an ISIS attack. Two police officers also were killed in the line of duty.

Our president then came out and said, "Can't we all get along," shit condemning both sides of the protest as if they were on equal ground. He bitched throughout his presidential campaign that President Obama wouldn't say "Islamic terrorism," which would have condemned a whole religion for actions committed by a tiny percentage. Yet he wouldn't call out the KKK, neo-Nazis, and other white supremacists for their treacherous and un-American thoughts and behaviors.

It was new information for me to learn that most of the Civil War monuments were erected, not after that war in the late 1870s, but in 1920 and forward through the 1960s. They were really erected as a protest to civil rights.

As a Jew, watching the demonization of the free press, neo-Nazis marching through the night with torches, overtly expressed anti-Semitism, and proponents of it serving in the White House, I feel as if I am living in 1936 Germany.

Oh, America, we have strived so hard for so long to live up to our own ideals, and now we are blowing it.

I was preparing for a dinner party in my kitchen, and my yard sprinkler repairman came in to give me a progress report and get paid for the work so far. He was standing at the end of my kitchen counter beside a cutting board on which was a large carving knife. He picked up the knife and said, "Swoosh," waving the knife in the air as if slicing something above him.

"I beg your pardon?"

"Swoosh," he said. "This is what I would like to do to him."

"Who's him?"

"Obama."

My mind started racing what to say or do. I had more sense than to fire him on the spot and tell him never to come back; after all he had a large knife in his hand. Should I call the FBI? This man would never get within five hundred miles of the president.

"Oh, Jim, shame on you."

I paid him off, and when he called to come back, I told him my son finished fixing it.

What's crazy about this is two things:

First, I have tacked on the wall of my garage back-door entrance my campaign yard signs for Hillary 2008, Obama-Biden, and Hillary 2016. Everyone who comes into my house knows exactly who I am and how I think.

Second, does his being white give him the privilege to think I would be okay with that? Could he not imagine how offended I would be? It was like the woman in New Orleans who assumed I was against the Civil War monuments being taken down.

Being on edge now about overt racism, misogyny, homophobia, and xenophobia, I have forgotten all my Panel of American Women lessons and have been way too quick to prejudge. Reading Gloria Steinem's latest book, *My Life on the Road*, I have been relating pleasantly with her tales of wrongly prejudging people, especially a biker couple she met, but you will have to read that for yourself.

I was on a train excursion in Alaska with my grandsons when a nice woman volunteered to take a picture of us. Somehow her husband struck me as being a redneck. He had leathery skin, as if he had been in the sun way too much, perhaps for his job. I thanked her, and then we ascertained we were both on the *Norwegian Jewel* cruise ship. She asked if the boys were enjoying the trip. I told her, "They really are."

"I didn't study for this trip as I should have, but I did read Michener's tome on Alaska, and our narrator on this train seems to be following his chapter on Skagway word for word. I tried to get the boys to read it, but I think the size of the book intimidated them. Michener even anthropomorphized the woolly mammoths, and I thought the boys would like it."

The husband said, "Anthropomorphized? What a big word."

He took me right back to being mocked on Berkley Street.

"Jocelyn uses big words, Jocelyn uses big words." Yep, he's a redneck.

"I've missed hearing your southern accent," he said. "I went to Arkansas State."

Yep, it's confirmed. He's definitely a redneck.

The next evening on the ship I went to a martini tasting. When I arrived, the train couple waved me over, and I quickly assessed they had the last available seat for me. Shit.

I learned they were from California.

"How did you get from California to Arkansas State?" Arkansas State University is in the northeast corner of Arkansas, about one and a half hour's drive from Memphis and in the middle of nowhere.

"I had an athletic scholarship. I ran track and was in the 1966 Olympics," he said.

"Oh, really?" I said. He became interesting.

"My life at Arkansas State was quite an enlightening experience for me. I met Black people for the first time. All my trackmates were Black, and all my roommates were Black. They were so nice to me. They introduced me to their friends and families, and I loved being included in their culture, so to speak. It was quite transformative for me."

My heart melted. His words touched me like the world-renowned philosopher Roberta Flack: "Killing me softly with his song, telling my whole life with his words, killing me softly."

"Please, please, tell me you're voting for Hillary!"

"Of course!" he said.

Chapter Forty-Two

We Know How to Do It

It's not as if we don't know how to do it. We do. We won't, but we could. Orchids to those who are trying like hell.

In Memphis, Tennessee, we have zip codes that beat all national statistics for bad things — infant death, low birth rates, addictions, low graduation rate, single parenthood, domestic violence, and rape. The list goes on and on. We have children having children.

Dr. Nancy Hart got fired from the University of Tennessee College of Medicine for identifying those zip codes and admonishing the community for ignoring the problems. She turned off the Downtown Rotary Club, a Memphis club with clout, big time when she talked about these ills from the podium. A member asked, "What can we do?"

"You know what to do, for God's sake. You Rotarians tried to eradicate polio off the face of the earth. You know how to do it," she said.

We need a "Manhattan Plan" to break the cycle. It would take seventeen years to undo all of these negative things. Just seventeen years.

Right after Hurricane Katrina, I went to New Orleans with the CSA. We toured the areas devastated by the hurricane and resulting floods. Fascinating for me was our visit to the Green School. This inner-city school used to be surrounded by a ten-foot cyclone fence and razor wire to keep the neighbors out. Those neighbors are no longer there, and the fence is now four feet high with numerous gates.

The school is now a charter school, but under heavy government regulation. The school day is twelve hours, and the school opens for breakfast at six thirty. It runs year-round with a few weeks off for each season. The most interesting thing about the school is that the children tend its edible garden, which feeds the students. When the kids are out of school, the gates open for the neighbors to water the plants and help themselves to the vegetables for their own kitchens. The chef Emeril built a kiosk and has staff periodically lecture on cooking for the parents and neighbors.

For kids in trouble, the teacher-to-student ratio is one to four. The kids are thriving. What was hurtful for me was that the principal was from Memphis! From Memphis!

A few years ago, Memphis had one Head Start program that took children at six months of age. The babies were held, sung to, read to, talked to, and fed well. It accommodated seventeen infants. Seventeen!

Enhanced care and education from age six months to age eighteen is enough time to break the underclass.

So why don't we? We can pay for it. We just don't have the WILL. Which is stupid. A permanent underclass in our midst costs us a bundle.

Sick people spread their sickness — and to my grandchildren — so it would be best that we cure their sickness. If we don't provide medical care, they go to the hospital emergency room. They can't pay for it, so ultimately we do.

If a pregnant woman — all too often now, a child herself — doesn't get prenatal care, she delivers a deficient baby that you and I are going to pay for the rest of its life.

A prisoner costs over $50,000 a year to house. Add in the cost of the legal system to put him there — the police, the prosecutors, the judiciary — and the cost is astounding. It's far more than the cost on the front end for good childhood education. The savings we get from incarcerating uneducated people, who turned to crime when there was no alternative, would pay for the preventative measures.

There used to be a conservative or liberal way to approach our country's problems. But we all understood there was a problem. I remained a Republican until the civil rights movement dominated my ethos. Capitalism needed to be "enlightened," and it wasn't behaving that way. My state's rights conflicted with civil rights for all.

We wouldn't stand for integrated education, so we stopped funding education for kids with whom we won't go to school. We barely feed the hungry or house the homeless. Many states won't teach sex education in our schools, so children are having children. Many states won't pay a living wage to those who believe in work. Philanthropy can't pick up the slack.

For some reason, we won't lift folks out of poverty, the very folks who would spend money locally in our stores if they had any money, keeping our local businesses open.

We have come to believe that the poor are poor of their own making and deserve our scorn. Our various bibles suggest differently, but that's another essay.

The body politic is failing us. We have reaped what we have sown. And it costs us a bundle.

While I want to say, "Okay, you up-and-comers, the ball's in your court," I don't have the luxury of getting off the case. Some of us elders have formed an organization we call Voices of Reason. I refer to us as the "Grandmother Brigade." We have been meeting at McDonald's on Mondays to bitch about Trump and have a pity party — and drink free coffee, although some of the women attending could buy the McDonald's. We tip well. This spontaneous gathering is interesting since some of the women have never been political, nor social justice advocates, before. I call our formation "The Trump Effect." Plagiarizing Jerry Garcia, "We are old and intend to be in the way!"

We disapprove of what we are seeing. Americans, we are not acting very American. We see us normalizing xenophobia as badly as we did against the Irish Catholics back in the 1920s. We see us normalizing anti-Semitism as badly as Adolf Hitler did in the 1930s. We see us normalizing racism as badly as Jim Crow in the 1940s. We see us equating radical Islamist terrorists with all God-loving Muslims. We see us normalizing misogyny as we always have since we blamed sin on Eve.

Fellow Americans, we are happy for you if there are federally funded social programs you don't need. You are indeed fortunate. But some of us who worked most of our lives — inside or outside the home — are dependent upon Social Security, Medicare, or Medicaid. Some of us would be bankrupt without them.

We have a benevolent government, America, and it is our friend. Our tax dollar provides us essentials; anything left over helps us buy things that keep the wheels of commerce turning. This is good!

To the next generation I ask, "Can we fix it?"

Yes! All we have to do is want to do it.

Chapter Forty-Three

Awards-R-Us

The Dr. Martin Luther King Jr. national holiday on Monday, January 20, 2014, commemorating King's birthday, was an extraordinary day for me. The mayor of Memphis, the Honorable A C Wharton, gave me an inaugural Martin Luther King Be the Dream Civil Rights Legacy Award. The award ceremony was held at the Mason Temple, the venue of Dr. King's "I've Been to the Mountaintop" sermon foretelling his death, and, in fact, this was his last sermon.

Seven of us received awards; my rabbi, Micah Greenstein, invited to give a prayer to commence the event, labeled us "the sensational seven." The exciting thing about that for me is that my journey, as revealed throughout this book, enabled me to be friends with each one.

My daughter Mindy attended, and music was a huge part of the program. Marvelous music! She announced to Rabbi Micah that she was converting to AME.

There I was, seventy-three years old, standing on the spot where my personal hero stood. The church, Mason Temple, ran a video of Dr. King delivering the speech. Overwhelming experience! I had a chance to grasp the podium where he stood.

Dr. King's assassination here in my town was the most transformative event of my life. It changed entirely everything about me. Who I was, what I was, what I knew about things. Was I supposed to be doing something about this? Damn, I had to challenge all my scripts.

Over the last few years, I have been honored multiple times; it has been an embarrassment of riches. The interesting thing is, since I've lived long enough, I have received honors for things folks hated me for back then.

I couldn't help but picture that twenty-eight-year-old me standing before the city council and demanding they bargain in good faith with the sanitation workers.

Fifty years later, in 2018, the City of Memphis is giving each of the remaining sanitation workers from the '68 strike $70,000. I'm conflicted. The "old me" says the gesture is admirable. The "new me" thinks, "Is that justice? That's only $1,400 a year to make up for all the ways the sanitation workers were mistreated."

A pricked conscience has no rest. But the "new me" is better than the "old me." Thank you, Dr. King.

Appendix I

Awards and Appointments

Youth Appointments

President of the Jewish Youth Council
Board of Directors of the Jewish Community Center
Shelby County Youth Commission
Editor of the Central High Yearbook

Appointments

Coordinator of the Memphis Panel of American Women, Esther Brown, 1968

Tennessee Human Development Commission, Tennessee Gov. Winfield Dunn, 1971

Comprehensive Employment and Training Act Board Advisory Committee

Tennessee Commission on the Status of Women

Commission on Social Action, Alex Schindler, president of the Union of American Hebrew Congregations, 1976

United States Commission for the Observance of International Women's Year, President Gerald Ford, 1976

Minority Resource Center of the Federal Railroad Administration, Secretary of Transportation William Coleman, 1977

Beale Street National Historic Foundation, Memphis Mayor Wyeth Chandler, December 1977

United States Commission on Civil Rights State Advisory Committee, Chair Arthur Flemming, January 1979

Tennessee Task Force on Church Arson, Gov. Don Sundquist, 1996
Tennessee Human Rights Commission, Gov. Phil Bredesen, 2005

Awards

Memphis Inter-Denominational Fellowship Award, 1971
National Conference of Christians and Jews Community Service Award for Women's Rights, 1981
Women of Achievement Award for Courage, 1990
Fifty Women Who Make a Difference, Memphis Women's News, 1996
Paul Harris Award, Rotary Club of Memphis, 1997
Outstanding Contributions to West Tennessee, University of Tennessee–Martin, 2006
Shelby County Diversity Award, Shelby County, 2008
YWCA Distinguished Community Leadership Award, 2009
Rhodes College Distinguished Alumni Award, 2009
Urban League Herman Ewing Award, 2009
Legend Award, Women's Foundation of Greater Memphis, 2010
Tennessee Human Rights Advocacy Award, 2010
Grayfred Gray Public Service in Mediation Award, 2012
Jocelyn Dan Wurzburg Civil Rights Legacy Award, Tennessee Human Rights Commission, 2013
Martin Luther King Be the Dream Civil Rights Legacy Award, Memphis Mayor A C Wharton, 2014
Tennessee Women's Hall of Fame, Tennessee Economic Council for Women, 2014
Cynthia D. Pitcock History Award, St. Mary's, 2016
The City of Memphis Heritage Trailblazer Award for Advancing Civil and Human Rights, December 2016
The Tennessee Tribune Person of the Year 2016, with Dr. Phyllis Qualls and Chancellor Zeppos
NAACP Service Award, 2017
Planned Parenthood Judy Scharff Lifetime of Achievement Award for the Panel of American Women, 2017
The Frances Wright Award, New Sardis Baptist Church, 2018

Appendix II

On the Other Hand

An article for *Memphis Bar Association* magazine

I read with interest David Caywood's two articles on mediation in our *Memphis Lawyer* publications (September–December), and was delighted that David is now bringing his forty-eight years of litigation clout to the field of mediation. On the other hand, I would like to share a totally different perspective my twenty-eight years of performing and teaching mediation bring to the profession.

But first, some mediation 101: The promise of mediation is to empower parties in conflict to consent to, with the help of a trained facilitator-mediator, an informed, fair, and durable agreement. Anyone can talk vulnerable, conflicted parties into some kind of agreement, but will the parties buy into it as fair?

Disputes fall under two categories. One is called "distributive," how much money for a tort, contract issues, etc., where funds are distributed from one party to another, and the parties never need further contact. Or, they are "transactual" whereby the disputants desire or require a continuing relationship after the dispute is resolved, such landlord-tenant, vendor-vendee, employer-employee, or divorcing parents.

All disputes, even fender benders, have three components — business, legal, and emotional — and a good mediator deals with all three. In transactual cases, there is hope that the mediation process can actually transform warring parties into problem-solvers.

After a decade of rejecting the use of mediation, the Memphis Bench and Bar finally came aboard, but immediately commenced lawyerizing it. They discounted the national paradigm and favored a model the TBA and the Tennessee Supreme Court Alternative Dispute Resolution exploration committees deemed too lawyer-like when it petitioned the Supreme Court to consider rules allowing judges to order folks to an alternate process for dispute resolution.

The Memphis goal was to close files, and our bar adopted evaluative, shuttle mediation, hardly allowing the parties, with help of counsel, to hash out agreements that will work for each of them. I never give my parties New Age, Aquarian, win-win stuff; I just work to help them arrive at something that each can live with.

Most of my practice has been divorce and family mediation as taught by trainers approved by the Academy of Professional Family Mediators. It is a heck of a lot harder than merely shuttling from one room to another, but the original founders of mediation as a profession (back in the 1970s) urged a process influenced more by the psychological sciences than the litigatory, adversarial system. We call that model "facilitative" where the mediator is trained to assist the parties to arrive at their own informed decisions, based on mutually agreed post-divorce budgets, proof of assets and debts (we trust, but verify), and needs-based parenting schedules. The parties are in the same room (attorneys are always welcome) examining the paperwork, questioning each other, approving line items in each other's budget for validity, and even mediating what additional discovery is necessary to have confidence everything is on the table.

Are parties emotional? Sure! They are dealing with divorce, one of the most emotionally potent experiences in their lives. They're usually hurt, scared (of being a bag lady or being taken to the cleaners), and functioning at their lowest. Sometimes they need a safe forum to vent their disappointment and anger at each other, before they can get into problem-solving mode. I have found it amazing how many lawyers can't handle emotional, conflictive behavior. By lawyering the proceedings, as David's articles denote, we hardly ameliorate the negative impact of the divorce process and the pain inflicted on the children or each other.

There are different styles of mediation: shuttle vs. facilitative, evaluative vs. transformative, hashers vs. bashers. A good mediator can do them all, and the skill is to know what style is best to use when and often in the same case. Because of the emotional impact of employment cases, the EEOC, the US Postal Service, and the Department of Justice engaged the facilitative divorce mediators to handle their workplace disputes and American with Disabilities Act claims.

What's most important is to distinguish the role of the attorney in the adversarial litigation system from the cooperative, advocate role in mediation. I tell my attorneys they are not potted plants here, but that we have now become team members trying to help our clients arrive at a satisfactory resolution.

With this preface, I would like to address some of David's points: Whether it is divorce or other civil cases, it is imperative that the parties meet together with the mediator at the same time, at least to hear the mediator's orientation, if for no other reason than being able to trust that the mediator is saying the same thing to each of them. This may be the first mediation these parties experience, so they start assessing their trust in the process immediately.

The parties, the mediator's true clients, always get to tell their stories first because they are the experts about their needs and feelings. The attorneys then brief each other and the parties on the legal issues involved. I have participated as a party in an evaluative, shuttle mediation expertly done. But our side asked if the attorneys and insurance adjusters would allow us to tell our story before we started assisted negotiation. The mediator said that was new for him, but since it was a case strictly on pain and suffering, the sharing of our experiences was indispensable to the outcome.

In my facilitative workplace dispute mediations, I tell the parties and their attorneys that mediation is free discovery. The attorneys are always assessing how the other party will come off in court. Sounds believable? Factual? Sympathetic? I tell employers that they are going to learn more about their businesses in this mediation than they could have imagined.

It's not about selling a mediator anything! The mediator is not a judge and will not make a single decision! If in private caucus with one side or the other (which I reserve for knocking someone up the head), a mediator can restate and reframe what they, as an unbiased participant, heard the other side say. Sometimes when you don't have a dog in the fight, you hear things differently and can give a kind reminder to disputant and counsel: "Now did you grasp what the complainant said about so-and-so?" Did opposing counsel's position on such and such resonate with you?"

If the mediator doesn't mind being somewhat evaluative, and only if asked, he or she might offer a thought his or her experience dictates. Or, "would you like to know what other couples decided in a similar situation?"

The mediator is not to be wooed or lobbied. The mediator is not supposed to be an advocate for either side over the other. Mediators are unbiased but often may have to balance the power in a room. If neutrally sitting there while one side beats the other up, that mediator is not a neutral. What's really hard for balancing is when one party comes without representation, but that was the party's choice.

I found litigating to be the zero sum game. It was all about winning at the expense of the other, and the failure to win could really hurt somebody. That's why I quit litigating early, and I am glad. I was able to get into mediation without decades of litigation practices contaminating the process.

Divorce mediation isn't about winning; this is about problem-solving and the problem here is how to get an uncontested divorce the least emotionally and financially expensive way possible. The problem here is how are we going to co-parent these children living apart almost as well as when we were living together?

The children are watching divorcing parents like hawks; everything a child learns about conflict resolution is from how the parents conduct themselves during the divorce. How we mediators, and counsel to mediating parties, conduct ourselves could affect a whole lot more than the case at hand.

Acknowledgments

Where do I begin? Bobby Bostick, my partner in life for thirty-five-plus years, was the victim of my writing this book, having been ignored during this process except at meals, which he had to prepare — and so well. Paula Casey, writer, organizer, authority on the Nineteenth Amendment, and good friend, gave me intellectual support and supplied me with alcohol.

My editors, Jacque and Jesse Hillman and Katie Gould, swelled my head telling me others besides family and friends might find this book interesting.

Three friends have told me I should put my stories to paper: Gail Murray, who has written about me in two of her books; Carolyn Cerbin, who is writing THE book about the Panel of American Women; and John Minervini, freelance journalist for NPR.

Happy Jones, my recently departed dear friend, and Jeanne Varnell have been my cohorts in crime and devoted supporters and rescuers in all my endeavors.

Pat Shaw, Modeane Thompson, Donna Sue Shannon, Mimi Rice, Patty Bladon, Mimi Dann, Anne Shafer, Mattie Crossley, Marcia Levy, Mary Collier Lawson, Nezie, Marilyn, Perre, Jo, Bernice, Callie, Joyce, Mattie Carol, Esther, (Lord, I love us all), all the Panel of American Women helped me grow.

So have Carol Berz, Marcia Bicks, Deborah Clubb, Daney Kepple, James Lawson, Ben and Frances Hooks, Maxine and Vasco Smith, Herm Ewing, Carol Lynn Yellin, Janann Sherman, Bonnie Ragland, Joyce Cobb, Jolene Saizow, and Patty Abraham.

I belong to three women friend groups: The Birthday Club, the Voices of Reason, and the Cava Girls. The Birthday Club consists of Deanna Kaminsky, Faye Marks, Suzanne Lazarov, Lynn Gruber,

Joyce Lazarov, Hallie Elliot, and Bobbie Shainberg. The latter three overlap with the Voices of Reason along with Sandy Lipman, Meryl Klein, Phyllis Levine, Lorraine Kroll, Iris Harkavy, and Mopsy Graber. We meet weekly to trash Trump. Meeting monthly to do the same and drink a lot of Cava as a remedy are the Cava Girls: Beverly Marrero, Beanie Self, Gina Sugarmon, Regina Newman, Jeanne Richardson, Rosalva King, Brenda Ofenheusle, Paula Casey, and Patty Dougherty. I love my girlfriends! Their friendships keep me grounded.

Al Vorspan, David Saperstein, Alex Schindler, Lynne Landsberg, Harris Gilbert, Evely Youdovin, and Si Dresner introduced me to real liberal Jews, sparse around Memphis at the time. They are my role models for social justice activism. A shout-out to my Memphis spiritual teachers: Micah Greenstein, John Kaplan, Feivel and Abbie Strauss, Valerie Cohen, Katie Bauman, Meir Feldman, Levi Klein, Sonia Walker, and Rosalyn Nichols.

My siblings Ray Dan and Libby Lavine, my in-laws Barbie and Mark, and my cousins Faye and Rose Merry have all been the glue to keeping the family attached. Thank you.

I self-published so my wonderful children, Cheryl, Mindy, and Richard, Michael, and Blair, and grandchildren forfeited some of their inheritance for me to do this. Josh, Noah, and Sydney helped me with my Bat Mitzvah, held just at the crucial phase of editing this book.

And of course, thank you to Dr. Martin Luther King. I share your dream.

Index

Editor's Note

Some capitalization in *Jocie* has been set as the author's choice due to her life experiences.

About the Author

Jocelyn Dan Wurzburg has always been a dedicated volunteer, at first in Jewish "civil service" and then in human, civil, and feminist rights activities after the assassination of Dr. Martin Luther King Jr. in her city. That tragedy transformed her position in a stable, secure Memphis Jewish lifestyle into a new existence with diverse and wider viewpoints. While enlightening, it was challenging. She has donated her time to numerous local, state, and national activities addressing these issues.

A late-in-life lawyer, she received her divorce and law degree about the same time. The combination told her there had to be an easier way to get conflict out of her life and for others, so Ms. Wurzburg became Memphis's first professional mediator.

Numerous books and articles have described her volunteer civil rights accomplishments: *Throwing Off the Cloak of Privilege: White Southern Women Activists in the Civil Rights Era*, by Gail Murray; *You Must Be From the North: Southern White Women in the Memphis Civil Rights Movement*, by Kimberly K. Little; *Tennessee Women: Their Lives and Times*, edited by Sarah Wilkerson Freeman and Beverly Greene Bond with her chapter written by Gail Murray; *Energized By Issues* in *Rhodes Magazine*, by Daney Kepple; and several doctorial theses using Ms. Wurzburg's Archive at the University of Memphis.

She is a lifelong fifth-generation Memphian and a graduate of Rhodes College '62 with a B.A. in sociology and anthropology, and University of Memphis Law School '79. She has a son and two daughters, three grandchildren, and one honey.

Rhodes Magazine: Energized By Issues
rhodes.edu/stories/jocelyn-dan-wurzburg-energized-issues

Women at Rhodes Panel — 10/27/2017
www.youtube.com/watch?v=8uq6xNO1j18

Rhodes Crossroads Video Interview:
www.crossroadstofreedom.org/view.player?pid=rds:1078

Ms. Wurzburg is an archivist for the Mississippi Valley Collection housed at The Ned McWherter Library of the University of Memphis. Access requires the permission of Ms. Wurzburg. Her ADR/Mediation materials are housed at the University of Memphis Law School.

Website: wurzburgmediation.com
Email: wurzburg@mediate.com

CPSIA information can be obtained
at www.ICGtesting.com
Printed in the USA
LVHW02s2236200618
580940LV00002B/2/P